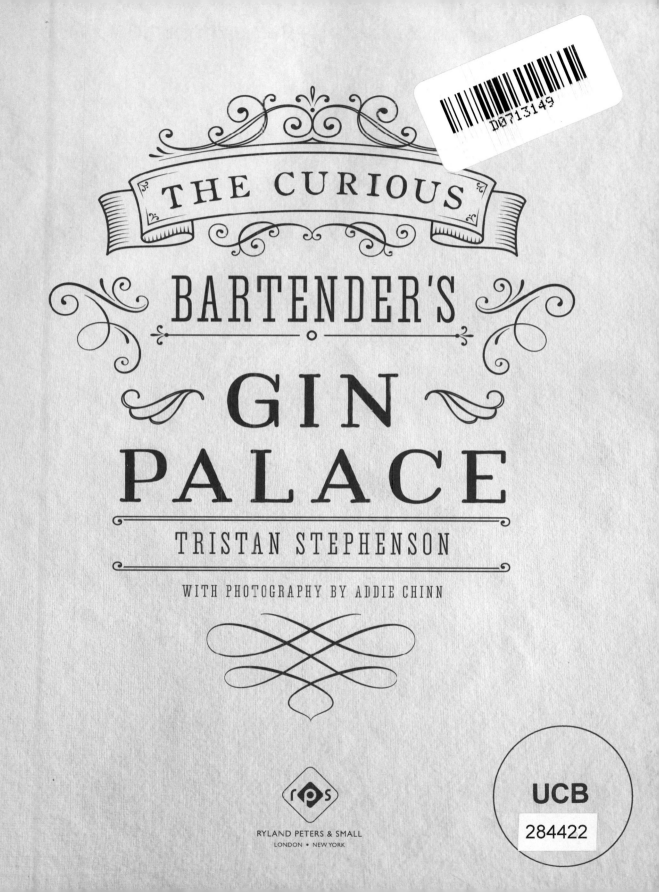

THE CURIOUS

BARTENDER'S

GIN
PALACE

TRISTAN STEPHENSON

WITH PHOTOGRAPHY BY ADDIE CHINN

RYLAND PETERS & SMALL
LONDON • NEW YORK

Designer Geoff Borin
Commissioning Editor Nathan Joyce
Production Manager Gordana Simakovic
Picture Manager Christina Borsi
Art Director Leslie Harrington
Editorial Director Julia Charles
Publisher Cindy Richards

Prop Stylist Sarianne Pleasant
Indexer Ingrid Lock

First published in 2016 by
Ryland Peters & Small
20–21 Jockey's Fields
London WC1R 4BW
and
341 E 116th St
New York NY 10029

www.rylandpeters.com

10 9 8 7 6 5 4 3 2 1

Text copyright © Tristan Stephenson 2016

Design and commissioned photography copyright ©
Ryland Peters & Small 2016 (see right for full picture credits)

ISBN: 978-1-84975-701-0

A CIP record for this book is available from the
British Library.

US Library of Congress CIP data has been applied for.

Printed in China

CONTENTS

INTRODUCTION
6

THE HISTORY OF GIN
8

HOW GIN IS MADE
44

THE GIN TOUR
74

GIN COCKTAILS
184

GLOSSARY OF DISTILLERIES
216

GLOSSARY
221

INDEX
222

ACKNOWLEDGMENTS
224

INTRODUCTION

Even before I was old enough to drink gin, I was thinking about it. My earliest memory of gin is my mother drinking a gin and tonic when I was nine, and, as it looked like a glass of lemonade, I thought it only right that I should be allowed one too. Even today I am known to react badly when refused a gin and tonic so my parents pacified me with a glass of tonic water. From the first sip I fell in love with its tongue-curling bitterness and that night I sneaked down to the kitchen and greedily swigged straight from a bottle. It would be a few more years before I could mix it with gin of course, but there was never any question that this heavenly mix of the sweet, bitter, boozy and botanical would become a big feature in my adult life.

Of course I never would have guessed that it would become this much of a feature. The most significant step was becoming a bartender, but when I got better at that I found myself delivering seminars on gin and judging gin competitions. Later, I appeared in advertising for a major gin brand, and opened two London cocktail bars – both heavily inspired by gin. After that I co-founded a (small) gin brand, and now I've written a gin book, having visited over 60 gin distilleries and sampled nearly 500 expressions. You could say I'm 'ginfatuated'.

And for good reason, too. In gin we have a spirit that is so specific in its flavouring, so chilling in its reputation, yet so far-reaching in its contribution to cocktails and mixed drinks.

From its origins as a medieval medicinal curative to becoming one of the world's first recreational spirits, gin, and its Dutch precursor, genever, soon became the go-to tipple for the British masses in the early 18th century. To say that party got out of hand would be playing it down somewhat. Juniper-scented gut-rot flowed through the streets of London, leading the poor and vulnerable into harm's way. But out of the ashes, something unexpected happened, and in the space of 100 years, gin journeyed from the backstreet bar rooms of London's inner-city slums to the cocktail lists of the most exclusive hotels in the world. Indeed, gin was the cocktail spirit, engulfing whiskey and brandy in a cloud of juniper-scented smoke by the beginning of the 20th century. Hundreds of dry gin cocktails were masterminded between 1900–1930. Not least of all, the Martini.

Who could have guessed that in the 50 years that followed gin's fortunes would change once again, fading away in to mediocrity becoming neither celebrated nor feared, but just unremarkable. The 1980s saw some of gin's most woeful times, where the cocktails of the golden era had been forgotten only to be replaced by vodka and a new era of cocktail culture where the concealment of a spirit's character through liberal use of sugar and fruit was the primary goal. Only gin's loyalest disciples kept the gin dream alive. Refusing to part company with their gin and tonics, keeping the fire burning and the ice stirring from bar room to home liquor cabinet.

Gin, as it stands today, occupies a curious position within the hearts and minds of drinkers. On the one hand there is 'mother's ruin', the degenerative scourge of 18th century English men and women, which has resonated through the centuries. On the other hand, though, gin has become a highly prized pinup of the craft revolution. Eschewing gin today is like sticking a finger up to local, artisan, independent businesses.

But the range of styles has also helped to a garner new admirers too. Assume the barstool position in any bar with a decent gin range and it won't be long until you hear that familiar sentence, 'I didn't used to like gin, but I like this one', signifying a new breed of gin drinker whose preconceptions have been squashed like a wedge of fresh lime. Pronounced flavour, credible provenance, botanical terroir and innovative packaging are just some of considerations that drive modern gin drinkers to buy one brand over another. This isn't just a renaissance of gin that we are experiencing right now – it's gin's golden time. Gin has never been this good and it might never be this good again, so enjoy it while you can, and be sure to enjoy this book with your gin drink of choice firmly in your hand.

THE HISTORY OF GIN

ALCHEMY, MAGIC AND THE ORIGINS OF DISTILLATION

Some scholars believe that it was the Chinese who first unearthed the secrets of distillation and that their findings were shared with Persian, Babylonian, Arabian and Egyptian merchants through centuries of trade along the old silk routes that penetrated in to the Middle East. These 3,200-km (2,000-mile) trails became well established in the 2nd century BC, and were used to trade gold, jade, silk and spices. However, it was as a hub of cultural networking that the silk route really came in to its own. It was, in effect, the information superhighway of its time.

Whether the Chinese got the know-how from the Indo-Iranian people, or the other way around, the mystic of ardent waters and botanical vapours was seething up in to the classical civilizations, where the preeminent physicians, alchemists and botanists took great interest in it.

The Greek philosopher Aristotle was certainly aware of distillation in one shape or another. One section of his *Meteorologica* (circa 340 BC) concerns experiments that he undertook to distil liquids, discovering that "wine and all fluids that evaporate and condense in to a liquid state become water."

In 28 BC a practising magi known as Anaxilaus of Thessaly was expelled from Rome for performing his magical arts, which included setting fire to what appeared to be water. The secrets of the trick were later translated in to Greek and published in around 200 AD by Hippolytus, presbyter of Rome – it turned out he used distilled wine. Around the same time our old friend Pliny the Elder experimented with hanging fleeces above cauldrons of bubbling resin, and using the expansive surface area of the wool to catch the vapour and condense it in to turpentine. Could Pliny have experimented with juniper distillates? Perhaps. But if he did, he didn't tell us.

The world's first self-proclaimed alchemist, Zosimos, an Gnostic mystic from Egypt, was also thought to be somewhat of a wizard with alcohol. He provided one of the first definitions of alchemy as the study of 'the composition of waters, movement, growth, embodying and disembodying, drawing the spirits from bodies and bonding the spirits within bodies.' It was Zosimos' belief that distillation in some way liberates the essence of a body or object that has lead to our definition of alcoholic beverages as 'spirits' today.

Up and until at least 900 AD these studies in spirit and alcohol were confined to the Middle East. Europe was still wallowing in a kind of post-Roman Empire hangover that had been dragging on for the better part of half a millennium. And while the Europeans passed the time burning witches and sharpening steel, Islam erected the Great Mosques of Damascus and Samarra,

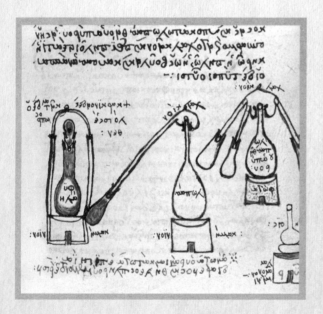

LEFT The first alembic stills designed by Zosimos of Panoplis use the same basic design as those made today.

and bred scholars and scientists. Under the ruling of the caliphate Muslim borders expanded, and so too did schools of mathematics, alchemy and medicine. During that time Abu Musa Jabir ibn Hayyan (who in time became known simply as *Geber*) emerged, in what stands as modern day Iraq, as the undisputed father of distillation. It was the research and observations of Geber that established the fundamental understanding of distillation throughout Islamic culture.

With knowledge came power, the Moors (a Muslim group from north Africa) persistently and systematically seized big chunks of southern Europe from the 8–9th centuries: Spain, Portugal, parts of southern France and Malta all fell to a force that was superior in every way.

In the 11th century the Europeans began to claw their way back however. Ranks were formed, the Catholic church rallied, and very slowly the 'Reconquista' groaned in to action. But this was a lengthy process, leaving some cities, like Toledo in Spain, under Muslim occupation for over 300 years. Once the Europeans moved in and noticed the rather impressive libraries, and the surprisingly well-educated people that inhabited the lands they had seized, the thirst for education and enlightenment became the new focus.

Universities of learning were established and one of them, *Schola Medica Salernitana*, in Salerno, Italy, would play an important role in the development of distillation. At that time the Principality of Salerno covered almost the entire western coast of southern Italy. Salerno had unprecedented access to Arabic materials thanks to regular interaction with the Byzantines (who liked nothing better than warring with the Arabs and Ottomans) but more importantly the Moors, who occupied Sicily from 902 AD through to the end of the 11th century, and regular skirmishes on to the Italian mainland would have taken them right up to the doorstep of *Schola Medica Salernitana*.

One of the school's primary functions was translation work from Arabic or Greek in to Latin. Arabic or Hebrew would be translated into Castilian by Muslim and Jewish scholars, and from Castilian into Latin by Castilian scholars. Knowledge blossomed. The scholars of antiquity who presided over this, Johannes Platearius, Bartholomew and Michael Salernus, outputted reams of material during the school's golden era, and within the dense volumes of their work we

ABOVE For the curious 12th century physician there was no better place to hone your craft than Salerno's medical school.

GEBERI PHILOSOPHI AC ALCHIMISTAE
MAXIMI, DE ALCHIMIA.
LIBRI TRES.

RIGHT The 1529 book *Geberi Philosophi ac Alchimistae Maximi, de Alchimia Libri Tres* features the works of pioneering alchemist Geber.

find the first inquisitions in to distillation by Europeans. One recipe book of herbal treatments, which was originally compiled by Platearius at some point in the 12th century, even includes a recipe for a tonic distilled from wine mixed with squashed juniper berries.

THE HISTORY OF MEDICINAL JUNIPER

Juniper has consistently been one of the most widely used trees in the whole of human history. It was essential to the survival of some primitive cultures who used the wood as a material to construct shelter, or shaped it in to utensils, weapons and furniture, or who simply burned it to provide heat and light. Societies have fed themselves with juniper (some Native American tribes were known to consume juniper berries in something resembling a fried juniper burger – I wouldn't advise trying it) and even the Bible makes reference to juniper as food, in Job (30:4) the King describes the desperation of his impoverished subjects as they 'cut up juniper roots for meat'. It lends itself better to being sustenance for livestock, and juniper is widely grown for decoration and landscaping purposes, and is a firm favourite of the bonsai tree-growing community.

THE WONDER-DRUG OF THE UNDEVELOPED WORLD

But juniper's greatest value has always been in its medicinal properties, where it has been held in high regard by medicine men and women for as long as medicine has been documented.

The Zuni of New Mexico would burn twigs of juniper then infuse them in to hot water, making a kind of tea that was administered as a relaxant to pregnant women during labour. The Canadian Cree made a tea from the root of the plant, while the Micmac and Malachite tribes (also of Canada) used juniper for sprains, wounds, tuberculosis, ulcers and rheumatism. The Shoshone boiled a tea from the berries and used it to treat kidney and bladder infections.

The Guna People, who occupy the San Blas Islands off the East coast of Panama, would smear ground-up juniper berries all over their bodies to fend of parasitic cat fish that would attack them when they went swimming, ironically, to catch fish.

In traditional Chinese medicine juniper is prescribed to tackle urinary infections and indeed any discomfort or disease centred around the lower or middle abdominal region. In central European folk medicine the oil extracted from the berries was regarded as a cure-all for typhoid, cholera, dysentery, tapeworms and various other afflictions you might associate with the poverty-stricken.

In Medieval times juniper berries were ground down and used as an antibacterial salve, which would be applied to cuts and wounds. For infections of the mouth you might be instructed to chew on juniper berries for a day to ward off microbial infection.

Juniper's more esoteric uses include its capability of driving-off evil spirits. Icelandic and Nordic tribes would wear sprigs of juniper about their person to protect the bearer from wild animal attacks. Wreaths made from juniper sprigs might also have hung above your door in efforts to protect the household from bad luck. All good shamans should turn to juniper when needing to cleanse or purify an area and drive away misfortune. Burning the leaves, roots, berries or twigs was common amongst Druids too. The Celts had similar ideas, fumigating the sick or possessed with juniper smoke until the subject recovered or died.

The Romans kept some in the their medicine cabinets, too. In the 2nd Century AD the Greco-Roman physician Galen noted that juniper berries 'cleanse the liver and kidneys, and they evidently thin

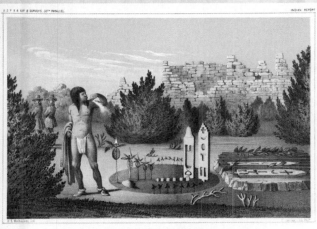

INDIAN ALTAR AND RUINS OF OLD ZUNI

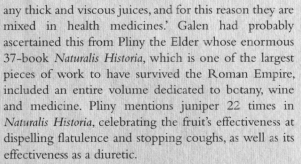

Juniperus Sabina

Published by Phillips & Fardon, Jan.1.1803.

ABOVE Juniper burgers were once all the rage in some native North American communities.

FAR RIGHT Juniper is one of mankind's oldest medicines. Alcohol is another...

RIGHT Cato the Elder is often considered to be the first Roman to have written in Latin. He was an avid juniper grower, too.

any thick and viscous juices, and for this reason they are mixed in health medicines.' Galen had probably ascertained this from Pliny the Elder whose enormous 37-book *Naturalis Historia*, which is one of the largest pieces of work to have survived the Roman Empire, included an entire volume dedicated to botany, wine and medicine. Pliny mentions juniper 22 times in *Naturalis Historia*, celebrating the fruit's effectiveness at dispelling flatulence and stopping coughs, as well as its effectiveness as a diuretic.

Pliny also makes reference to Cato the Elder for juniper-based know-how. Cato (b. 234 BC) was the consummate Roman statesman, an accomplished soldier, as well as a farmer who did a good job at playing doctor to his family and veterinarian to his livestock. If we're to believe Cato, a vineyard was the best sort of agricultural estate to possess, but even better if you can use that wine to make medicine. He lists a lot of botanical recipes in his book *De Agri Cultura* 'On Agriculture' (c. 160 BC) mostly derived

from his garden such as hellebore and myrtle, one recipe however is for a wine-based juniper infusion used to cure gout and urinary infections. Cato lived to the ripe old age of 85, an achievement that many attribute to his fondness for his self-prescribed farm tonics.

The oldest reference to juniper's use as a medicine takes us back almost 4,000 years, to Ancient Egypt. A number of important medical scrolls were written between 1800–1500 BC, including the Eber Papyrus and the Kahun Papyrus, the latter of which is the earliest known medical text in existence. Many of these treatments relied on a healthy measure of magic, chanting, or some very unusual ingredients (e.g. cat's fat), so suffice to say that they are not all as firmly rooted in scientific principle as each other. Juniper was used to treat digestive ailments, soothe chest pains and soothe stomach cramps. The Eber Papyrus lists a recipe that is used to treat tapeworms that calls for 'juniper berries five parts, white oil five parts, taken for one day.'

THE SPICE TRADE AND THE ORIGINS OF JUNIPER SPIRITS

When the distillation of wine was first discovered by European alchemists, the fiery, volatile liquid that emanated from the alembic still was dubbed *aqua vitae* (water of life). It was genuinely believed by Arnaldus de Villa Nova, a 13th-century professor from the University of Montpellier and the godfather of medical chemistry, to be a cure for mortality: 'We call it *aqua vitae*, and this name is remarkably suitable, since it really is the water of immortality. It prolongs life, clears away ill-humours, strengthens the heart, and maintains youth.'

The knowledge of distillation steadily disseminated through Europe, via monasteries and new-fangled universities, evolving in to regional variants, made from barley, grapes, rye and wheat. Over the coming centuries these distillates would graduate in to the spirit categories of whisky, brandy and vodka that we recognize today.

At some point, probably in the early 13th century, *aqua vitae* arrived in the Low Countries, an area comprising 17 individual states covering modern-day Holland, Belgium, Luxembourg, and parts of France and Germany. At that time the Low Countries were enjoying a prosperous period. Towns were designed and built from scratch, rather than being bodged together from existing settlements. Canals and waterways provided a broad and efficient trade network for goods and materials. The city of Antwerp, in its centre, was fast becoming a spiritual and intellectual hub, and by the middle of the 1400s, it was the richest city in Europe.

The population swelled as a result and it didn't take long for physicians, chemists and Cistercian monks to begin documenting the newest and trendiest findings in the world of science and alchemy. One of the earliest

of these comes from *Der Naturen Bloeme* by Jacob van Maerlant. Published in 1269. This work was a translation of a slightly earlier volume of books titled *Opus de Natura Rerum* (A Collection of Natural Occurrences) – by a theologian called Thomas de Cantimpré, who was born in 1201.

Spread over twenty volumes, and written entirely in rhyme, it took de Cantimpré fifteen years to write what was, at the time, probably the most exhaustive text on natural history in existence. An entire volume of the text is dedicated to medicinal plants and their various uses, and included within that is provision for boiled rainwater or wine containing juniper berries, used to treat stomach pain.

By the end of the 14th century, juniper wines and spirits were stocked in the medical cabinets of any physician worth their salt. A 1578 translation of Rembert Dodoens' *A Nievve Herbal* (A History of Plants) celebrates the juniper berry's properties as 'good for the stomacke, lunges, liver and kidneys: it cureth the olde cough, the "gripinges" and "windinesse of the belly", and "provoketh brine"'. The passage finishes with instructions, 'to be boiled in wine or honied water and dronken'. Thanks to books like *Constelijck Distilleerboet*, by Phillip Hermanni, an Antwerp-based physician, the knowledge required to make these spirits was in the public domain. Hermanni's 'distillation for doctors' handbook included a recipe for *geneverbessenwater* (juniper berry water) that saw the berries crushed, sprinkled with wine, and distilled in an alembic pot still. Hermanni goes on to describe how the liquid can

ABOVE This 1506 engraving depicts the alchemist and astrologer Arnaldus de Villa Nova picking grapes for wine.

be used for digestive disorders, colds, plague and to treat bites from venomous animals.

The 14th century also saw the first murmurings of a very important and necessary (for the purposes of this book) shift in the way that spirits were perceived and consumed. The first example of this in the Low Countries (where we would soon see the birth of genever) comes from a manuscript written by Flemish alchemist Johannes van Aalter, in 1351. The text was copied from an earlier piece, the author unknown, but the lucid appraisal of alcohol's social effects is quite uncanny: "It makes people forget human sorrow and makes the heart glad and strong and courageous."

For a well-motivated 15th-century alcoholic, spirits would soon become a quick and easy route to inebriation. By flavouring these *aqua vitae*, one could mask some of that rough-hewn temperament, offering a delicious in-road into botanical spirits. The fact that many of these so-called botanicals were also endowed with impressive medicinal benefits was just an added bonus. A change was clearly afoot and all the cogs were beginning to align.

The only problem now was that many of these fruits and spices were still quite expensive. Nutmeg, for example, was worth more than its weight in gold, and many of these products could only get to you via the complex spice trade routes that ran through the Middle East in to Europe via Constantinople and Venice. When the Ottoman Empire took control of Constantinople in 1453 they imposed huge levies on spices that passed through the city. It was demand for these spices (ginger, cassia, cardamom and pepper) that triggered the age of discovery, as European nations were forced to find new routes over sea to the sources of these commodities. They were incredibly expensive for an average European to purchase however, and any access outside of medical circles was rare and really only the preserve of the rich and powerful, which is what makes the next part of the story so incredible.

RIGHT The complex process of distillation as depicted in the 1519 book, *Liber de Arte Distillandi, Simplicia et Composita.*

BELOW Aided by good town planning, Antwerp was Europe's most prosperous city in the 15th century.

ANTVERPIA

THE BIRTH OF GENEVER

In 1495 a wealthy merchant from a region known as the Duchy of Guelders (now a part of The Netherlands, near Arnhem) decided it would be a good idea to have a book written for him. Being a household guide, the book documented some of the lavish recipes he and his family were enjoying at the time. Included was a brandy recipe made from '10 quarts of wine thinned with clear hamburg beer.' After distillation the liquid would be redistilled with 'two handfuls of dried sage, 1lb of cloves, 12 whole nutmegs, cardamom, cinnamon, galangal, ginger, grains of paradise' and – crucially – 'juniper berries.' The spices were placed in a cloth sack and suspended above the distillate, allowing the vapours to extract their flavour. Grinding diamonds over white truffle is as close a comparison as I can imagine to expressing the extravagance of such a recipe during that period. It's for this reason that it's highly unlikely that the drink was intended for anything other than sinful pleasures.

This was the dawn of a new era of spirits, where recreational delight superseded medicinal comfort. Juniper was cheap, readily available and tasty. It quickly assumed its modern role and became the poster-boy for the flavoured spirits movement.

LAWS & WARS

The early 16th century saw consecutively poor grape harvests in the Low Countries that lasted over two decades. The price of wine went up, so distillers turned to beer instead. The fermented grain mash of rye and malted barley quickly became known as *moutwijn* (malt wine) and its distillate, *korenbrandewijn* (grain burnt wine), which was later shortened down to *korenwijn* – a term that is useful to know when navigating genever styles. In English it's a common mistake to associate *korenwijn* with corn, but it can in fact be made from any cereal, and would not have been made with corn until at least the 1880s.

Any flavoured spirit made from flavoured *korenwijn* would adopt the name of its chief ingredient to avoid any confusion as to what it was. It's not known who first used the term genever (the French word for juniper) or if indeed anyone prior to 1495 had experimented with it. The van Dale dictionary, The Netherlands' equivalent of the Oxford English Dictionary, first listed the word (in reference to the drink) in 1672, but production of juniper spirits in Holland and Belgium had already been galvanized some 100 years prior to that.

The 16th century was a tumultuous time for the Low Countries. The year 1568 marked the beginning of what would later be known as the 80-years war. In the briefest of summaries, the war was a Protestant uprising centred around the Low Countries and aimed at their then sovereign ruler, Spain. During the considerable period over which the war lasted the city of Antwerp was eviscerated of its populous, as its panic-stricken residents fled to the north, to France, to neighbouring German cities, or to the safer towns of Hasselt and Weesp. Some 6,000 Flemish Protestants had already fled to London by 1570, paving the way for the genever/gin boom that followed later. The fall of

LEFT This reproduction of a copper engraving shows the sack of Antwerp by Spanish forces on 4th November 1576.

Antwerp in 1585 is seen by many as the turning point in relations between the northern and southern Low Countries, drawing a line in the sand between the areas that would one day form the Netherlands and Belgium.

Consistent with most wars of the era, next, inevitably, came a ban on distilling from fruit or cereal, imposed in 1601 by a government dealing with a very apparent national food shortage. The ban wouldn't be lifted until 1713, a full 112 years later. But the dictate was not recognized in the north, so for a down-on-his-luck distiller the northern towns posed a tempting prospect. As the south was torn apart, the new Dutch Republic in the north accepted swarms of skilled refugees from Antwerp, laying down the foundations of the 'Dutch Golden Age'.

EMERGENCE OF AN INDUSTRY

Many of the fresh-off-the-cart brewers and distillers gravitated towards Schiedam, a neighbouring city to Rotterdam, and a place whose name would become synonymous with spirits production over the next 200 years. Included amongst the folk on the move was a Flemish family by the name of Bols (meaning 'arrow'), who fled to Cologne initially, then eventually settled just outside of Amsterdam in 1575. They set up a distillery called 't Lootsje ('the little shed') and began making spiced spirits and liqueurs. Later, in 1664, they added genever to their portfolio. Bols is now the oldest spirits brand in the world.

Amsterdam gratefully took on the mantle of Europe's premier trading port and in 1602 the Dutch East Indies Company (VOC) was founded. More a roving nation than a business, the VOC would soon become the biggest company in the world, and with over 30,000 employees spread across the globe, the world's first multi-national corporation. The VOC traded in everything: spices, precious metals, tea, coffee, cotton, textiles and sugar. It also minted its own currency, waged wars, imprisoned slaves and established colonies. It turned Holland into a 17th-century superpower. Genever travelled to all the four corners of the world and was used for trading, or just to provide a familiar taste of home. Most Dutch sailors were entitled to between 150-200 ml (5–7 fl. oz) of genever every day. In the colonies it was popular too, where residents would down *soopjes* (shots) of colloquially named

The fable of Dr. Sylvius

Franciscus Sylvius de la Boe was a professor of medicine at Leiden University, Holland, between 1658 and 1672. During his time at the University, Sylvius cooked up no small quantity of juniper-based tonics, and prior to that he had worked as a plague doctor, where juniper had no doubt featured in his arsenal of preventive remedies. It's fair to say that Dr. Sylvius is historically one of juniper's most reliable advocates. Nowadays, however, he is widely and erroneously credited as the man who invented genever.

There are plenty of reasons why Sylvius couldn't possibly have been the inventor of genever, or juniper spirits. The previous pages of this very book can attest to the preliminary work of such things having taken place years before Sylvius appeared on the scene. The fact that Sylvius was only born in 1614 – late enough to have entirely missed the Flemmish spirits boom of the 16th century – should be proof enough, but just to be sure, it's worth pointing out genever was never mentioned in any of his surviving research, nor was he ever cited more than once regarding his distilling expertise. Oh, and did I mention he was German, born in Hanover?

Case closed.

proto-cocktails, like *papegaaiensoep* (parrot soup), *hap snert* (bite of pea soup) and *dikop* (fat head).

Spirits were stored by the barrel back then, meaning that all of the spirits distributed abroad, and most of those drunk at home, would have undergone some degree of barrel ageing. This would place them closer in style to a light whisky than a modern-day gin.

With the trade network established genever production in Holland boomed. Schiedam had 37 distilleries at the beginning of the 17th century, but it was more like 250 by the turn of the next. By the 1880s, there would be nearly 400 and the industry was employing over three-quarters of the city's 6,000 residents in milling, malting, brewing, distilling and barrelling. Twenty enormous windmills were the backbone of the Schiedam spirits machine, grinding the huge volumes of cereal that entered the city, piled high on Dutch flute boats that navigated along the

gridlocked river Nieuwe Maas. The tallest and widest windmills in the world were all in Schiedam at that time (a fact that remains to this day) grossly miss-proportioned in their efforts to capture their share of the city's breeze.

But the slick sheen of well a well-oiled industry also concealed a grave defilement of the city and its people. The coal-field distilleries polluted the air and died the city black – awarding Schiedam its label as the 'Black Nazareth' – off-spill from the still's condensers poisoned the water. And what with all that booze, alcoholism ensued, perpetuated by the squalid living conditions and low pay received by the distillery workers. Schiedam became a sprawling workhouse of industry, bolstered by a new global demand for genever.

Five original windmills can still be seen in Schiedam today. They are the five largest windmills in the world (the biggest, De Noord, is 33.3 m (110 ft) high) and have recently been joined by a sixth windmill that was rebuilt in 2011 on the site of an original 1715 mill.

THE FASHIONABLE
LONDON DRINK

The Dutch-born William of Orange (William III) arrived in England in 1688. His seizure of crown was a surprisingly peaceful affair in an otherwise bloody period of history. In fact parliament more or less propped the door open for him. The man he ousted, James II, the last Roman Catholic monarch to reign over the Kingdoms, was very much in the dog house as far as popular opinion went. Dethroned and desolate, James skulked off to Catholic France, and all things French became deeply uncool.

William's first act as King was to declare war on France, which included banning the import of French brandy outright. William also lowered taxes on cereals, earning him a big 'thumbs-up' from the landed gentry who owned most of the countryside, and loosened up the laws concerning distilling to encourage more people to buy home-grown grains. It was a wicked cocktail of policies and the result, as with any good cocktail, was total inebriation.

It's for the reasons above, along with William's Dutch origins, that he is often credited as the man responsible for making genever (and gin) fashionable in England. William's relaxing of the rules meant that more or less anyone could bag themselves a distilling licence with nothing more than an administration fee and ten days to see if anyone objected. Of course 'King Billy' (as he was known to the Scots) never intended the outright anarchy that ensued (he wouldn't live to see the worst of it) and to some extent he achieved what he set out to, but in the process condemned London to sixty years of drunken carnage.

But gin, or as it was still known then, genever, was already reasonably well established in London before William came along, in fact it was doing quite alright before William's father was born, too. Distillation was

not as widespread in England as other European countries like the Low Countries, but had long been the preserve of curious monks and crackpot alchemists as far back as the 14th century. Henry VIII's dissolution of the monasteries in 1534 forced great numbers of the well-informed monks from the sanctuary of their chapels out into the badlands of civilisation. Many of these learned men developed trades in activities consistent with their previous monastic practices: carpentry, weaving textiles, baking bread, brewing beer and distilling spirits. One hundred years after Henry VIII founded the Church of England there were over 200 distilleries in London.

It was during the Eighty Years War (1568–1648) that juniper spirits would have first appeared in

RIGHT London's lust for gin was in place before William III's accession. But his policies lit the fuse that ignited the gin explosion.

London taverns. In December 1585, Elizabeth I sent 6000 armed men to the Low Countries to provide support against Spanish forces. They failed to suppress the Fall of Antwerp, but during their time travelling and fighting alongside their Dutch comrades the English noticed the Dutch men partook in a certain strange ritual. This took the form of small bottles on their belts, like hip flasks, which they would customarily swig back before wading in to the battle. The English observed the courage exhibited by their Dutch compatriots, later coining the term 'Dutch Courage'. It wouldn't be the last time that the Dutch and English fought side by side. During the Thirty Years War (1618–1648), which was one of the bloodiest and nastiest in European history, the English and Dutch troops once again fought side by side in opposition to Spain and the Holy Roman Empire. On that occasion it's quite likely that both the English and the Dutch were knocking back bottles of 'courage'.

As is consistent with other parts of Europe, juniper spirits were also a favourite of English doctors and physicians. Gervase Markham's 1615 guide to household management, *The English Housewife*, included a recipe for eyedrops that featured juniper,

fennel and gromwell seeds. London's pre-eminent 17th-century chronicler, Samuel Pepys, wrote in 1663 that he had been advised by a friend to take 'strong water made from juniper' to cure a severe case of constipation.

But one of the earliest and perhaps improbable sources of early juniper spirits in England terminated not from the physicians table, but the kitchen table. Sir Hugh Plat (inventor and sometime hero of the housewife) published Delightes For Ladies, in 1602, which included a whole section dedicated to recipes for distilling in the home. One recipe, for a drink called 'Spirits of Spices' calls for 'cloves, mace, nutmegs, juniper, rosemary' in no specific quantities. This was mixed with 'strong and sweet water' then distilled over a bain marie or hot ashes. The result? According to Plat you can hope for a 'delicate spirit of each of the said aromatical bodies.' If we resist being too critical of the recipe, Plat's 'Spirits of Spices' could be regarded as England's first proto-gin.

BELOW This etching shows spirit drinking and pipe smoking in 17th-century Holland. The liquor wasn't to everyone's tastes, as the chap on the right would attest to.

GIN AT THE TURN OF THE 18TH CENTURY

While the likes of Plat and Markham served a purpose, at least as far as the enterprising housewife was concerned, England was in dire need of some practical instruction relating to the art of distillation. It arrived (almost exactly as requested) in 1692, in the form of The Whole Art of Distillation Practically Stated, by William Y-Worth. Y-Worth, an immigrant from Holland, made no bones about it: his was the only credible work concerning distillation available. Sadly, only one recipe in the entire book uses juniper, and the spirit is intended for medicinal purposes.

Following Y-Worth's book, The Distiller of London by Thomas Cademan was published in 1698. This distilling manual was actually a private handbook for London's Worshipful Company of Distillers. As a Livery Company of the City of London, this group was founded in 1638 to oversee and regulate the production of spirits in London. Caveman's book is an important one, because it lists a number of recipes (by number rather than name) which include juniper, and some where juniper is the chief ingredient. The recipes are often extravagant, incorporating expensive imported spices (such as nutmeg and cloves), dried citrus peels and fresh berries. They were labour-intensive too, but the eventual outcome would have been a product of exceptional quality for the period.

As the gin craze began to kick hard (page 23) things began to turn sour. The books that followed approached the subject of juniper and genever more cautiously. Ambrose Cooper's The Compleat Practical Distiller (1757) includes a simple recipe for gin that calls for 'three pounds of juniper berries, proof spirit ten gallons, water four gallons' which is distilled in the classic way.

The law meant it was cheap and easy to buy alcohol, and not difficult to produce some imitation genever. A lack of distilling expertise lead to the gin makers casually disregarding Dutch genever practices (including the all-important malt wine) and focus on infusing poorly-made neutral alcohol with botanicals, the latter to mask the impure and unpleasant flavour of the neutral spirits. Gin became as cheap as beer, but packed a much bigger punch. In time, the botanicals too would be considered an unnecessary expense.

In Cooper's book he also informs the reader that the 'common sort of gins' are made using oil of turpentine, a compound extracted from pine tree resin that bears some resemblance to the piney aroma of juniper. He seems more confused than disgusted by the this practice adding that, 'it is surprising that people should accustom themselves to drinking it for pleasure.'

'Common Gin' or 'Gineva' production was a two-part process in your average slum setup. No-one distilled their own spirit from scratch, so it first had to be bought in from a larger distillery. These distilleries would take beer and run it through pot stills a couple of times to make 'proof spirit'. This was a time before the continuous still had been invented, so the proof spirit would not be entirely neutral in its character, but quite likely entirely awful. A large chunk of this proof spirit came from Scotland, where the game was to run your still as fast as possible, heedless of any negative effects it might have to the taste or safety of your spirit.

Once the proof spirit arrived at your door, all that was left was to flavour it. The gentry were all drinking imported genever, so the smart move would have been to hash together some pseudo-genever of your own. Unfortunately botanicals were seen as time-wasting and expensive. Far better to compound salts, acids and toxic extracts in to your product, right? One gin recipe from the 1740s from the firm of Beaufoy, James and Co., doesn't even mention juniper: 'Oil of vitriol, oil of almonds, oil of turpentine, spirits of wine, lamp sugar, lime water, rose water, alum, salt of tartar.'

It was gin that fuelled the gin craze, but in its guise as inexpensive fire water, consumed without restraint.

LEFT When the River Thames froze over in 1814, you can bet that Londoners turned to gin and gingerbread to warm themselves up.

BELOW An 18th-century gingerbread seller displays his wares on the streets of Mayfair.

Not the aromatically balanced botanical spirit that we recognize gin as today.

It might have tasted bad, but that didn't stop tenacious types knocking it back. But not everyone swigged straight from the flagon. Mixing gin with sweet cordials, like peppermint or lovage, took the edge off and made a kind of pseudo-liqueur. Another one of the more popular ways of drinking gin was with a side helping of gingerbread. Ginger really was the flavour of London in the early 18th century (along with gin of course) largely thanks to colonies in India and the Caribbean doing a damn fine job of growing the stuff. This made ginger comparatively cheap compared to other spices and stalls selling fermented ginger beer lined many of the traditional market streets of London, like Petticoat Lane. In 1740 Joseph Stone, a prominent spice merchant based on High Holborn, loaned his name to the Finsbury Distillery Company, and Stone's Green Ginger Wine was born. But it was perhaps in the form of gingerbread, coupled with a measure of warm gin, that ginger truly excelled itself. When the Thames froze over and there was little else to do, other than spectate over executions and get drunk, it was gin and spiced gingerbread that filled a Londoner's belly.

THE BROKEN PROMISE

Britain's grand conquests abroad made London an enticing prospect for starry-eyed immigrants. But on their arrival in to London's docks reality would have hit quite hard. Those who brought a trade with them stood some small chance of a normal, honest existence. Those who didn't found themselves forcefully strained through convoluted layers of bedlam and poverty, coming to rest, broken and dejected, only once they reached the guts of one of London's inner-city slums. And it would be in the slums that 'gin' would rally its forces. It would be the sympathizer to the impoverished, and would lead to ruin for all of those who went near it.

THE GIN CRAZE

The word 'gin' didn't appear in the Oxford English Dictionary until 1714. Defined as 'an infamous liquor' it had clearly made its mark already. During the early days of the 'craze' gin was known as geneva or 'Madame Geneva'. Probably no coincidence that gin's entry in to the dictionary coincided with Bernard Mandeville's 'Fable of the Bees', a poem that was published in 1705, followed by a book, which first appeared in 1714. In his frank and detailed description of London's various vices and corruptions Mandeville gives us one of the earliest insights in to gin as a purely ruinous force, as well as one of the earliest uses of the word 'gin'.

'Nothing is more destructive, either in regard to the Health or the Vigilance and Industry of the Poor than the infamous Liquor, the name of which, deriv'd from Junipera in Dutch, is now by frequent use and the laconic spirit of the nation, from a word of middling length shrunk into a monosyllable, intoxicating GIN'.

Slowly at first but gathering pace, the overconsumption of gin became endemic, far removed from the blithe alcoholism associated with beer and wine, it was perceived by those lucky enough to escape its clutches as perfectly abhorrent. Gin was the widespread social drug of the time that preyed on the poor and vulnerable, gutting London from the inside out. Dr Stephen Hales, an anti-gin campaigner wrote in 1734 that 'Man, has unhappily found means to extract, from what God intended for his refreshment, a most pernicious and intoxicating liquor.' In the 1730s around five million gallons of raw spirits were being distilled in London every year, and less than 10% of it would ever leave the city.

The population of London as a whole was relatively stagnant between 1725 and 1750, but this was only due to the steady influx of migrants. The death rate in London during the mid-1700s exceeded the birth rate. In the worst areas, a newborn had less than an 80% chance of making it to the age of two. Many families were forced to live in single rooms in ramshackle tenements or in damp cellars, with no sanitation or fresh air. Drinking water was often contaminated by raw sewage and garbage was left rotting in the street. Problems with the disposal of the dead often added to the stench and decay. Many London graveyards became full to capacity, and coffins were sometimes left partially uncovered in 'poor holes' close to local houses and businesses. It's little wonder that the poor turned to gin as a release from the hardships of survival.

Imagine every single newsagent, store, supermarket and street vendor in central London turning their hand to selling gin. Then imagine that it's cheaper than bread or milk and that anyone can buy it: violent drunks, the elderly and infirm, children. Finally, imagine that it's not only highly addictive, but poisonous, laced with added 'flavour-enhancing' properties that when consumed in large quantities cause blindness, death or the loss of one's mind.

It's easy to imagine widespread turmoil throughout the entire city, but 'dramming' was really only centred around the poorest districts. In 1700 London had a population of 575,000, which made it the largest metropolis in Europe. While the residents of St Giles got drunk for (literally) a penny, the city could press on with business as usual, preoccupied and only vaguely aware of the horrors taking place around the corner. Gentleman, politicians, merchants and scholars wouldn't venture in to fleshpots of Holborn or Shoreditch. They would meet in nearby Cornhill to drink coffee and discuss politics, trade, the colonies, science or poetry. Perhaps some might have indulged in glass of gin on occasion, but it would be imported Holland's Gin, not the ghastly stuff produced in some squalid basement. The single biggest reason that the gin craze lasted so long and its effects were so brutal is ignorance of the upper classes to what was taking place under their noses.

If the gin craze was a storm then the area of St Giles in the Fields, near Charing Cross Road, was the centre of the deluge. Renowned as one of the country's biggest slums, for the 20,000 people living there gin

was a simple, cheap and accessible solution to all of their problems.

As you might expect, there is no shortage of harrowing stories from the period. As a researcher it becomes a macabre process of selection, sifting through the fallout and singling out the accounts that best represent the grim horror of the gin craze. William Hogarth's 'Gin Lane' etching might seem like a grizzly exaggeration of events, but the true plight of the people embroiled in the gin craze was perhaps even worse than his famous depiction (see right).

One of the most disturbing and notorious tales from the period is of Judith Dufour. In 1734 Dufour deposited her unclothed two-year-old daughter, Mary, at the workhouse where she was employed, then returned the following day to claim her. Now fully clothed, she stripped the child of her clothes, then strangled her to death, dumped her body in a ditch. She then sold the clothes for 1 shilling and 4 pence and used her earnings to buy gin.

Spare a thought too for Joseph Barret – a 42-year-old labourer, who was hanged in 1728 for beating his son to death. Barret's final confession is a harrowing account of how his son (James) spent his days begging for money and his nights 'drinking until

he appeared worse than a beast, quite out of his senses.' Barret apparently had 'no evil intention' and planned only to 'reclaim [James] from his wild courses.' Barret's punishment was too savage however, and James died in his bed. He was eleven years old.

By 1751 half of all the British wheat harvest was used to make spirits. There were reportedly 17,000 'private gin shops' in London and almost half of them were in Holborn. That's approximately one shop for every black cab in Greater London today. And that figure only represents the gin specialists! It doesn't include all the taverns and public houses that also sold gin by the bucket load. Neither does it include the street markets, grocers, chandlers, barbers, barrows and brothels that also did a roaring trade. Some estimates – and they can really only be estimates – suggest that over 10 million gallons of gin were consumed in London that year. A worthy effort for a population of only 700,000, helped along by the fact that many factory workers were partly paid in gin. Follow the maths down and you're looking at a pint of gin per week for every single London citizen. The novelist Henry Fielding argued that there would soon be 'few of the common people left to drink it' if the situation continued.

GIN LANE

Poets, playwrights and journalists turned their attention to the scourge, publicly voicing their concerns over the parasite that was gnawing at London's underbelly. It was in 1751 that William Hogarth unveiled his remarkable 'Gin Lane' etching. Burdened with ghastly imagery, the scene was designed to shock all who laid eyes on it, serving as a morbid checklist of gin's capacity to induce social decay, drunkenness, starvation, depression, violence, suicide, infanticide and madness.

The motives behind Gin Lane are a little more convoluted than the simple intentions a respected artist performing a much needed public service. The Treaty of Aix-la-Chapelle of 1748, marked the end of the War of the Austrian Sucession, the upshot of which would see the return of around 80,000 soldiers who had been fighting abroad. That's a lot of soldiers to feed and water, and knowing the ease with which fighting men could be drawn in to Madam Geneva's embrace, public tensions were strung tight. Hogarth produced Gin Lane and the sister piece, Beer Street, in response to the public's demand for another Gin Act (pages 26–27). There have been suggestions that Hogarth was in cahoots with the brewers, and that the pieces were pure propaganda, diverting the masses away from their demon water, and promoting the drinking of good, clean, honest beer. Either way, Gin Lane is the most prominent piece of satire to emerge from the gin craze, and one of the more effective weapons in gin's undoing.

Gin Lane is certainly worthy of a few minutes' close inspection, where the most observant amongst you will find countless sub-plots in the wider story of gin's destructive force. In the foreground we are naturally drawn to the image of the inebriated mother, cheerfully oblivious to the fact that she has dropped her child in favour of a snuff box. In front of her sits a skeletal man, clutching a flagon of gin and a ballad

entitled 'The Downfall of Madam Gin' – its objective plainly fallen by the wayside. Behind and to the right an elderly woman is fed gin from her position in a barrow, while a pair of St Giles orphans share a dram while people riot outside a gin distillery. The pawnbroker on the left of the scene is doing a roaring trade as the three-sphered sign doubles up as a cross above the distant Bloomsbury church spire. The message is clear: the people of Gin Lane have placed their faith in an altogether different kind of spirit. The middle distance is a picture of more tumultuous behaviour: dilapidation, death, and a man beating himself over the head with a pair of bellows while holding aloft a dead child on a spike. The detail of the composition even stretches to the silhouetted figures of a funeral procession working their way through the rubble at the far end of Gin Lane.

RIGHT The illustrations of George Cruikshank vilified the gin shops for their role in the moral and physical decay of the lower classes.

THE GIN ACTS

In the 1720s, the government finally took notice of the effect that London gin was having on its poorest inhabitants declaring that 'the drinking of spirits is… very common among the people of inferior rank and the constant and excessive use thereof tends greatly to the destruction of their healths, enervating them, and rendering them unfit for useful labour and service.'

The first of six Gin Acts, spread across a 30-year period, was made law in 1729, in the wake of the doubling of the spirit's production in the previous 10 years. The purpose of the First Act was to curb the manufacture and consumption of gin by imposing a higher tax of five shillings per gallon on 'compound waters'. The price of a retail licence also went up to £20 (US$30), around £1,800 (US$2,670) in today's money. Targeting the troublesome compounders should have been a good tactic, but the Act failed to deal with the two dozen-or-so distillers who were the ones making the spirit in the first place. It didn't work. Consumption continued to rise and taxes were left unpaid.

The second Act, in 1733, did away with extra duty on 'compound waters' and banned the sale of gin in the street altogether. If you were caught a £10 (US$15) fine would be imposed, and if you assisted in a conviction a £5 (US$7.50) reward would be granted. This was quickly followed by the Third Act, in 1736, which raised the fine for unlicensed retailers to £100 (US$150) and the fine for street-selling to £10 (US$15). The price of a licence more than doubled, to an exorbitant £50 (US$75), and a 20 shilling per gallon tax was applied to gin sold in small quantities. The cost was so extreme that it should have crippled compounding altogether. But only two applications for licences were ever filed. The trick now was not to get caught. Around 4,000 rewards were claimed over the next two years, but known informants were beaten bloody in the streets or thrown into the River Thames. One poor man was 'set upon an ass' and paraded down Bond Street while having stones and mud thrown at him.

Enterprising gin sellers developed new and elaborate methods to inconspicuously deliver their payloads to wanting customers. The best example of this is the 'Puss and Mew' contraption, pioneered by Dudley Bradstreet. These human-operated gin vending machines were denoted by a wooden carving of a cat on a wall. Those in need of a fix would approach the cat and whisper 'puss'. If anyone was listening, and gin was available (which it surely was) the response would come back 'Mew' to which the patron would place a penny in a drawer and gin would be dispensed out of lead pipe protruding out of the wall.

Soon though the number flouting the law was so tremendous that the time for discretion had passed. The next Act, in 1743, took a different tack. Duty on spirits was raised, but the cost of a licence was slashed to £1 (US$1.50) and the duty on compounded spirits was cut to a fraction of its previous rate. Anti-gin campaigners saw this as surrendering to popular demand but it had the desired effect, with thousands of licences issued over the following years. But this was not just about finding salvation for the lower class, the tax revenue was desperately needed to fund the war effort overseas. As the courtier Lord Hervey put it, 'This Bill

ABOVE In this 1829 etching by George Cruikshank, gin shop patrons don't realize that ruin, poverty and death surround them.

To those Melancholly Sufferers (by a late Severe Act) the DISTILLERS this Plate is most humbly Inscrib'd by a Lover of Trade.

The Funeral Procession of Madam Geneva Sep.r 29.1751.
Publish'd according to Act of Parliament.

Genera, Brandy, Rum, Arrack,

ABOVE A satirical funeral procession for Madame Geneva. But was she really dead?

is an experiment of a very daring kind… to find out how far the vices of the population may be made useful to the government [and] what taxes may be raised upon poison.'

The Fifth Act became the undoing of the fourth however as, in 1947, the ever-powerful distillers revolted and were granted £5 (US$7.50) licences and the opportunity to sell direct from shops. The effect was clear to see as, in 1950, gin consumption was nearing an all-time high.

Finally, in 1751, the Sixth Act was introduced, which successfully tackled all of the issues contributing to mass consumption. Distillers were banned from selling gin in shops, workhouses and prisons were

banned from distributing gin amongst their residents. Licence fees were doubled and were only granted to public houses. Perhaps the most effective blow was the withdrawal of rights to the distillers concerning debt collection. The distillers had, until then, had the full force of the law behind them when it came to unpaid invoices from compounders. The Fifth Act stated that debts of less than £1 (US$1.50) could no longer be legally recovered, so the prospect of dealing with these small-time operations, whose credit barely stretched beyond a few shillings, became quite unappealing.

THE GENTLEMEN OF GIN

The 1751 Gin Act suppressed the public appetite for gin by keeping check of the compounders' production capabilities. That alone might have been enough to keep Madame Geneva down, but disastrous grain harvests in 1757 meant that she wouldn't be getting back any time soon. As corn was held back for more important things (like food) its use in distilling was outlawed from 1757 through to 1760. That didn't stop distillers importing molasses, but trickle of liquor was a fraction of what it had been. By 1761 gin consumption in London was down to less than 20% of the level it had been ten years previously, at around 2 million gallons. By that time most of the small distillers and compounders with their limited buying power had already been squeezed out of the marketplace. The price of gin went up in reflection of the elevated production cost and the relative scarcity. Gradually the lower classes turned their attention to relative safety of beer and porter. The whole point of gin had been that it was cheap, but it wasn't cheap anymore. Now, if the gin category were to survive at all, the quality would have to go up.

Fortunately, Britain was on the cusp of the industrial revolution and it was time for gin to go industrial too. Emerging from the ruin of the gin craze, the first families of gin would establish themselves during this era. A name, rather than a brand, flagons of Booth's and Gordon's spoke of

reliability and accountability in a marketplace that had been previously full to the brim with anonymity.

Clerkenwell would soon become ground zero in London's next explosive phase of gin production. Named after the Clerk's Well (but also featuring the Skinner's Well and Sadler's Well) this area had been known since medieval times as the best source of clean water in all of London. It's for this reason that some of London's biggest breweries had already set up shop there. The Clerkenwell and Goswell Road proved popular with the distillers and rectifiers of the day.

One of the earliest purpose-built distilleries was John & William Nicholson & Co, who started making gin there in 1736, on St. John Street. Later, they acquired another distillery in Mile End and began producing their Lamplighter Gin, a product that would remain popular right up until the 1970s.

Langdale's on London's Holborn Hill was established in 1745. Langdale's Gin became extremely popular in London over the next few decades, although it was often diluted by bootleg sellers. Sadly the distillery was gutted on the sixth day of the anti-Catholic Gordon Riots of 1780.

The Booth family, who were established wine merchants as far back as the 16th century, added distilling to their repertoire in 1740. They built a distillery at 55 Cowcross Street in London, next to present-day Farringdon Station. From their base in Clerkenwell, Booth's grew to be the biggest distilling firm in the UK, and another distillery was built by Sir Felix Booth in Brentford, Essex, in 1817.

Booth's is currently owned by spirits giant Diageo, and as of 2006 is manufactured under the supervision of 'Booth's Distilleries of London' in Plainfield, Illinois. But putting the inconvenience of geography aside, Booth's is still the oldest gin brand in production today.

LEFT By 1900, the Gilbey's Distillery in London, covered over 8 hectares (20 acres) of land.

The year 1769 saw perhaps the biggest name in gin establish a distillery in Bermondsey, south London. Deciding it was better to keep his competitors closer, Alexander Gordon moved his entire operation to 67-68 Goswell Road in 1786. By the end of the 18th century Gordon's was producing over half a million gallons of gin from Goswell Road. Despite mergers with Tanqueray and a sale to the DCL, which went on to be known as Diageo, production remained on the same site at Goswell Road right up until the late 1980s (pages 139–143).

One of the oldest and most significant families of the age (at least as far as the history of gin is concerned) was Boord. The Boord distillery was built in 1726, just on the cusp of the gin craze proper. But it weathered the storm and later became famous for its brand of Old Tom gin which, in 1849 started to feature the 'Cat and Barrel' trademark on the label. Boord was actually the first gin to be trademarked and its use of the cat is thought to be the springboard for the Old Tom style of gin (page 71).

Now with respectable names on the bottles and a higher standard of liquid inside them, the idea of gin was slowly becoming more palatable to the public. For business operators, there was commercial value in making gin too, which meant that it was attracting the attention of distillers outside of London too.

James Stein (father of Robert Stein, inventor of one of the first continuous stills) installed a gin plant at his Kilbagie distillery in Fife, Scotland. New distilleries in Bristol, such as the one on Cheese Lane, which was established in 1761, leveraged the nearby docks which had historically handled the lion's share of Britain's wine and sherry imports. By 1825 Bristol would have five distilleries and if they weren't making gin themselves, they would certainly be selling the spirit on to be re-distilled as such. Similar things were going on in Liverpool. The Vauxhall Distillery was founded in 1781 by Robert Preston, followed by the Bank Hall Distillery, the original site being located very near the present-day Liverpool Gin Distillery in Kirkdale.

Meanwhile, in one of Britain's most important commercial shipping ports, Plymouth, one Mr. Coates joined the Fox & Williamson Distillery in 1793. He bought the operation some time after, renaming the distillery Coates & Co and began selling his own Plymouth Gin.

ABOVE The gentlemen of gin brought advertising clout, drawing attention to their (supposed) history and accolades.

THE RISE OF THE
GIN PALACE

As we move in to the 19th century, it's worth reviewing the drinking habits across the entire class spectrum at that time. The upper classes, free from the constraints of cost, continued to enjoy anything imported: wines, spirits, genever (or 'Hollands gins'), rum, brandy, and in the not-too-distant-future, cocktails. The high price of these products was often more about availability rather than quality, but being expensive they at least gave the illusion of quality and earned the imbiber some valuable ranking points amongst their peers.

The middle classes stuck mostly to ales and porter (notwithstanding the occasional imported spirit or liqueur, you understand) enjoying them in their taverns, public house and clubs.

For the poor, as Patrick Dillon's book *The Much Lamented Death of Madame Geneva* puts it 'Freed from the tyranny of Madame Geneva the poor seemed to eagerly embrace middle class virtues.' Beer had always been the drink of the poor, but the cut-price gin touted during the craze period had been an opportunity too great to miss out on. Following the gin craze, home-grown liquor options like gin and whisky were still many people's first (or only) available option, so consumption remained steady but not outrageous. Things were set to change, however, as the beginning of the 19th century saw the price of beer rise quite sharply.

This wouldn't have been too much of a problem if it weren't for some disastrous legislation in the pipeline (seeing a pattern here?). The early 1800s saw the British government fight a long and dirty war with smugglers and illicit distillers, many of whom were born into the game of making and moving contraband items into and around the country. Whisky smuggling was dealt with in the 1823 Excise Act, which successfully curtailed the 14,000 illicit operations thought to be operating in Scotland at the time.

Gin was next on the list and the solution came two years later, in 1825, when the government slashed the cost of a distilling licence and cut duties by a whopping 40%. This was partly in efforts to legitimize (and tax) all the illicit operations, and partly to ameliorate the economic impact of the grain surplus that Britain was experiencing. But with the lower classes already on the hunt for a high-strength, low-cost alternative to beer, it didn't take long before, with tails between legs, the poor flocked in the direction of their old friend Madame Geneva.

Between 1825 and 1826, gin consumption doubled from 3.7 million gallons to 7.4 million gallons. Once again, a pint of gin was cheaper than a pint of beer, and for the present time, even easier to get your hands on, too.

Distilleries caught on quickly and some bought up taverns in central London, which they fitted out with ornate panels of cut glass, gas lighting and long polished bars. Frequented by all classes save for the higher echelons, gin palaces became the grand meeting halls of apathetic gin drinkers, and the pit-stop for those after a quick fix or a 'flash of lightning' before heading home or on to the theatre.

Going on appearances alone, the gin palace was as far removed from the shady goings-on of a gloomy gin house as one could imagine, and a spectacular piece of 19th century mass marketing at the point of sale. From the outside, the gin palace must have appeared a jewel amongst the sooty gloom of London's urban landscape. The comparatively large frontage would be clad with plate glass windows adorned with stucco roses. Gas lamps hung from the walls and the signage was embellished with golden flourishes.

Appearances can be, and in this case, were, deceiving though. Looking every bit the sumptuous playground for pleasure seekers and gin connoisseurs, this gilded dram shop was more a toxic sump, an

RIGHT The gin palace was a melting pot of inebriety, where gin was stacked high and sold cheap with little concern for class, age or gender.

George Cruikshank

enabler, designed and built with large volumes of people, gin and profits in mind. Gin was stored in enormous wooden vats, which were stored above the bar, ready for administration to the poor creatures that jostled around, with children and animals underfoot, like cattle to a trough. Brandishing seductive names like 'Cream of the Valley' and 'Best Butter Gin', the marketing engine was hard at work. There were no seats. This was fast-food liquor. In truth, the gin palace was nothing more than a gin shop with a facelift. The product of a political mistake more than the need for decadent surroundings to drink in.

The popularity of the gin palace was as fervent as it was short-lived. The government corrected their legislative blunder in 1830, reducing the tax on beer, provoking a mass exodus from the gin palaces as the taverns and public houses resumed normal service. But the legacy of the gin palace persisted. Taverns upped their game, taking some design cues from the gin palaces and cutting the template for the Victorian pubs that can still be seen in London and beyond.

NEW STYLES EMERGE

By the mid-19th century, gin in England had, with heavy steps, left behind the turpentine-laced gut-rot of the gin craze, and settled upon the still-rough-around-the-edges-but-just-about-drinkable gin palace tipple. The 'gentlemen of gin' deserved a pat on the back. Salt of vitriol and alum were crossed off the shopping list in place of more 'natural' options like angelica root, which cemented the status of these dependable family-owned brands and improved gin's marketability no end. The gin palaces had been a nasty bump in the road in terms of category credibility, but no one could deny that they did a sterling job of placing the product in the consumer's hands. Now, if gin was going to have any kind of future challenging the superior character and quality of genever, sherry and brandy, it was going to have to face up to some hard truths.

Firstly, gin had always been a bit of a patch-up job in that botanicals were used as an 'air freshener' to cover up the 'bad smell' of the base spirit. The production methods of the base spirit hadn't evolved in three centuries. It was still produced in batches using large pot stills and little consideration was given to how it actually tasted. Dealing with the problem at the root was needed, so the pursuit of a higher-quality base spirit that could be produced at scale became a driving force for many entrepreneurial distillers of that time.

One of the first of these was French chemist Edouard Adam, who developed and patented the first type of column still in 1804. Unrecognizable from previous stills, Adam's column was a horizontal arrangement that linked together a series of what Adam called 'large eggs', with pipes that would route alcohol vapour from one to the next. The strength of the spirit increased in each subsequent egg, whilst the leftover stuff was recycled back at the start again.

Next came the Pistorius Still, patented in 1817, which was the first still to be arranged in a column shape. Steam was pumped up from the bottom and beer from the top and distillation took place on a series of perforated 'plates' arranged through the length of the column. This design worked best because it allowed for a smooth graduation of temperature change from higher at the bottom to lower at the top. Since ethyl alcohol boils at exactly 78.3°C (172.9°F), in theory you could extract spirit vapour off the column at a height that corresponded to that temperature and capture a very high-strength spirit, leaving most of the (undesirable) residual flavour behind.

Subsequent iterations were developed by the French engineer Jean-Baptiste Cellier Blumenthal and then Robert Stein, who owned the Kilbagie Distillery in Fife, Scotland. By 1830 the final design had been settled upon, fully realized in a design patented by the Irish excise officer, Aeneas Coffey. The 'Coffey Still' or 'Patent Still', as it would be later known, was a truly continuous process, where beer was pumped in and high-strength alcohol drawn off. It was quite energy-efficient for its time, using the cool pipes that fed beer in to the system as condensing coils for the hot alcohol vapours exiting it. It was a work of genius for its time, so much so that the basic design is used all over the world today. Coffey's company was registered in 1835, but later, in 1872, under the management of Aeneas' son, Aeneas, the company was handed over to the site foreman, John Dore. John Dore & Co. continue to make stills today, awarding them the title of the 'oldest manufacturer of distillery equipment in the world'.

The promise of a higher-strength, more neutral-tasting base spirit, was the secret to the next stage of the evolutionary process. Better spirits meant that fewer botanicals were needed in the cover-up job and it also meant that less sugar — which was by no means cheap at the time — was required. Gin would become drier, more delicate and — dare I say it — aromatic. And good gin couldn't have come at a better time either. Genever from both Holland and Belgium was under a trade embargo during the Napoleonic Wars (1803–1815), so Britain was forced to turn to native options.

It was around this time that England's first truly credible gin style emerged: Old Tom. Steeped in legend (quite literally as some might have you believe) this style could be described as a slightly more botanical heavy, and perhaps slightly sweeter, 'cordial', version of the London Dry Gins that we drink today. Theories on the Old Tom name are bounteous and colourful, including a tall tale of a tom cat falling into a vat of gin, imparting its 'flavour' in its death throws and lending Old Tom another slang name, 'cat's water'. The more plausible claim for the name comes from Hodge's Distillery in the London Borough of Lambeth. The proprietor was one 'Old' Thomas Chamberlain, who helped fund the opening of a gin palace in Covent Garden. The owner was Thomas Norris, a former employee at Hodge's. Norris bought a particular recipe from Chamberlain, which was reserved only for his top customers. Norris's gin palace kept it in big barrels above the bar marked with 'Old Tom's Gin'. Old Tom would go on to become a catch-all term for the style of gin that was drunk during that time.

Adulterations Detected, an 1857 manual on how to detect fraudulent spirits compares recipes for both London and Plymouth gins, where the recipe for 'Plain or London Gin' includes '700 gallons of the second rectification, 70 lbs German juniper berries, 70 lbs coriander seeds, 3.5 lbs almond cake, 1.5 lbs angelica root, 6 lbs liquorice powder' whereas 'West Country Gin, known as Plymouth Gin' is made from the same quantity of spirit and only '14 lbs German juniper berries, 1.5 lbs calamus root and 8 lbs sulphuric acid'. The London Gin recipe appears, at first, to be closer in style to the gins we drink today and would certainly have produced a more concentrated product. But it's possible that, even though both recipes contain no sugar at all, the London Gin would seem more like an Old Tom than a London Dry thanks to its high concentration of botanical ingredients. Plymouth omits the sweet botanicals, but also uses less juniper too, which gives weight to the brand's claim of being the world's first 'dry gin'.

New distillation methods did not go unnoticed in Holland and Belgium. In 1830, a revolt by the southern Low Countries established the borders for modern-day Belgium and The Netherlands. The first move of the sovereign Belgian government was to ban the importation of genever from Holland and lower taxes on their own home-brew. Belgium was finally entering a well-earned genever renaissance after 250 years of war, embargo, prohibition and underrepresentation.

The Belgians were quick to adopt new practices, such as Cellier Blumenthal's column still, and

ABOVE This magazine advert from the 1920s makes it clear which version of the Old Tom story it's going for.

production capability quickly reached eye-watering levels. The late, great Meeus Distillery, established in Antwerp in 1869, could output 50,000 litres (13,200 US gallons) of spirit a day. 1912 saw an all-time record of 100,000,000 litres (26.4 million US gallons) of Belgian spirit flow off the stills. To put that in to context, it's roughly the same volume of liquid as Gordon's, Tanqueray, Beefeater and Bombay Sapphire sold together in 2014.

The Dutch on the other hand were slower to adopt the distillation column, which meant their product still relied heavily on malt wine and sat very much in the Oude style, for now at least. Fortunately, the Dutch were pretty good at making malt wine, so good, in fact, that English, German and French distillers imported it for use as the base for their own spirits and liqueurs. The 20th century would be a very unkind period for genever, however, with the Great Depression and World Wars around the corner.

GIN IS JUST THE TONIC

To discover the distant origins of the G&T, we must first investigate the roots of tonic water, or the 'bark' of tonic water, to be more specific. Tonic is little more than sweetened and acidulated fizzy water, but it contains one key ingredient: quinine. Quinine is an effective painkiller, a good antipyretic (fever-reducer) and a particularly proficient antimalarial.

Quinine is naturally produced by the *Cinchona* tree. There are 90 or so varieties of this red-barked tree, which also happens to be a relative of the coffee tree. Peruvian cinchona bark was first brought to Europe in or around 1631, during a time when even the best medical minds were completely clueless when it came to both the cause and treatment for 'marsh fever' or 'the ague' as malaria was then called.

The miraculous story of cinchona's discovery goes something like this: some time in the early 17th century, the Countess of Chinchón, the wife of the Viceroy of Peru, became very sick with tertian fever (a form of malaria that recurs every second day). The

Countess was a popular celebrity of her day so this spelled bad times for Peru, and stories of the Countess' sickness spread from Lima through to other colonies, including the Andean hill town of Loxa. The Prefect of Loxa travelled to Lima, met with the Viceroy and prescribed a special remedy to the Countess, derived from the bark of an indigenous tree. The countess recovered and the tree from which the bark originated was renamed 'cinchona' in her honour.

There's only one tiny problem with that story, though: it's a complete fabrication. Indeed, the Countess was never even ill in the first place, that is, until she died suddenly in 1641 on a trip to Madrid. Detailed diaries left by the Viceroy's secretary make very little reference to malaria at all, and offer no clues of magical remedies made from tree bark.

Another possible scenario sees the Incas passing on their knowledge of the tree (under duress, or otherwise) to the Spanish conquistadors. The best and oldest reference we have to cinchona's medicinal properties comes from an Augustinian Friar by the name of Antonio de la Calancha, who wrote in 1638: 'A tree grows which they call the fever tree in the country of Loxa whose bark, of the colour of cinnamon colour, made into powder to the weight of two small silver coins and given as a beverage cures the fever and tertianas; it has produced miraculous results in Lima.'

Another priest, Bernabé Cobó, wrote a similar account the following year, describing the tonic as 'a bit coarse and very bitter' and advising that 'those powders must be taken […] in wine or any other liquor'.

What we know for sure is that by the turn of the 18th century, cinchona bark powder was being used widely as an antimalarial drug, often being added to wine and sherry to mask its intensely bitter flavour. Bernardo Rammazzini was the chief physician to the

LEFT Cinchona revolutionized the art of medicine and gave us tonic water for our gin!

Duke of Modena, and in 1707 he wrote that 'Cinchona revolutionized the art of medicine as profoundly as gunpowder had the art of war.'

The Spanish controlled all of the world's supply of quinine up until the 19th century, and it wasn't until the Dutch managed to plant trees in Java, and the British in India, that the medicine became widely available among the colonies. Quinine was first isolated in France, in 1820, and quinine pills were made available by the Philadelphia-based firm Rosengarten & Sons, in 1823. For most people, this advancement meant a huge sigh of relief, as it eliminated any need to drink the bitter tonic any longer. But by that time British troops in the Indian colonies had already developed a work-around. By mixing their tonic with sugar and gin, the whole thing became not just tolerable, but enjoyable. West Indian workers digging out the Panama canal half a century later did a similar thing, mixing their quinine pills with pink lemonade and gin. This would have seemed every bit the double-bonus in the eyes of the recipients. Gin was still regarded as a health drink in the 19th century. Not a cure-all, but perhaps equivalent to a daily dose of multivitamins. In 1890, The London Medical Recorder made no bones about where they stood on the matter, 'Our attention has been recently called to the "Original Plymouth Gin". As this Medical Recorder will circulate amongst the profession in India, we have no hesitation in calling attention to its value for medicinal, as well as general use.'

Erasmus Bond marketed the first commercially-available tonic water brand in 1858. He was quickly followed by Jean Jacob Schweppe, who had previously launched the world's first carbonated water in 1770. Schweppes original seltzer waters were available in no less than five varying degrees of fizziness, each purported to offer different medicinal benefits. Schweppe's have been masters of fizz for nearly 250 years now.

When I first explored making my own tonic water, back in 2004 (pages 189–190), the only mixers available in the UK came from Schweppes and Britvic. There are now over a dozen options that are readily available to buy online or in supermarkets. The growth in this category began with the launch of Fever Tree, who quite rightly recognised that 'when ¾ of your gin and tonic is tonic, make sure you use the best'. Whether the best tonic is Fever Tree or another brand is a

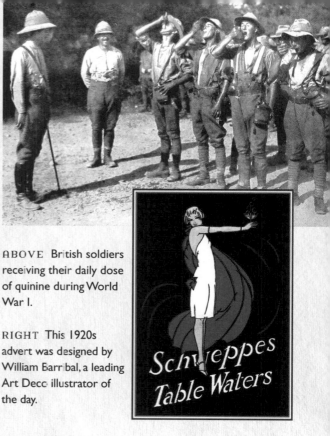

ABOVE British soldiers receiving their daily dose of quinine during World War I.

RIGHT This 1920s advert was designed by William Barribal, a leading Art Deco illustrator of the day.

Schweppes Table Waters

subjective matter – the refreshing reality of the situation may be that there isn't a one-size-fits-all tonic brand and that, just as each gin has a unique botanical profile, so too does it have an ideal tonic partner. An antidote to match the poison, if you like – but it would be Fever Tree and East Imperial (which has quite possibly the best standalone flavour) that get crosses on my ballot paper. With 'craft tonic' in high demand, and bartenders coming under increasing pressure to diversify their tonic water stocks, the natural evolution was flavoured tonic water. You can now take your pick from familiar sounding and naturally fitting flavours as elderflower, lemon and liquorice/licorice or the more esoteric options like 'Mediterranean' and 'herbal'. Amazingly, cinchona trees remain the only economically practical source of quinine, and even cut-price brands of tonic water are still made from quinine extracted from cinchona bark.

But perhaps one of the most unrecognized factors in choosing good tonic is how damn fizzy the thing is. Ice and gin will suck the fizz right out of your tonic, and in my option no other brand can match Schweppes for sheer face-melting carbonic impact – impossible volumes of CO_2 tenant every bottle.

A PUNCH AND A KICK

By the time Harry Craddock's *The Savoy Cocktail Book* was published in 1930, gin had become the most dependable weapon in the cocktail bartender's arsenal. Craddock's 'masters thesis' lists 750 cocktail recipes and over half of them contain gin of one sort or another: gin; dry gin; Plymouth gin; and Old Tom gin. Martinis were in full flow, Slings in full swing, and Fizzes showing no signs of fizzling out. Gin was experiencing its golden age.

But it hadn't been all plain sailing to get there. Gin's graduation to cocktail stardom featured all the distasteful experiences and dirty encounters of any awkward adolescent period. Hampered by the inconvenience of being a second rate product, and used to ill-effect in various examples of early bartending explorations, gin was by no means the original cocktail spirit – that honour went to brandy and whisky – but it was perhaps the bartender's most capable test subject.

George Cruikshank

The punch pre-dates the cocktail by at least 200 years, but 'Gin Punch' would have a somewhat oxymoronic term in the 18th century. Punch, which contained such lavish ingredients as lemons and oranges shipped in from Asia, spices and sugar from the Caribbean colonies, as well as imported brandy or rum, was, at up to 8 shillings a bowl, very expensive indeed. English gin, on the other hand, was the widely abused crack of the scrabbling masses, and as we have already learned, incredibly cheap to boot. Needless to say, throwing gin in to a punch was an act of madness, like dropping a spoon of heroin in to a glass of Burgundy. But they did it, and in doing so opened up the world of punch to a whole new middle class audience who were happy to fit the 1 shilling bar tab for a tainted taste of high society. There are no known recipes for Gin Punch from the 18th century (a fact for which we should probably be grateful) but since gin punch may have been mixed from either imported Holland's gin or inferior English gin the intended purpose of the concoction seems to have varied widely. One English journal from 1749 suggests that Gin Punch (made, presumably, on this occasion from English gin) might not have even been fit for human consumption, recommending that a 'hornful of gin punch' be used in a recipe that cures 'distemper among cattle'. References to its use in non-bestial medicine become more frequent towards the end of the 18th century, where gin punch is used to treat kidney stones, promote perspiration, fix weakness, cure beriberi (nutritional deficit) and many other things besides.

Higher quality punches were of course available and it's more likely that the punch consumed in 1776, by James Boswell, the Scottish lawyer and biographer of Samuel Johnson, was made from the imported stuff. Boswell wrote in his diary a favourable account of a nighttime encounter with gin, and more specifically with, the gin punch, 'I drank rather too much

LEFT The frightfully agreeable and convivial goings-on of a punch bowl caucus room.

gin punch. It was a new liquor to me, and I liked it much.'

As the Georgian period drew to a close and the gin palaces opened for trading, we begin to see recipes penned for gin punch. The earliest of these come from neither the gin palaces nor the physician's handbook, however, but from London's tobacco-stained gentlemen's clubs like Limmer's Hotel and the Garrick Club and, curiously, from Oxford University.

Oxford Nightcaps (1827) was a 30-page pamphlet commissioned by Oxford University, which lists various weird and wonderful recipes. It has a strong case for 'the world's first cocktail book' – or book dedicated only to mixed drinks – and in it we encounter a recipe for 'Gin Punch' made using 2 pints of gin, oranges, lemons, capillaire (a kind of sugar syrup aromatized with orange flower water) and white wine. That's it. Nothing out of the ordinary there… oh, wait… it also called for calves-feet jelly, which was a kind of primitive gelatine substitute made from boiling up the feet of baby cows. Delicious.

A more approachable drink came in the form of the Garrick Club Punch, which emanated from the Leicester Square club of the same name that opened in 1831. The club's manager, an American by the name of Stephen Price, was an early advocate of iced soda water, which would have seemed a strange combination at the time, as David Wondrich notes in *Punch* (2011) 'soda water [was] a popular hangover cure… seen as an antidote to punch, not an accomplice.' The Garrick Club Punch recipe – which includes 'half a pint of gin, lemon peel, lemon juice, sugar, maraschino, a pint and a quarter of water, and two bottles of iced soda water' – was published in *London Quarterly* in 1835 and over the years that followed it became an international sensation, laying the foundations for the Limmer's Punch and eventually the John Collins and Tom Collins single-serve equivalents that took America by storm in the 1870s.

There are eight recipes for Gin Punch in William Terrington's *Cooling Cup and Dainty Drinks* (1869) including the Punch 'à la Garrick' and Terrington's own 'Gin Punch à la Terrington', which replaces Maraschino in the Garrick Club Punch with Green Chartreuse. Here is a book that was clearly intended only for those with some serious capital to dispose of on their drinking pleasures, listing such luxury commodities as pineapple syrup and green tea, and

ABOVE The Garrick Club was 'where actors and men of refinement and education might meet on equal terms'. They also drank punch.

even going as far as to distinguish between German seltzer water, 'aerated lemonade' and Vichy water, then providing instructions on how to make and source various types of ice. Terrington's inclusion of gin in the book is a striking indicator of how much the English gin category had accomplished in the decades that precede the book. And his specification of 'good unsweetened gin' leaves us with little doubt that this was probably not genever, but English gin. The shift from sweet through to dry, in England at least, was finally gathering pace.

The punch bowl served as the perfect societal seasoning to witty, high-spirited gatherings among friends, and genial discussion on politics with business associates. Punches scribed out a playing field on which the sport of mixing drinks could be enjoyed, but the invention of the cocktail put an end to it being a team game. Despite featuring a good array of punch drinks, both Terrington's book and *Jerry Thomas' Bartender's Guide* focused more on the single serve punch than their predecessors did, before deviating entirely to cocktails, which would be the modus operandi for cocktail authors over the next 50 years. There's a certain sadistic pleasure that can be taken in witnessing the manifestation of one's own, personal drink through the deft movements of a trained bartender. And so it was that the future of mixed drinks lay not in the murky waters of the English punch bowl, but in the icy embrace of an American cocktail glass.

THE AMERICAN DRINK

America stuck to genever for most of the 19th century. This was thanks, in part, to the large numbers of Dutch immigrants (Manhattan was New Amsterdam before it was New York), bringing their higher-quality spirit and superior distilling skillset with them. During the 19th century, five times as much 'Holland's Gin' was imported in to the US compared to English gin. The gin distilleries that were established in the US during this time followed suit, and mostly copied the 'Holland's Gin' approach, even labelling their product as such, which on more than one occasion landed them in legal bother. America needed gin, as a growing trend towards cocktails, thanks in part to the availability of ice from the 1830s and the invention of the cocktail shaker in the 1840s, meant that America was thirsty. That most patriotic of American spirits, whiskey, was

top of the mixing list, followed closely by imported brandy, but gin distilleries sprung up too to meet demand and establish a market, and by 1851 there were six distillers in Brooklyn, producing a combined 2.9 million gallons of grain spirit, most of it destined for rectification into gin.

The American distilling manual, *Hall's Distiller* (1813), which boasts an entire chapter on 'Full and particular directions for imitating Holland's gin', provides us with an insight into the state of gin and genever in America during the early 19th century: 'The use of spirits of turpentine has unfortunately become too common, and is one great cause of the badness of American gin', then asking 'why can we not make gin equal to Holland? The superiority of their gin is generally attributed to some secret, known only to themselves.' In the book, Hall offered detailed practical advice to distillers on how best to adjust their practices towards the Dutch style.

In 1870, the first dry gin distillery opened in North America. It was founded by Charles and Maximilian Fleischmann, a Czech family of distillers and brewers who emigrated to the US in the 1860s. Based in Cincinnati, Ohio, the brothers had already became quite famous for their compressed yeast, and became the biggest yeast manufacturer in the world. Charles' son, Julius, became Mayor of Cincinnati at 28, and their gin, along with every other branch of their rapidly growing empire, enjoyed great success. The gin is still available today, and owned by the Sazerac Co.

The switch to dry gin in America was ploddingly gradual. The earliest cocktail books, like *Jerry Thomas's The Bartender's Guide* (1862), specified 'Holland's gin' and 'Old Tom', but where no specification is made one can be assured that genever was the implied ingredient. And I'm talking proper genever, 100% malt wine, with no short-measure oak influence in the mix. For the contemporary, conscientious bartender, whose

LEFT American brands like Fleischmann's were liquid proof of the nation's shift towards drier, steely spirits.

profession relies on an understanding of the flavour profile of classic cocktails like the Gin Fizz and Tom Collins, this revelation throws everything into disarray, fundamentally altering these bastions of the cocktail world. As spirits writer David Wondrich notes, 'This makes perfect sense: in the days before the dominance of the Dry Martini, when gin was drunk in slings, simple punches or cocktails (the original kind, with bitters and sugar), the mellow, malty roundness of the "Hollands", as it was known, was preferable to the steely sharpness of a London Dry Gin, or even an Old Tom, which stood somewhere between the two styles.'

Harry Johnson's Bartender's Manual (1888) has 19 gin drinks, 11 that call for Hollands, eight with Old Tom. One of those eight is for a 'Martine Cocktail', which is considered by many to be a typo on the 'e', and therefore the first recipe for a Martini (page 186). William Schmidt's *The Flowing Bowl* (1892) has 11 genever drinks in it and only five with Old Tom, and by 1908, the transformation to dry was in full flow, with the publication of Bill 'Cocktail' Boothby's *The World's Drinks and How to Mix Them*, which featured nine genever drinks, nine Old Tom drinks and six drinks that called for 'dry gin'.

The Volstead Act of 1919 brought about national prohibition in America between 1920–1933 and forced the closure of thousands of saloons, cocktail bars, breweries and distilleries. It could have marked the end of the cocktail, and it certainly set the American cocktail back by a decade or so, but it also forced it to become a global entity, as talented bartenders exported their trade to Europe and beyond. The upshot of this sudden and imperative propagation of knowledge and skill elevated bars like those at The Savoy and The Café Royal in London and The Ritz in Paris to historic

standards. The bartenders who ran these operations became the next generation of superstar drinks mixers, and the names of Harry McElhone and Harry Craddock secured their positions in drinking history.

The early 20th century saw the conception of some of the classic gin cocktails, like the Bronx (1905), the Dry Martini (1906) and the Aviation (1916). Then, in Europe and abroad, the Negroni (c. 1920), the Singapore Sling (c. 1922), the Hanky Panky (c. 1925) and the Pegu Club (c. 1927).

From British gin's perspective, prohibition was not all bad news. Determined distillers explored new means and ways of bootlegging their product on to US soil, fuelled by a desire to secure the gin industry (which by this time had become heavily reliant on the lucrative American market) while at the same time scoring valuable kudos points that would be cashed in during the 1930s when Gordon's and Gilbey's both established distilleries on American soil. Prohibition saw enterprising smugglers transport gin by way of the Bahamas and Canada, but the risks involved meant that product fetched a high price. Meanwhile, those who couldn't gain access to the contraband product, or couldn't afford it, set about making their own. Gin was the obvious DIY candidate, as history had already proven, so turpentine once again assumed the role of the juniper berry, and bathtubs the role of the still.

GIN'S DARK AGE

The return to cocktails after prohibition was an uneasy experience for Americans. Prohibition had brought out the worst in drinkers, and forced them to explore the depths of drinking depravity that they never would have thought possible. How could things go back to the way they were when all the artistry of the cocktail had been so easily forgotten? America sought shelter in that most trusted and iconic of all cocktails, the Martini. The 'Cocktail Hour' was conceived, or rather concocted, in an effort to encourage Americans back into bars and ordering cocktails. Even though the Martini was experiencing its glory days, and would continue for some time to do so, even after World War II, the creativity and showmanship of the bartender was nowhere to be found. Not a single decent gin cocktail was invented between 1935 and 1980. But for the time being, gin had bigger problems to contend with.

World War II saw restrictions on the sale of spirits imposed across all sides of the Atlantic Ocean. In Great Britain, gin distilleries were requisitioned to produce industrial acetone, which was used in the manufacture of cordite, an essential propellant used in shell and rifle cartridges. Rather fittingly, the best product to extract acetone from is that most lethal of playground weaponry, the horse chestnut, or 'conker'. In the US, many distilleries were seized and repurposed to produce industrial alcohol to use as fuel for submarines' torpedoes, although some would argue that the American whiskey industry benefitted greatly from a few extra years of maturation in their casks. Despite Belgium and The Netherlands' early attempts to remain neutral during World War II, much of the copper in their stills was seized by the invading Nazi forces and used for the manufacture of munitions. Some distilleries employed ingenious

tactics to protect their equipment. Filliers (pages 156–157), for example, hid their copper in nearby lakes to keep it safe from the German war effort.

In Belgium, a radical ban on selling genever in Belgian bars as a means of combating excessive alcohol consumption was enforced in 1919. It would go on to last for a remarkable 66 years. This coincided with the US embarking upon their 'noble experiment' that saw Prohibition law imposed for a full 13 years. The Belgian genever ban more closely mirrored the absinthe ban of 1915 in France, however, where the government took the misguided approach of victimising and driving out the most popular drink, blind to the fact that alcoholics will drink anything they can get their hands on. With no genever available the Belgians turned to beer instead.

RIGHT The end of Prohibition saw drinkers return to bars, but the damage was done – the cocktail's golden era was coming to an end.

But genever's loss was beer's gain, and it was during this period that the Belgian beer industry rose up to become the best in the world, as it still remains today. It seems incredible that entire generations of drinking-age Belgians lived out their lives with very limited access to their country's national spirit.

The memory of Belgian genever began to fade from the minds of drinkers, both at home and beyond the country's borders, while the Dutch spirit surged on in popularity. It's for this reason that we tend to associate genever with The Netherlands, rather than Belgium. Having said that, in time the Dutch too would stumble. Aggressive genever price wars during the late 1960s caused the industry to cannibalize itself, forcing distillers to cut corners and ultimately allowing the jonge style to rise as the victor.

In the UK, Brits turned back to the G&T, but it quickly fell out of fashion through the 1960s, replaced by cheap and sweet continental wines, blended scotch and sherry. The G&T became the preserve of the aristocracy, the perception being that they were only consumed at garden parties, on board yachts, or on the occasion that 'one' visits the queen for afternoon tea. Meanwhile, in America, drinkers once again returned their attentions to the Martini, which had become consistently drier over the past couple of decades.

The post-war drinking milieu was reflected in the progressive changes in culture that the war had brought about. Sweet and flabby Old Tom was fast becoming old-hat, and its exit made way for the stiff and steely London Dry style – named after the city which first campaigned the style – and it became the new hero of the highball. But the legend was short-lived, as a new player was about to enter the game.

Just like Ian Fleming's legendary secret-service agent who helped to make it famous, vodka was packed full of delicious anonymity and seasoned with no short measure of thrilling danger. Coinciding neatly with the Cold War period, Russian vodka offered something exotic and non-conformist to the latest generation of drinkers. Brands such as Smirnoff first landed on American shores in the 1940s, sporting the marketing tag line 'It leaves you breathless', a clever ploy aimed as much at those wishing to conceal a sneaky drink under odourless breath, as it was to those people looking for a

ROD ALEXANDER AND BAMBI LYNN DOBS, ROD ALEXANDER

IT LEAVES YOU BREATHLESS! Let nobody try to tell you all vodkas are the same! There's only one flawless Smirnoff. Charcoal-filtered to incomparable smoothness, Smirnoff has virtually no taste of its own. It never "takes over" in your drinks. It leaves no whisper of liquor on your lips. Make sure you get Smirnoff, the *Vodka of Vodkas*. At liquor stores, settle for nothing less. At bars, just mention our name!

Smirnoff
THE GREATEST NAME IN **VODKA**
80 AND 100 PROOF. DISTILLED FROM GRAIN. STE. PIERRE SMIRNOFF FLS. (DIVISION OF HEUBLEIN), HARTFORD, CONN.

ABOVE Vodka was the white warrior, the Soviet slayer, the faceless phantom. It exploded during the 1950s.

stimulating social lubricant. The campaign had the desired effect, and vodka sales in the US increased 100-fold between 1950 and 1956, from 40,000 cases to an eye-watering 4 million cases. Vodka was leaping past gin and, in time, would go on to surpass even whiskey too.

And so the battle was lost. Gin was perceived to be old-fashioned and its marketing had been comprehensively outclassed. Even though sales remained steady in America throughout the 1970s and 1980s, there was no question that this period of the 20th century belonged to vodka. All that was left was for gin to hunker down, assess the damage, watch and wait. Its time would come again.

THE RETURN OF GIN

These days gin remains a quintessentially British drink, although it is probably with the English that the strongest association lies. According to the International Wine & Spirit Record (IWSR) though, Brits are not the biggest consumers of gin – we quaffed a paltry 400 ml/13½ fl. oz. of gin per person in 2014. If, like me, you're known to put away similar quantities on a single afternoon, you may be surprised by that figure, but still, it places us (I am a Brit) at 5th in the world per capita.

In 4th place is Spain, which has, for some time, been an important market for premium gin brands like Beefeater and Tanqueray. In 3rd place is The Netherlands where roughly one standard 70-cl (24-fl. oz.) bottle is consumed per person, per year. Then it's Slovakia in 2nd with 1.2 litres (41 fl. oz.) per person. First place goes to the mighty Philippines, who drink more gin by volume than any other nation, drowning in a very respectable 1.4 litres (47 fl. oz.) of gin per person every year – around six times that of the USA. (If all this is beginning to sound a bit boozy keep in mind that the Russians put away a whopping 14 litres (3⅔ US gallons) of vodka per person every year.)

Gin has reached the most exciting period along what has been, by any standards, a highly tumultuous journey. From its origins as a medieval cure-all tonic, to the tables of the wealthy and powerful, on to battlefields and into new kingdoms. It has gorged on the poor and cruelly seduced the vulnerable, then risen up to become the most trusted of cocktail ingredients, before succumbing to the worst of all fates: obscurity.

There are many threads that support the gin revival story. There can be no doubt that a certain blue glass bottle marked the beginning, though; Bombay Sapphire did a number on all of us with a double jab of luxury and authenticity, followed by an upper-cut of fresh, accessible flavour. As the 1990s drew to a close, the cavalry began to gather. Backed up by the stalwarts of Beefeater (pages 83–84), Tanqueray (pages 141–143), Seagram's and Gordon's (pages 139–141), Citadelle (pages 152–153) from France and Hendrick's (pages 144–145) from Scotland became the next heroes of the tale, quickly followed up by Junípero (page 176), Martin Miller's (page 106), Hayman's (pages 88–89) and Sipsmith (pages 116–117).

For new distilleries and products to flourish so

effectively and repeatedly, there must first be a market. That market came about largely through the rediscovery of classic cocktail culture, along with 1930s and 1950s couture, which in turn has led to the new wave of bars where the emphasis is on quality of drinks and service, as well as provenance and authenticity of the ingredients used. Bartenders are more aware of their ingredients than they have ever been, and certainly in terms of technique and professionalism, they are better trained, too. This awareness of product, as well as inquisition in to the history of mixology has formed a gap in the market for dynamic, young products that aim to either innovate the category, or re-create the past.

The craft distilling movement has altered the landscape of the spirits world, which was only until quite recently dominated by large, cumbersome, corporations. Craft distilling (as with brewing, and indeed, any other craft activity) works on so many levels, supporting the small guy, supporting local industry, exercising freedom for the producer to innovate and broadening the scope of the category. In the US and UK alone, an average of two distilleries a week opened in 2015. But the craft movement is by no means limited to these markets. Spirits enthusiasts, brewers, engineers and crackpot scientists are establishing gin distilleries across virtually every developed nation on the planet. I recently heard that there are now seven gin distilleries in Portugal, a country that had none only 10 years ago. Many of

these new operations are unashamedly using gin as a go-between to help with cashflow while they age whisky, rum or brandy stock. But many others see gin playing a pivotal role in their future businesses.

Gins are now being made in over 30 countries, and in numerous different styles, incorporating hundreds of unique botanicals. London Dry, as vague as the term is, remains the supreme champion of gin styles, but past favourites like Old Tom and barrel-aged gins have been dusted off and tarted up, often revisited with unerring loyalty to their original recipes. Super and ultra premium gins now adorn our liquor store shelves, encased in cut-glass packaging and adorned with various bells and whistles (the former being a true story). With price tags high enough to make your eyes water, these same bottles would have prompted laughter only a few years ago. In the 'New Western' style gins, we're seeing an exaggeration of the category through explorations away from juniper and into floral, citrus, spice and fruit. Some new brands have adopted cutting-edge distillation processes and state-of-the-art extraction methods in pursuit of the most faithful possible liquid representation of the product. Botanicals are now foraged, juniper origin and terroir is scrutinized and production processes are laid bare for the benefit of consumer transparency.

BELOW A selection of some of the finest gins around today, in all their shapes, colours and sizes.

HOW GIN IS MADE

THE BASICS

Most spirits are distilled from some kind of fermented agricultural product. Whether it's a cereal, fruit or grass, the natural starch or sugars in the plant provide yeast with the fuel it needs to make fermentation possible. Even through distillation, where newly formed alcohol molecules are expanded apart then wound back together again, the biological ancestry of the base product usually carries through to the liquid.

Tequila, for example, is a product of the agave plant, which lends the drink its peppery, vegetal disposition. Brandy is made from grapes, which bestow a wide range of fruit flavours upon the liquid. Malt whisky often retains some link to its humble origins as a barley grain. Bourbon's round and sweet aromas can, in part, be attributed to corn, and even that most neutral of spirits, vodka, pays some small homage to the cereal, sugar, or starch, from which it was created. Gin is the exception to this rule. The material gin is distilled from is of virtually no consequence. What is of consequence is what it is distilled with.

Gin belongs to a large family of mostly colloquially flavoured spirits and liqueurs. These spirits, which, besides gin, include a range of regional anise-flavoured spirits, as well as the caraway- and dill-flavoured akvavit of Scandinavia, are not shaped by the raw material that they were made from, but by supplemental flavours, introduced in the latter stages of production. All of these spirits are, in effect, flavoured vodkas, distilled from the fermented sugars of cereal, fruit or other plant matter. Any trace of origin is for the most part overshadowed by the botanical characteristics of fruit, vegetable, spice, grass or herb. Producing spirits in this manner bestows upon the spirits maker superior levels of control over what flavours are allowed in or out of the product and is generally a more cost-effective means of carrying flavour into the final product. Flavoured spirits like these can be manufactured using any one or combination of three distinct methods. The first is by a simple maceration. Liqueurs are traditionally made in this way, where the subject matter (seed, bark, etc.) is steeped in spirit – usually neutral – to extract its flavour. This method extracts both flavour and colour of course, the latter of which may or may not be desirable. In the case of gin, it's a clear spirit that producers are after, so the maceration is distilled.

The second method is, technically speaking, a re-distillation, since the product has already been distilled at least once to produce a neutral spirit. During re-distillation, the vapours that boil off the maceration carry only a selected frequency of flavour through from the macerate and no colour whatsoever. The result is a concentrated perfume of volatile aromatic compounds and alcohol in a crystal-clear liquid.

The third method is to use 'off the shelf' compounded flavours to flavour a neutral spirit. Rather like mixing a cocktail, this process takes a lot of the hard work out of making a flavoured spirit by letting someone else do all the ground work for you. There's nothing wrong with this, of course.

Flavouring a spirit with any of the above methods results in a sharper expression of the subject than it would by fermenting and distilling it from scratch. Also, many of the botanicals used in gin production contain little or no sugar/starch, rendering them impractical or impossible to distil in the first place. For those that do, there is also a cost and practicality element to consider.

Most of the gins in this book use a combination of the first and second method. Gabriel Boudier's Saffron Gin, for example, is a distilled gin that undergoes a maceration of saffron before bottling, awarding it its golden hue. Some gins use a combination of the second and third methods. Hendrick's, for example, has a dash of compounded cucumber extract added to it after its distillation.

There are no gins in this book that rely solely on the third method; this tends to be reserved for cheap supermarket brands. You could argue that they are frauds; scheming imposters who, behind all the herbal-scented bravado, are nothing more than a bunch of flavoured vodkas.

NEUTRAL SPIRIT

All gins begin with neutral spirit. It's the blank canvas upon which the botanicals sit, the empty plate that the dish is served on, the silent space that the music fills.

Neutral spirit can be made from any starch or sugar-rich agricultural product such as cereals, potatoes, grapes or molasses. Neutral spirit made from fermented cereals – corn and wheat are most common – is called sometimes called GNS (grain neutral spirit). If the starting point is a cereal or potato it is first cooked to break down the starch in to sugar, but in all instances yeast is added and it is fermented in to a strong beer or wine known as wash.

The distillation of neutral spirit is done in a column still. As the name suggests these workhorses of the distilling industry are big; sometimes towering many floors high. They work with a continuous feed of low-alcohol wash, which is heated by steam and forced through a series of perforated plates. Each plate acts like a still in its own right, fractioning the vapour at different levels based on its boiling point. The end result is a steady flow of nearly pure ethanol, along with plenty of waste product which is recycled back in to the start of the system, to be unceremoniously stripped of its last remaining remnants of alcohol.

In a modern pot still, it's only possible to make a spirit of around 85% alcohol by volume (ABV) and that requires multiple time-consuming distillations. 85% might sound pretty strong, and it is, but remember that if 85% percent of your spirit is alcohol it means that 15% is other stuff, namely water and various residual impurities left over from fermentation. In whiskies and brandies these 'impurities' give the product character, but in gin it's the botanicals that are the stars of the show, so a clean and uncontaminated spirit is what's required.

A column still should produce a spirit of over 95% ABV (190 US proof). At that strength, so little of the character of the base material remains that the product can be deemed 'neutral'. Dilute neutral spirit with some water and you have vodka. While many vodka manufacturers will tell you that their product is not neutral in character – and as it happens, some are not – vodka is legally required to be made in this manner.

If purer is better for the purposes of making gin, why don't distillers make 100% pure alcohol? This is because at 96.48% the ethanol and water form an azeotrope – a phenomenon that occurs when the vapour of two mixed liquids has the same composition as the liquid mixture. No amount of repeated distilling will change that, although there are other means and ways of achieving 100% ethanol.

Most distilleries buy their neutral spirit in, either in large containers or drums, delivered by the tanker load. There are only a handful of gin distilleries that make their own neutral spirit, though, and most of them are featured in this book: Cameron Bridge (Tanqueray/Gordon's), Chase, Adnam's, Langley, Girvan (Hendrick's), G'Vine and Nolet's.

It's a matter of contention amongst distillers as to whether the base that the neutral spirit is made from has any bearing on the overall quality of the finished liquid. In the case of vodka I would say that a potato, grape, rye or barley base does produce a more nuanced liquid, but if that liquid is being distilled with a range of flavourful botanicals, I'm not convinced it makes much difference.

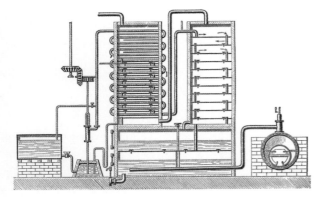

LEFT A 19th-century diagram of the distillation apparatus called a column still, also called a Coffey still, after its creator, Irishman Aeneas Coffey.

STEEP AND BOIL

Macerating ingredients in spirit and boiling it into aromatic vapour is the oldest and most basic form of concentrated flavour extraction via distillation. All London Dry Gins are made in this manner, and all distilled gins will undergo some degree of pot distillation where botanicals are steeped in spirit then boiled off. The heat of the boiling spirit cooks the botanicals, breaking down cell structure that holds the plant together, splitting chemical bonds and releasing aroma. The same thing happens when you cook a curry on a stove and the result in both cases is similar: the release of volatile aromatic molecules in to the surrounding atmosphere. In gin distillation the lightest of these fragrant compounds are carried upwards by the rising vapour currents. As they reach the top of the still they are drawn downwards in to the lynearm (also known as the swan neck) and into the condenser. Cold water is pumped through the condenser and as the spirit vapour cools, it returns to its liquid phase forming a miscible compound of alcohol, water and aromatic components. From start to finish the process may take anywhere from a couple of hours to the better part of a day. The rate of the distillation depends on a number of factors including the shape and size of the still and how aggressively the master distiller chooses to run it – all factors that will impact flavour.

The first crystal-clear drops of liquid that fall from the condenser are known as the heads, or foreshots. Because gin is made from pure neutral spirit (see left), unlike whisky or brandy, where the first 15% of the distillate may be set aside, in gin production the heads pose no significant danger. Heads can, however, contain water-insoluble compounds, derived from residual film on the inside of the still and leftovers from the previous distillation run. Traditionally distillers 'cut' the heads away based on a series of 'demisting' tests, where water is added to the spirit to see if it turns cloudy. Once the mixture remains clear the spirit can be deemed 'potable' (drinkable) and the distiller starts collecting the hearts, or the middle section of the run. This is the first of two 'cuts' that take place during distillation,

ABOVE Gin making involves macerating botanicals in neutral spirit and boiling off the aromatic vapour.

marking the beginning and the end of the spirit's recovery. Besides the gin recipe itself, the cutting of the spirit is probably the most important determinant of gin character. Some distillers claim to make these cuts with their noses, and some by feeling the liquid with their hands. In the more automated distilleries, the first cut is made routinely, at a specified time.

Once the heart of the product is distilling, the distiller can 'nose' the product. Some botanicals emerge more quickly than others. Juniper, for example, typically presents itself near the start of the spirit run, whereas coriander emerges nearer the end. As time goes on, the strength of the distillate will diminish and the aroma will lose its brightness and finesse. If left long enough the distillate would turn to cooked botanical water vapour. Naturally it's in the best interests of the distiller to collect as much alcohol as possible, but also for it to be tasty. The timing of the second cut marks the end of spirits collection and the flow of liquid will be diverted in to the feints receiver. The feints won't make it as far as the bottle, but most distilleries still collect them and re-distil them in subsequent batches, or send them away for recycling into neutral spirit.

VAPOUR INFUSION

It's good to visualize the steep and boil process (page 49) as like making a cup of tea. The teabag represents the botanicals, the water the neutral spirit and the aromatic vapour rising off the mug is the gin. But what if the teabag was suspended above the mug, out of contact with the liquid? This is the analogy that I like to use to explain how vapour-infused gins work.

Vapour infusion in gin production was first introduced in the mid-19th century, and first documented in the French distillers' handbook, *Traité des Liqueurs et de la Distillation des Alcools*' (1855). Despite what Bombay Sapphire may have you believe, the method was more than likely born out of necessity and convenience rather than flavour innovation.

The introduction of the column still in the 1830s generated a notable leap in spirit quality thanks to its rectifying column and steam-powered design. Other stills were conceived during the era that borrowed elements from the traditional pot and hybridized it with pieces from the column still. One such still was the 'Carter head', designed by a coppersmith of the same name who worked for the renowned still manufacturer John Dore. The Carter head still was simply a pot still heated by a steam jacket with a rectifying column plonked on top. Just like a regular pot still, it could only produce spirit batch after batch, but thanks to the column it could produce a higher strength, purer spirit than with a copper pot.

One of these stills was installed at Bridge Street Distillery in Warrington, England, in 1836. It was a useful bit of kit for purifying low-quality alcohol, but when someone tried to make gin in it they found that the column was too efficient, and the spirit stripped of all its botanical character. The solution was to attach a sealed drum, fitted with perforated baskets, at the far the end of the lynearm. The baskets were filled with gin botanicals, which would infuse in to the spirit vapour as it blasted towards the condenser. It worked exceptionally well.

From a distiller's perspective there is one major advantage to distilling this way, and that is the speed of turnaround. In a traditional steep and boil scenario, the distiller has to clean all the cooked botanicals out from the bottom of the pot in between batches, and sometimes a caustic wash is necessary. Refilling and cleaning pots is time-consuming, laborious and messy.

In a still with a vapour infusion chamber, the botanicals never come in to contact with the still, or indeed the liquid spirit. The botanical 'magazines' are simply slotted in to place and ejected out again once the work is done. The still itself requires little or no cleaning since it has only had to deal with ethanol and water, both of which are cleaning products in their own right! Using vapour infusion, a distiller could, in theory, make their tails cut, replace their botanical racks, and recharge the still in a matter of minutes.

LEFT This 'rack' of botanicals at the Balmenach Distillery features perforated drawers containing each botanical.

DISTILLATION

With neutral spirit in hand, now it's time to get on with the real gin-making process. As we have already learned, there are various rules that govern how gin can be labelled, and that not all products labelled as gin are as romantically agreeable as we might wish them to be. Here, we delve in to the methods and instruments used to make gin flavour compounds and distilled botanical spirits, as well as the cutting and bottling of gin.

In all instances, gin-making is overseen by the master distiller. In the make-believe distillery wonderland that resides only in your head, this man probably wears a boiler suit and steel toe-capped boots, he has hands like shovels coated in boiled leather and his nose and palate have been honed to a rare state of superhuman sensory perception.

I do know of one or two gin distillers that fit that brief, but for the most part the people who make gin are a very diverse bunch, from moustache-toting hipsters, to wizened old gentlemen, with everything in-between. And don't make the mistake of assuming this is only a job for men. Women are proven to have a superior sense of smell over men, and around half a dozen of the distilleries in this book have leading ladies of the drinks business at the helm.

The master distiller's primary responsibility is to produce a quality product and to ensure consistency in the product through continued monitoring and management of the distillation process. Distilling an aromatically desirable product that is both balanced and complex is not as simple as turning on the still, any more than baking a wedding cake is as easy as turning on the oven. An understanding of alcohol and botanicals is essential, but mastering the impact of temperature and vapour pressure in the still and how it impacts flavour extraction and gin composition, along with capturing only the best of the liquid for bottling, is what makes a truly great product.

RIGHT This kind of pot still is common among newer 'craft' distilleries. The spirit can be directed through the central rectifying column if a higher-strength distillate is needed.

LOW-PRESSURE DISTILLATION

Low-pressure distillation has its origins in the science lab, where pieces of equipment like the rotary evaporator (or rotavap) are used in organic chemistry to split and concentrate liquids with different boiling points. Put simply, a rotavap is a type of still with a rotating glass flask that sits in a heated water bath. The pressure of the system dictates the boiling point of the liquid mixture, and the water bath is adjusted to meet this. The rotation of the flask increases the surface area of the liquid mixture and encourages a faster distillation.

Given that the rotavap is a still in its own right, it's ironic that it has had to travel via kitchens and bars before anyone explored the possibility of commercially distilling flavoured spirits with one. The main reasons for this are size and cost. Even a 1-litre (¼-US gallon) rotavap can easily set you back £5,000 (US$7,400) and the largest 20-litre (5¼-US gallon) set ups can easily approach six figures.

Crucially, by lowering the boiling point of the liquid, the quantity of heat-sensitive compounds that may otherwise have been de-natured or destroyed at traditional temperatures, are preserved. Of course, lower temperatures also mean that some less volatile compounds that might feature in steep and boil gins might not distil over in a low-pressure environment. All botanicals contain a complex array of compounds with differing degrees of volatility. The beauty of low-pressure distillation is it allows the distiller to find the ideal temperature to boil the botanical to showcase the best bits of its aromatic profile. In general, it's soft and delicate botanicals (flowers, fresh herbs and fruit) that benefit most from low-pressure, low-temperature distillation. Hard spices, roots and barks are more inclined to give up the goods at higher temperatures.

There are two gins in particular that have become synonymous with low-pressure distilling, Sacred (pages 112–113) and Oxley (pages 124–125). The latter uses a one of a kind vacuum still that operates at a near-perfect vacuum. Such a low pressure means that the boiling point of the liquid is below 0°C (32°F), dripping through at around -6°C (21°F). This still requires no heat, since the surrounding atmospheric temperature is enough to trigger the evaporation of the spirit. It does however require significant amounts of energy to run the cooler and vacuum pump.

ABOVE Some distilleries use table-top rotary evaporators to distil under low pressure. Others, like Sacred, build a room full of interconnecting glass vessels.

ONE-SHOT AND MULTI-SHOT

If you hear a gin geek moaning about a 'multi-shot' gin, rest assured that they're not referring to a drinking ritual or an intensive tasting procedure. The topic of 'one-shot' and 'two-shot' (or 'multi-shot') is actually a matter of grave controversy which has resulted in disparity amongst distillers.

One-shot gins are prepared by distilling a given volume of neutral spirit with a given weight of botanicals (page 57). The resulting distillate is then cut down to bottling strength with water and that's the end of the story. With multi-shot gins, which make up the vast majority of the London Dry Gin bottles in your local liquor store, the weight of botanicals is multiplied up, but the quantity of spirit kept the same. The result is a kind of gin concentrate that is then cut back with both neutral spirit and water before being bottled.

The advantages of multi-shot are obvious to see; in a single distillation run you can produce many times the quantity of finished product that can be delivered in a one-shot batch. But those of the one-shot camp see multi-shot as both non-traditional, non-craft, and, well – cheating.

The proof is of course in the pudding, and if the blind tastings are anything to go by there's little to tell apart between a cut-back multi-shot and a classic one-shot. Going under the assumption that a still loaded up with botanicals doesn't reach some kind of botanical vapour saturation point, one has to concede that – assuming the maths is correct – a bottle of gin made either way will contain the same quantity of spirit, water and botanical extract in either instance.

While we're on this subject, and for what it's worth, I would like to convey my distaste for the terms 'one-shot' and 'multi-shot'. They are, in my eyes, both vulgar and inapt, but for reasons unknown to me they have regrettably become the standard convention in distillery-speak.

Some common multi-shot gins include: Gordon's, Tanqueray, Beefeater, Jensen's and anything produced at Langley and Thames. Some common one-shot gins include: Bombay Sapphire, Sipsmith, Dodd's, Thomas Dakin and Tarquin's.

BELOW Gin labels are not legally required to state whether they're made by a one-shot or multi-shot method.

COMPOUNDING

Compounding has long been a dirty word in the gin world. And sure enough it's not the most glamorous way to manufacture gin, nor does it require a great deal of artistic flair. A compounder is, by definition, a blender, and that's exactly what's going on here. Individual gin flavours – obtained from sources, natural or unnatural – are mixed with neutral spirit and water to create a product that looks, smells and tastes like gin. And it is gin! According to the law that is. The vast majority of flavoured vodkas are made in the same way, and so too are all the suspicious-looking supermarket own-brands you've seen labelled only as 'gin'. There is no master distiller as such (their title would more likely be master-mixer) and the only skill really lies in the blend's recipe, and its effectiveness at making a chemical cocktail smell and taste like a London Dry Gin.

I viewed compounded gins in this way for many years, but one day an interesting thing occurred to me. If compounded gins are a mixture of concentrated flavours and neutral spirit, isn't that the same as a multi-shot gin? Sure, multi-shots are distilled, but so are a lot of compounded flavour extracts, so how do the two differ?

The truth is that they don't and the problem here lies in terminology confusing itself with classification. We naturally assume that a compounded gin is not a distilled gin, because the process suggests a degree of corner-cutting and cost-saving. We also take it for granted that a gin brand that speaks of provenance, craft and flavour is a one-shot London Dry. Most of the time these conclusions are valid, but it is absolutely not the case all of the time and it's for this reason that we should refer to the gin's classification (page 70–73) to better understand its production process before drawing conclusions from the authentic look and feel of the bottle, or some other similarly cunning distraction.

Let's take Sacred (see pages 112–113) and Hendrick's (see pages 144–145) as a pair of examples. Sacred is a made from top-quality botanicals that are individually macerated and distilled in to super-concentrated liquids using a home laboratory. These extracts are then sent away to be blended (read: compounded) with a lot of neutral spirit then cut down with water before bottling. Sacred is a compounded gin, but it is also a London Dry Gin because it adheres to all of the requirements of the classification. Hendrick's on the other hand, is distilled in a copper pot and packaged in a legitimate fashion, but it also contains cucumber and rose extract that are added after distillation. For this reason it is not a London Dry Gin.

In summary, yes, some – perhaps most – compounded gins are a bit nasty. Mixing one part juniper extract with 1,000 parts neutral spirit will never produce a gin that boasts the aromatic and textural finesse of a copper distilled one-shot product.

LEFT Sacks of botanicals are evident at Hendrick's Distillery, but the gin is flavoured with compounded essences, too.

CUTTING AND BOTTLING

The heart of the product, now a high-strength gin of at least 70% (for a London Dry) and possibly as high as 90% ABV, is ready for the next stage of the process.

For a compounded or multi-shot gin, it's time to be cut back with neutral spirit. This is the stage where de-mineralized water is added to dilute the product down to bottling strength.

In the EU, gin has to be a minimum of 37.5% ABV, while for the US it's slightly higher, at 80 proof (40% ABV). Premium gins tend to all be a minimum of 40% ABV and some are much higher. In fact, if you glance over a selection of premium gins you'll probably find that they all differ in strength – 41.4%, 43.7%, 45.2% and so on. This is not a case of more booze means a better product, nor is it a desperate attempt to claim ownership of a specific alcohol content (although some brands do appear to have achieved this).

Gin presents its botanical aroma quite differently depending on the strength of the product. The molecules carrying aroma are more chemically similar to alcohol molecules than water so they tend to latch on to alcohol molecules. This means that a drink that is high in alcoholic strength tends to sequester its aroma molecules away in the liquid of the drink, giving very little away on the aroma side of things. Add some water, a common practice amongst malt whisky drinkers, and suddenly the aroma is revealed. In the case of gin, honing in on a particular ABV can amplify or suppress certain botanical characteristics, allowing the distiller to divulge just the right amount of the drink's aromatic properties.

The irony of all this is of course that very few people drink gin straight from the bottle. It's mixed, with either tonic water, or in a cocktail, and once mixed all that detail goes out of the window. Even if you drink gin on ice – and you're really in the minority there – the drink will be diluted, and consequentially its aroma will have been adjusted. Even if you are one of the 20-or-so people in the whole world who drinks neat gin at room temperature, the shape and size of your glass will also have some bearing on aroma perception, too. The point is that, besides the controlled tasting room scenario, the ABV of the product is not particularly important unless it comes with precise instructions explaining how to mix it.

RIGHT AND BELOW At G&J Distillers, in Warrington, England – the oldest continually operating gin distillery in the UK – supermarket gins (right) and super-premium gins (below) are all made and bottled under the same roof. It's an enormous operation featuring all sorts of technical wizardry, with only six or so employees needed to check that everything's going to plan.

HOW GENEVER IS MADE

Genever production guidelines are vague, so the process differs from one distillery to the next. Unlike gin, which is a botanical distillate that is sometimes blended with neutral spirit, a bottle of genever comprises at least three components (as well as water) and sometimes many more. Based on the ratio of components, a bottle will labelled as *Oude* (aged), *Jonge* (young), *Corenwijn* (grain wine) and so on (see below), but there's some confusion surrounding these terms, most specifically with *Oude* and *Jonge*. Most of us associate 'old' with 'aged', and since many genevers undergo maturation in oak casks, it's an obvious connection to make. However, oak-ageing is not a pre-requisite of the *Oude* style (it is for *Corenwijn*), but it does often happen. A better title for *Oude* and *Jonge* would be 'old-fashioned' and 'new' respectively.

The first and most important of the components is *moutwijn*, or 'Malt wine', which is a richly flavoured cereal-based pot-still distillate. The mash of cereals can be made from any combination of rye, corn, wheat and barley, the combination of which will dictate character in the finished genever. Of all the malt wine produced in Belgium and The Netherlands, 99% is made by the Filliers Distillery (page 156–157) who tailor the recipe to the requirements of their clients. If wheat and corn are being used, they are mixed with water and cooked at a high temperature to loosen up the starch. As the mixture cools, the rye is added, followed by the barley. If the barley is malted, it releases enzymes that break the cereal's starches down in to simple fermentable sugars. Unlike malt whisky production, the law permits the diastase enzyme to be used in its pure form in place of malted barley grain. The sweet and bread-y liquid 'wort' is then drained from the mash and yeast is added to promote fermentation, which converts the sugar in to alcohol. This takes anywhere from 3–7 days to complete and because the speed of the process has a direct impact on flavour, it is again tailored to the recipe and the brand. The fermented mash, or beer, is then stripped of its alcohol in a continuous still, then redistilled two or three times in linked pot-stills. In some distilleries, like Zuidam (pages 168–169), the distillation is done entirely in pot stills, which results in a fruitier, drier spirit as opposed to the nutty, cereal notes that come from the column-still method used at Filliers.

If a column is being used the first spirit will be drawn off at around 48% ABV. After subsequent distillations it may be as high as 80%, but is typically closer to the 70% mark. The first distillate, which comes off the continuous still, is called *ruwnat* ('rough wet'); the second distillate (from the first linked pot-still) *enkelnat* ('single wet'); and the third distillate (from a second linked pot-still) *bestnat* ('best wet'), otherwise known as malt wine. For the optional fourth distillate (from an optional third linked pot-still) you get *korenwijn* ('grain wine'), which should not be confused with the finished product *Korenwijn* (also spelled *Corenwijn/Corenwyn*) (see below).

A portion of the malt wine is then re-distilled with juniper and (optionally) other botanicals, like coriander seed, caraway seed or fennel seed. The concentrated *habaida* (berry) *moutwijn* is then blended with unflavoured malt wine. Sometimes a botanical distillate made from neutral spirit is mixed in too.

All genever was made this way up until the mid-19th century, but the invention of the continuous still in 1831 changed everything. The availability of cheap, neutral, flavourless spirit gave economically minded genever distillers the option to dilute their flavoursome malt wine and 'stretch' it out a lot further. This gave rise to the individual styles of genever that we recognise today: *Moutwijn* (100% malt wine), *Corenwijn* (at least 51% malt wine), *Oude* (between 15–51% malt wine), and *Jonge* (under 15% malt wine but typically less than 5%).

After malt wine, botanical spirit, and neutral spirit have been mixed the distiller needs only to add water to achieve the correct bottling strength – this is how all *jonge* genever is made. Alternately, the spirit can be aged in oak casks no bigger than 700 litres (185 US gallons) for a period of no less than 1 year.

BOTANICALS

Botanicals are an essential component of gin (and genever) production as they give the product its aroma and flavour. Simply put, botanicals are substances obtained from plants, or anything that grows: fruit, seed, root, bark, flower, leaf or grass. The range of options is infinite, and I see this as one of the driving forces behind the revitalization of the gin category as new distillers customize their recipes to a specific profile of flavours.

Generally speaking, gin is made in the same way as an essential oil, where a solvent (in this case alcohol) is heated and the vapour used to carry the volatile aromatic components of the plant. All botanicals contain a range of compounds, some of which we can taste and some that we can smell. Molecules that are geared more towards smell (pine, cinnamon or lemon, for example) are much lighter than those we associated with taste, and it's for this reason that we are able to smell them in the first place – they carry to our noses with a greater ease. We describe them as being more 'volatile' – which is apt, since 'volatiles' are interesting, unstable and often elusive.

Gin making is all about extracting a desirable range of these volatile aromatic molecules from a selection of botanicals. In addition to the recipe, the presses used to extract them along with the quantity of botanical used will go on to dictate the style of gin. It gets more interesting when you consider that some gins' most desirable compounds can be present across many different botanicals. The compound *pinene* (which gives gin its sweet, woodsy, pine aroma) for example, is found in juniper, coriander seed, angelica, cinnamon and many other botanicals besides. It's in this manner that, historically, a variety of botanicals were used to bolster the juniper flavour of gin through their own

pinene content, but also augment it with other, harmonious flavours.

These days things have moved on somewhat and even though many brands stick to the classic juniper-driven style, the options that the world of botany presents us with has led others to experiment with all kinds of weird and wonderful botanical combinations. Over the next few pages we will explore some of the more classic examples, but The Gin Tour (see pages 74–183) delves deeper in to the contemporary scene.

RIGHT Once a botanical recipe has been formulated, it's up to each distillery to ensure that the quality of these natural ingredients is consistent from batch to batch.

JUNIPER

The common juniper tree (*Juniperus communis*) is a coniferous plant and a member of the Cupressaceae (cypress) family. It can grow up to 10 m (30 ft) tall and live for over 100 years, but those cultivated for gin production are engineered to be much shorter and bushier. Common juniper has the widest geographical range of any tree in the world, taking up residence in western Alaska, throughout Canada and northern parts of the USA, in coastal areas of Greenland, Iceland, throughout Europe, north Africa, and in northern Asia and Japan. It's quite content in either acid or alkaline soils and can be found across a variety of landscapes.

Juniper is a slow-grower, taking a leisurely 10 years before the plant produces flowers and fruit. Individual plants are either male or female, unlike most tree species, where both male and female flowers occur on the same tree. Male flowers present themselves as yellow blossoms near the ends of the twigs in spring and disperse pollen into the wind. Female flowers look like very small clusters of scales, and after being pollinated, they become tiny cones, which soften and grow into juniper berries.

Shaped like irregularly-sided spheres, juniper berries are green at first, but ripen only after 12–18 months to a dark, blue-purple colour. They are about 0.5–1 cm (¼–½ inch) in diameter when fresh. Each berry contains 3–6 triangular seeds, which are dispersed by birds that eat the berries. Given that it takes so long for the berries to ripen, it's normal to see ripe and unripe fruit at any one time. This means the same tree may be harvested three times over a two-year period.

Most of the juniper used to make gin is sourced from Italy or Macedonia. Juniper can still be found in the UK, especially Scotland, but the fungus *Phytophthora*

BELOW **A juniper tree overlooks the barren slopes of the Annapurna mountain range of the Himalayas in Nepal.**

austrocedrae has decimated up to 70% of Britain's juniper in recent years and, in general, the tree is at risk of extinction throughout the British Isles.

Considering that the industry uses an extraordinary quantity of juniper every year, it's surprising to find that most juniper trees are not farmed or cultivated and picking is more akin to foraging than harvesting. Traditionally, pickers will circulate around a tree, beating the branches and catching the falling berries in a round flat basket. On a good day, an experienced beater can collect their own bodyweight in berries.

The earliest recorded use of juniper medicinally dates back to ancient Egypt and around 1500 BC when the brown coloured fruit of *Juniperus phoenicea* was used as a poultice to treat joint and muscle pain. Athletes in Greece's ancient Olympic Games gobbled up juniper berries, believing they would improve performance. The Romans used juniper for a range of digestive ailments, and famous medieval herbalist Culpepper used juniper infusions for the relief of trapped wind, for which juniper oil is still used today.

The volumes of juniper oil and its constituents can change dramatically according to a berry's ripeness, the age of the plant, period of harvesting and terroir. In general, the essential oil content of juniper cones peaks at around 3% just before the fruit reaches full ripeness. Over 70 different components have been identified in the oil, but it is largely made up of five flavourful compounds called terpenes. Pinene is the main terpene in juniper, and there are no prizes for guessing the aroma that it imparts. There are actually two types of pinene in juniper. Alpha-pinene, the principal of the two, has a woodsy cedar-like aroma. Beta-pinene is found in much smaller quantities, and can be distinguished by a green, Christmas tree-type aroma.

Other important terpenes in juniper are myrcene, which gives a lingering herbal, mossy aroma; sabinene, offering a warm, slightly nutty aroma; and limonene, which provides freshness and citrus notes.

Typical cost per 10 kg (22 lbs.): £70 (US$104)

Particularly prevalent in: Adnam's First Rate (p.79), Dodd's (p.129), Sipsmith (p.117), Sipsmith VJOP (p.117), Tanqueray (p.143), Beefeater (p.84), Gordon's (p.141), Tarquin's (p.119), Whitley Neil (p.107)... the list goes on.

Flavour profile: pine, leather, fruit, citrus, grassy, peppery, sweet.

RIGHT Juniper berries in the first year of their growing cycle. The berries have formed but they are hard and green in colour.

ABOVE TOP Ripe juniper berries, most likely in the second year of their growing cycle.

ABOVE Juniper is usually dried for use in gin production. This takes about 3 weeks, or a few days in a dehydrator.

~ CORIANDER ~

The green leaves of the coriander plant (*Coriandrum sativumis*) are used liberally in some Middle Eastern, Asian and Central American cuisine. North Americans have adopted the Spanish word for coriander leaves – cilantro - due to the plant's habitual use in Mexican cuisine. The leaves and stalks have a highly perfumed, bright, and grassy flavour, and those who dislike coriander/cilantro (approximately 15% of the world) tend to do so vehemently thanks to a genetic predisposition that causes some people to detect a sickly 'soapiness' in the aldehydes present in the plant.

In the production of gin, it is not the leaves that are used, but the seeds – or I should say, fruit. The fruit of the herb tastes quite different to the leaves, as it is dried during preparation, removing much of the vibrant green characteristics of the fresh plant. And it's these perfect little sand-coloured spheres that you will find in the spice section of your local market, as well as your gin. Coriander fruit has a far more diverse range of abilities when compared to the leaves, thanks to a symphony of active flavour compounds that play nicely with other ingredients. The seeds are used extensively in the curry dishes of India (where they are called *dhania*), as a pickling spice for onions and cucumbers, as a sausage spice for the South African *boerewors*, as well

as in the production of some citrus wheat beers, herbal liqueurs, and are second only to juniper in gin botanical rankings.

Coriander seeds have a distinct lemon aroma, more lemony than lemon itself I would argue. It's coriander seed that contributes the citrus aromas to many of the world's best gins that mysteriously have no lemon or orange zest on their botanical shopping list. The citrus characteristic of coriander can be attributed to the combination of four terpenes: linalool, thymol, pinene and geranyl acetate. Linalool's highly desirable spiced floral aroma is synthesized in huge quantities and is thought to be used in over half of the world's scented cleaning products. Thymol gives us a warm and woody incense; geranyl acetate is floral and feminine; and pinene is found in high concentrations in pine needles and nuts. It is also a major player in juniper, so does a neat job of binding the two botanicals together with a fresh, potent cedar wood aroma.

As with any other botanical, the aromatic profile of the seed will vary according to its specific variety and origin. It's widely accepted that the best coriander seed comes from the *microcarpum* variety. These plants flourish in eastern Europe, Russia and Scandinavia (all places that, ironically, use relatively little coriander in their cuisine) and is famed for its small fruits that pack a big punch. The alternate is the sub-tropical variety, *vulgaris*, which can be found India, parts of Asia and northern Africa.

Typical cost per 10 kg (22 lbs.): £40 (US$60)

Particularly prevalent in: Dr. J's, Tanqueray London Dry (p.143), Cremorne 1859.

Flavour profile: Sweet spice, lemon balm, sage, cedar, white chocolate, lemon curd, lemonade, earl grey tea.

LEFT Coriander seeds lose their potency very quickly once ground up, so are better stored whole.

CARDAMOM

Cardamom is the third most expensive spice in the world after saffron and vanilla, and since those two are scarcely seen in gin it makes cardamom the most expensive for our purposes. Cardamom is painfully difficult to process, requiring specific quality standards at every stage.

Cardamom is native to Southern India and is grown commercially in its surrounding countries, but today the world's largest grower is Guatemala. Guatemala has the German coffee planter, Oscar Majus Kloeffe, to thank for the 30,000 tons of cardamom they now produce annually – he took cuttings from India and planted them there at the end of the 19th century.

Two genera of cardamom grown commercially for flavouring and both belong to the ginger (Zingiberaceae) family. *Elettaria Cardamomum* is the common green cardamom (also known as true cardamom) and *Amomum cardamomum* is the black (or brown) type. Green cardamom, which can be found in a lot of Indian food and medicine is more aromatic, 'greener' and fresh tasting than black, which takes on a spicy, smokey quality useful in Asian cooking. Both pack a serious punch, so only a little is required to reach a desirable effect.

While still on the plant, the pods resemble pale green olives, growing low to the ground and often creep along the ground like a necklace of beads. Once picked they are washed and dried at exactly 50°C (122°F) for about 6 hours. Stalks are removed and the pods are then graded by passing the pods through different sized apertures, which aims to weed out underdeveloped or overripe pods. Most often the pods are hand-graded too, where shrivelled or diseased pods are discarded. Quality is paramount and it's not unusual for cardamom to undergo additional screening before being packaged for sale. In India and Sri Lanka the pods are graded in three categories: Alleppey Green Bold (AGB), Aleppey Green Extra Bold (AGEB) and Alleppey Green Superior (AGS). The greener the pods the more expensive the cardamom is. The pods can

ABOVE The more vivid the colour of your green cardamom, the more money it's worth.

then be ground whole, hulled for their seeds, or used whole for gin production.

Both green and black cardamom share a group of terpenes: cienol, which is a major contributor to the fragrance of eucalyptus; and fragrant and fresh terpinyl acetate, the same stuff that can be found in the leaves of some citrus trees and pine oil. Both of these terpenes are found in rosemary and basil, too. What differentiates the two cardamom genera is a healthy measure of the citrus-scented terpene, limonene, in green cardamom, whereas black cardamom favours beta-pinene, giving it a woody, green note.

Typical cost per 10 kg (22 lbs.): £300 (US$445)

Particularly prevalent in: Dodd's (p.129), Professor Cornelius Ampleforth's Bathtub Navy Strength Gin (p.82), 209 Gin, Sacred Cardamom Gin and Opihr (p.96).

Flavour profile: Spicy, herbal, minty, green, ginger, grapefruit, fresh, warming.

❧ LIQUORICE ❧

LEFT Liquorice/licorice root is quite expensive, so should never been confused with kindling!

The liquorice/licorice plant (*Glycyrrhiza glabra*) is actually a legume, so, like lentils and peas, it produces a kind of podded fruit. The pods are next to useless, and I haven't found a single reference of anyone using them for anything. It is of course the root of the liquorice/licorice plant that gets flavorists excited, valued for its intense sweetness, and earthy anise qualities. Liquorice's/licorice's medicinal uses stretch back as far as medicine itself. Ancient Chinese pharmacists positioned it amongst the highest class of drugs for its adeptness tackling fever, thirst, cough and respiratory ailments. The Ancient Egyptians enjoyed liquorice/licorice recreationally, turning the root into a sweet non-alcoholic drink that must have tasted something like watered-down molasses.

These days, liquorice/licorice is still used medicinally, but can also be found in a wide range of soft drinks, food products and cigarettes. It's been estimated that over half of the world's liquorice/licorice root is used to flavour tobacco products. It would seem that the sweet, earthy flavour of liquorice/licorice does a good job of enhancing the flavour of tobacco while softening its harshness. My father was, at one time, a staunch follower of liquorice-/licorice-flavoured papers in his 'roll-up' cigarettes.

Liquorice/licorice root contains a powerful natural sweetener called glycyrrhizin [glis-eer-riz-in], taken from the greek words *gluku* (sweet) and *rrhiza* (root). Glycyrrhizin is a tooth-softening 50 times sweeter than table sugar (sucrose) but before you send lilies to your dentist, know that much of the brunt of the force is perceived as a lingering sweetness rather than a full frontal assault. Liquorice/licorice root can contain anywhere from 4–25% glycyrrhizin by dry weight, so it can pack a serious sweet punch.

When I worked at the Gordon's Distillery in Cameron Bridge for a day (see pages 139–141), liquorice/licorice was the only one of the gin's 10 botanicals that was not automatically deposited into the still. This meant taking a heavy bag (around 10 kg/22 lbs.) of ground liquorice/licorice root and bundling the contents through the hatch. I can still remember the sensation of the oleaginous dust fixing to the surface of my tongue as I inhaled, turning in to a sweet glue on my palate. The flavour stayed with me all day.

Besides fenchone, which is the ketone that gives camphor its distinct aroma, liquorice/licorice root has a hefty dose (around 3% of the dry weight) of the compound anethole. Anethole is a compound that contributes a large part of the 'aniseed' flavour of fennel and anise – plants that belong to the Apiaceae family – and it is the missing link between the aromatic similarities of these plant species and liquorice/licorice.

Typical cost per 10 kg (22 lbs.): £100 ($148)

Particularly prevalent in: Adnam's First Rate (p.79), Beefeater 24 (p.84), Spirit of Hven, William's Chase London Dry (p.89).

Flavour profile: Earthy treacle, molasses, anise, woodsy, herbal.

ORRIS

The *Iris pallida* is native to Croatia's Dalmatian coast and is a hardy plant with sword-shaped leaves that produces purple to white flowers. The flower is thought to be the basis of the French 'fleur-de-ly', but it is the root of the plant (or rhizome) that botanists have a greater interest in. The plant has been cultivated for its root since Roman times, which, when dried, is prized for its perfume and its usefulness as a fixative – an odour that assembles and supports other aromas. Today, *I. pallida* is grown in surprisingly small quantities, mainly in Italy and especially in Tuscany – where it is known colloquially as 'giaggiolo' – along with its descendant *I. germanica var. Florentine*, found in Morocco, China and India, and *I. germanica 'Albicans'*, which is also used in orris production.

Three-year-old plants are proven to provide the best yield of rhizome development, as the rate of growth of the rhizome slows after that period. Harvesting during dry spells is preferred, as the skin of the root tends to fall away naturally due to dehydration. The root is cut from the leafy plant, and the plant is then inserted back into the ground where it grows fresh roots. The root itself is washed, peeled and dried. Because there's less than 80 hectares (200 acres) of commercially grown orris in the world, this process is generally very hands-on. Also, it takes almost 1 metric ton of orris root to make 2 litres/½ US gallon of orris essential oil (known as orris butter).

The fresh roots smell of little more than earth. The development of desirable floral characteristics is only possible through a drying period of up to five years, which sees some of the root's duller constituents oxidize into a group of closely related aromatic compounds called irones and ionones. Orris's unique combination of irones and ionones results in a complex floral and woody quality that is as prized amongst perfumers and gin manufacturers as it is expensive – a reflection of orris's lengthy preparation process.

Typical cost per 10 kg (22 lbs.): £250 (US$370)

Particularly prevalent in: Martin Miller's (p.106), London Hill.

Flavour profile: Woody, sawdust, iris, violet, rose, raspberry, powder and the overriding smell of 'purple'.

BELOW With a flower that pretty, it's only fair that Iris pallida has an ugly (but brilliantly perfumed) rhizome.

CINNAMON & CASSIA

Cinnamon and cassia are commonly confused with one another, and in North America especially, there are a great deal of products sold as cinnamon that are in fact cassia. Although both belong to the Lauraceae family and the *Cinnamomum* genus, cinnamon and cassia do not come from the same plant. Both are harvested in a similar manner, however, wherein strips of inner bark in young trees are dried in the sun and rolled in to the familiar sticks of spice.

The *Cinnamomum* genus has over 300 species, but scientifically speaking, there is only one true cinnamon. Commonly known as Ceylon cinnamon, named for the fact that it is found almost exclusively in Sri Lanka, it comes from the *Cinnamomum verum* plant, which literally translates as 'true cinnamon'. This stuff is the Champagne of the cinnamon world and the rolled quills of its highly aromatic bark are distinguishable by numerous layers of soft, thin, velvet-textured wafers.

Cinnamomum cassia (also known as *C. aromaticum*) is more like the Pinot Grigio of tree bark spices. It's readily available and passable. Most of the world's cassia heralds from China (it's also known as Chinese cinnamon) and Vietnam, but it is grown widely across Southeast Asia and Madagascar. Cassia takes its name from the Hebrew word *qātsa*, meaning 'to strip off bark'.

If you look down at the cross-section of a cassia quill, you will see that only one or two, thick layers of bark make up the furl.

The aromatic oils of cinnamon trees are used extensively to flavour meat and in fast-food seasonings, sauces and pickles, baked goods, confectionery, soft drinks, tobacco flavours and in dental and pharmaceutical preparations. They are also used to flavour a number of spirits and liqueurs.

Most gins opt for cassia, and even most of those gins that state they are using cinnamon are in fact sourcing it from cassia trees in China or Vietnam. There are a few exceptions to the rule, however. Sipsmith use both cassia, from China, and true cinnamon, from Madagascar in their gin recipe.

That familiar cinnamon flavour comes from the flavour compound cinnamaldehyde. Ceylon cinnamon trumps cassia in the cinnamaldehyde stakes, but the lesser known Saigon cinnamon (*C. loureiroi*) which is grown exclusively in Vietnam, beats them both. It can contain up to 3% essential oil by dry weight, of which over 80% is cinnamaldehyde. Other compounds consistent to all cinnamon species are pinene, linalool, limonene and camphene – all familiar names (see pages 58–61).

FAR LEFT These quills are recognizable as cassia because of their hollow, brittle structure.

LEFT All of the world's cassia and cinnamon is still stripped and rolled by hand.

The flavour that cassia contributes to gin is somewhat spicier than the soft and round flavour that you might associate with cinnamon, mostly thanks to a terpene called alpha-guaiene, which contributes a woody heat to the product. But I believe that slightly spicy botanicals like cassia can have the effect of softening the alcohol burn in the finished product, whereby the presence of a cinnamon aroma justifies a slight burn where it would otherwise be austere or unexpected. In other words, the burn becomes acceptable because the flavour permits it.

Typical cost per 10 kg (22 lbs.): £60 (US$90) (cassia) £150 (US$220) (true cinnamon)

Particularly prevalent in: Opihr (p.96), Blackwood's and Professor Cornelius Ampleforth's Bathtub Navy Strength Gin (p.82). Although more nuanced, Langley's No. 8 Gin (p.106) also has a distinct cassia-induced twang on the finish.

Flavour profile: Sweet spice, wood sugar, warmth, smoke and a headily aromatic, medicinal quality.

TOP Cinnamon trees are harvested during the wet season when the bark is softer.

ABOVE This etching from 1671 shows workers peeling cinnamon bark in Ceylon (modern-day Sri Lanka). In Sri Lanka, cinnamon quills are still graded according to the diameter of the roll.

ANGELICA

Angelica belongs to the Apiacae (carrot) family of hollow-stem aromatic shrubs, making it a cousin of coriander, anise, fennel, dill, celery and parsnip – to name but a few.

There are over 60 known species of angelica. Some, like *Angelica sinensis* (Dong Quai), are used in Chinese cooking and medicine, while others are indigenous to Europe and the West coast of the US. The Eurasian species of angelica, *Angelica archangelica*, is the one that we are most interested in.

A. Archangelica takes its name from the Greek word *arkhangelos* after the myth that it was first introduced to mankind by the Archangel Gabriel. The plant flourishes across Scandinavia, where it stands as a respected medicinal herb used to treat respiratory ailments, and as a digestive aid since as far back as the 10th century. It also features in the traditional cuisine of Iceland and the Faroe Islands, where it is known as *hvonn* and is consumed like a vegetable. Its uses were not limited to the physical either; in the Middle Ages it was common for children to wear angelica leaf necklaces to ward off evil spirits and it was widely believed that witches gave it a wide berth.

In 17th century *arkhangelos* was required to live up to its name. The bubonic plague was taking its toll on

Europe's population and it was claimed that chewing on the plant helped ward off the plague. This, in turn, meant the countryside in Britain was stripped almost entirely of angelica. If you're thinking about foraging your own, you should be very careful because the plant is very similar in appearance to water hemlock, which possesses a deadly cicutoxin.

These days, the stem of the plant, which looks a lot like a stick/rib of celery (*A. archangelica* is also known as wild celery) is sometimes candied in to a baton of sickly-sweet acid-green mulch that's widely used to decorate cakes and flavour puddings – although it's somewhat less fashionable than it might have been thirty years ago. The tiny fruits (seeds) of the plant are sometimes used to flavour absinthe and occasionally crop up in gin, too.

It's the angelica root that we are mostly interested in, however. When dried, the root has a wonderful herb and musk character to it and when brewed in to a tea can be used medicinally. It's for this reason that it crops up in many, if not *most*, of the better known herbal

LEFT Dried angelica root is visually indistinguishable from any other dried root. It tastes quite root-y too.

LEFT Angelica grows in the wild in many parts of the UK, but should not be confused with similar-looking water hemlock or cow parsnip.

BELOW Angelica stems are perfect for being candied or for brewing a sweet, peppery tea.

liqueurs, *amari* and bitters, including Chartreuse, Benedictine, Fernet and Galliano. The roots are harvested while the plant is still young and tender, typically in its first year, before it even has a chance to seed a new generation.

I've always been told that angelica's role in gin is to bind the other botanicals together, rather than contribute an original flavour of its own. Indeed, angelica is on the inventory of every single gin containing at least four botanicals. By itself, the root tastes generically herbal and warming to me — much like the aroma of a health food store. That green, herbaceous note comes partly from a terpene called phellandrene, which, when isolated, has a peppery, minty and slightly citrusy aroma. Couple that with limonene (lemon oil) and our old friend pinene (pine) and you have a botanical that fits in to the gin family rather nicely. Having said that, in this author's opinion, angelica root doesn't taste wildly different to other aromatic roots, like orris, burdock and dandelion. I'd like to see the latter two used more in gin production.

Typical cost per 10 kg (22 lbs.): £160 (US$237)

Particularly prevalent in: Plymouth (p.111), Martin Miller's (p.106), Gordon's (p.141), Beefeater (p.84), Tanqueray, No. 3. (p.143)

Flavour profile: Warm herbal, fresh yet slightly peppery, earthy musk.

LIGHT

GREENALL'S ORIGINAL LONDON DRY
37.5% ABV p.95

JUNIPER GREEN
37.5% ABV p.124

FLAVOUR MAP

This chart shows a selection of gins featured in this book and where they sit in terms of style and depth of flavour. 'Classic' gins include more traditional juniper-forward offerings, whereas 'contemporary' gins may lead with citric flavours or focus on unconventional ingredients.

BOMBAY SAPPHIRE
40% ABV p.87

BEEFEATER 24
45% ABV p.84

BOMBAY EAST
42% ABV p.87

PLYMOUTH
41.2% ABV p.111

GORDON'S LONDON DRY
47% ABV p.141

CITADELLE
44% ABV p.151

BOMBAY ORIGINAL
37.5% ABV p.86

EAST LONDON LIQUOR CO. LONDON DRY
40% ABV p.91

CAORUNN
41.8% ABV p.134

STAR OF BOMBAY
47.5% ABV p.87

CLASSIC

BEEFEATER LONDON DRY
40% ABV p.84

TARQUIN'S
42% ABV p.119

WARNER EDWARDS HARRINGTON DRY
44% ABV p.130

FORD'S
45% ABV p.123

ZUIDAM DUTCH COURAGE DRY GIN
44.5% ABV p.169

SIPSMITH
41.6% ABV p.117

PORTOBELLO ROAD NO. 171
42% ABV p.126

TANQUERAY LONDON DRY
43.1% ABV p.143

QUININE 1897
45.8% ABV p.82

RUTTE DRY GIN
35% ABV p.155

HAYMAN'S LONDON DRY
40% ABV p.99

BURLEIGH'S
40% ABV p.131

OLD RAJ
55% ABV p.146

PICKERING'S
42% ABV p.148

FINSBURY PLATINUM
47% ABV p.105

CREAM
43.8% ABV p.81

JENSEN'S BERMONDSEY DRY
43% ABV p.101

DOROTHY PARKER
44% ABV p.181

SIPSMITH VJOP
57% ABV p.117

G'VINE NOUAISON
43.9% ABV p.162

HEPPLE
45% ABV p.109

BURLEIGH;S DISTILLER'S CUT
47% ABV p.131

FIFTY POUNDS
43.5% ABV p.122

HAYMAN'S OLD TOM
40% ABV p.99

DODD'S
49.9% ABV p.129

HAYMAN'S ROYAL DOCK
57% ABV p.99

PERRY'S TOT
57% ABV p.181

HERNÖ SWEDISH EXCELLENCE
40.5% ABV p.163

MARTIN MILLER'S
40% ABV p.106

GIN DE MAHÓN
38% ABV p.159

PROFESSOR CORNELIUS AMPLEFORTH'S BATHTUB NAVY STRENGTH
57% ABV p.82

MARTIN MILLER'S WESTBOURNE STRENGTH
45.2% ABV p.106

SILENT POOL
43% ABV p.115

BROKER'S
47% ABV p.104

WILLIAMS CHASE GREAT BRITISH EXTRA DRY
40% ABV p.89

JENSEN'S OLD TOM
43% ABV p.101

THE LAKES
43.7% ABV p.103

OLD ENGLISH GIN
44% ABV p.107

HEAVY

LIGHT

BLOOM
40% ABV p.95

SACRED
40% ABV p.113

OXLEY
47% ABV p.125

FILLIERS DRY GIN 28
46% ABV p.157

HENDRICK'S
41.4% ABV p.145

GILPIN'S WESTMORLAND
EXTRA DRY
47% ABV p.123

THE BOTANIST
46% ABV p.149

AVIATION
42% ABV p.177

DEATH'S DOOR
47% ABV p.178

EDEN MILL ORIGINAL
42% ABV p.136

G'VINE FLORAISON
40% ABV p.162

GIN MARE
42.7% ABV p.161

WHITLEY NEILL
42% ABV p.107

ST. GEORGE BOTANIVORE
45% ABV p.182

EAST LONDON LIQUOR CO.
BATCH NO. 2
47% ABV p.91

DARNLEY'S VIEW
40% ABV p.121

ST. GEORGE TERROIR
45% ABV p.182

WILLIAMS CHASE
EUREKA CITRUS GIN
40% ABV p.89

THOMAS DAKIN
42% ABV p.96

TANQUERAY NO. TEN
47.3% ABV p.143

BERKELEY SQUARE
40% ABV p.94

MONKEY 47
47% ABV p.165

PICKERING'S 1947
42% ABV p.148

EDINBURGH GIN
43% ABV p.138

LANGLEY'S NO.8
41.7% ABV p.106

FEW AMERICAN GIN
40% ABV p.179

HALF HITCH
40% ABV p.97

NOLET'S DRY GIN
'SILVER
47.6% ABV p.167

WILLIAMS CHASE
ELEGANCE 'CRISP'
48% ABV p.89

ADNAM'S COPPER HOUSE
40% ABV p.79

ZUIDAM DUTCH COURAGE
OLD TOM'S
40% ABV p.169

PROFESSOR
CORNELIUS
AMPLEFORTH'S
BATHTUB GIN
43.3% ABV p.82

ADNAM'S FIRST RATE
48% ABV p.79

OPIHR
40% ABV p.96

NOLET'S RESERVE
52.5% ABV p.167

HEAVY

CONTEMPORARY

CLASSIFICATION

Before we tackle the complexities of production it's sensible to first define what gin and juniper-flavoured spirits actually are. Fortunately for us, the rules that govern gin labelling are set out by the European Union, first in 1989 then updated in 2008 to the current Spirit and Drink Regulation, snappily titled '*110/2008*'. Similar regulations are set out in the US (1991), Canada (1993) and Australia (1987), and it's these that we work from today.

JUNIPER-FLAVOURED SPIRIT DRINKS

The most general and non-specific of all the categories of juniper drinks, think of this as the placeholder within which all other categories sit. Over the coming pages, we will explore in detail the two major players within this group: gin and genever.

Any product labelled 'Juniper-Flavoured Spirit Drink' must be a minimum of 30% alcohol by volume (ABV) and it must have a discernible flavour of juniper. Besides that you can do pretty much whatever you want: colourings, sugar, flavourings (artificial or natural) – take your pick.

GIN

It's surprisingly easy to make and sell a product called 'gin'. Only one minor variation on the rules distinguishes a *gin* from a *juniper-flavoured spirit drink*, and that is the strength. In Europe gin must be a minimum of 37.5% ABV (40% for the US). The rest of the rules remain unchanged; it must contain juniper flavour – be it from natural sources or otherwise – and juniper must be the predominant taste. The latter is a grey area to say the least, as taste is a subjective matter. There are a growing number of juniper-deficient products that are merrily marketing themselves as gin and indeed, *London Dry Gin* (see below). Many of these products are delicious citrus, spicy or herbal-tasting spirits. But are they gins? According to the law, no. But since there's no 'gin gestapo' out there kicking down doors, those brands will no doubt carry on with business regardless. I don't blame them for wanting to

create a great product that doesn't taste predominantly of juniper, but perhaps a new category of gin is required to house these renegades (see New Western Gin, below).

So gin is a loose term. You can add colouring, artificial flavouring and as much sugar as you like. In short, you could walk in to your local liquor store, buy a bottle of vodka and chuck some juniper berries in it and by the time you get home you would be well within your rights to legally market it as gin – in fact, it'll probably taste better than some of the other products out there calling themselves gin.

DISTILLED GIN

Distilled gin, as set out by the EU, is a gin with one significant difference: it has to be made using distilled botanicals. Now, what that means in practical terms is that the juniper element of the gin, as a bare minimum, must be re-distilled ('re' because the neutral spirit will have already been distilled at least once) in neutral spirit of a starting strength of at least 96% and water.

This appears to be good news then, right? Wrong. Rules are made to be bent, and there would be nothing to stop me distilling two or three juniper berries in some neutral spirit then diluting it with more spirit, water, sugar, colourings and natural or artificial flavourings *including* juniper. Revelations such as this do generate distrust in gins labels as such, but on the flip side of the coin we have respected brands like Hendrick's and Martin Miller's, which both sit in the *Distilled Gin* family because both products have additional flavours added after distillation.

The truth is that some brands packaged as 'Distilled Gin' will be stretching the concept of what a gin should be, but they will remain a *Distilled Gin* nonetheless. Others will be 99% adherents to the *London Dry* classification (see right) but refinements to their process grant them a 'demotion' to the lower league. My opinion is that without more specific definitions this entire category is rendered a little bit worthless.

OLD TOM

Old Tom is the oldest style of English gin still in production. It is not recognised by the European Union, so it comes with no directions on how to make it. In fact you could bottle and sell a product called 'Old Tom' bearing no resemblance to gin whatsoever and nobody could do a damn thing about it. But in the hearts and minds of bartenders, Old Tom is hallowed liquid, present at the birth of some of the world's best-loved cocktails and interspersed among the pages of the great cocktail books of the past 150 years. Of the few examples of Old Tom currently in production, all of them generally follow a sweeter path, either through the liberal use of sweet botanicals and/or the addition of sugar.

LONDON DRY

Finally we arrive at a gin definition that can be trusted. Well, except for the London bit that is, because the designation is not geographical and London Dry can in fact be made anywhere in the world. At one time the confusion around where London Dry Gins were made was a bug-bear for some distilleries (unsurprisingly for those based in London), but for the most part the industry has gotten over this terminological entanglement, mostly because those sitting at the discerning end of the table are aware that London Dry has little to do with the city of London.

The London Dry style became popular in London shortly after the column still (also called the continuous still) was invented, eventually replacing Old Tom as the dominant style. The purer spirit that the continuous still offered made a cleaner gin, which could be sold unsweetened, hence the 'dry'. While sugar is desirable in many mixed drinks and cocktails, it is, or at least was, an expensive route to make something taste palatable. If you could get away with not adding it, either because your product was good enough without it or because your target market were too drunk to care, you would have done. Sugar also takes its toll on the drinker, cloying up on the palate and softening the teeth. When the end goal is total and absolute inebriation, it's the dry spirit that will get you there faster.

But London Dry is an important destination in gin production, requiring more rigorous procedure and guaranteeing some degree of proficiency in the gin's

ABOVE It's becoming more common to find gins that list their full botanical array on the bottle. This (along with this book of course!) is your best guide to gin flavour.

RIGHT Some distilleries, like Jensen's, produce more than one style of gin.

production. London Dry Gin follows all the same rules as *Distilled Gin* but must be flavoured exclusively with distilled, natural botanicals. No additional flavourings can be added after the distillation process – in fact nothing at all can be added except for neutral spirit, water and a maximum of 0.1 g sugar per litre.

PLYMOUTH GIN

A category and appellation all of its very own. Or it was, at least. Until 2015, Plymouth Gin was legally bound to be made in Plymouth, Devon, using water from Dartmoor. Since there are no other gins being produced in Plymouth, the gin produced at the Plymouth's Blackfriars Distillery was the only gin in the UK with a geographical indication (GI). This changed in February 2015 however as, somewhat regrettably, this old and outdated classification lost its protected status. Although driven by the European Union, the decision to withdraw support for the appellation came from Plymouth Gin themselves, who had until February 2015 to submit a dossier outlining the 'particular geographical and organoleptic characteristics' of their product, and they didn't.

On the face of it, the GI seems a harmless relic of the past and a unique selling point for the Plymouth Gin brand, so the motives behind dropping it are not entirely clear. That is, until you consider how circumstances might play out if a brand new distillery opened in Plymouth, declaring compliance to the Plymouth appellation, and demanding a share of the GI-pie – a scenario that could be detrimental to the sales and marketing clout of the existing brand. Unfortunately it's already too late now for that storyline to play out.

One final thought on this matter: the fame and prestige that the GI confers upon Plymouth could also be seen as a prison cell. Giving the GI the heave-ho grants Plymouth gin the ability to distil their product anywhere they like, using any water they like, in the future.

OTHER GEOGRAPHICALLY INDICATED JUNIPER SPIRITS

The European Union currently recognizes 18 juniper-flavoured spirits that are protected by GI. Around half of these are types of genever from The Netherlands, Belgium, France and Germany. The rest can be loosely classed as gins, or juniper brandies, from Spain, Lithuania, Germany and Slovakia.

Gin de Mahón is not a well known style of gin, but it is perhaps the best known of these outlying examples. Originating from the Spanish island of Minorca, Gin de Mahón must be made in the island's capital city, Mahón. Only one brand, Xoriguer (*sho-ri-gair*), is currently protected by this status and it traces its history back to the 18th century. Minorcan gin hasn't made much of an impact internationally, but it certainly makes its mark if you happen to be holidaying on the island. Xoriguer is made in a wood-fired still from eau de vie (wine-based spirit) and locally sourced juniper, then rested in used American oak barrels before bottling.

Vilnius Gin (Vilniaus Džinas) comes from the Lithuanian capital Vilnius. Vilnius is the only gin currently brandishing the Vilnius Gin byline, and how and why the city of Vilnius was granted protected status I'm not entirely sure. The Vilnius Gin brand is only 30 years old, a mere pup compared to the likes of Plymouth and Xoriguer, so it seems unlikely that any other product will be jumping at the chance to share the GI any time soon. Vilnius meets all the requirements of a London Dry, and is made using juniper, dill seed, coriander seed and orange peel, to name but a few of its botanicals.

Steinhäger is a type of German gin originating in the Westphalian municipality of Steinhagen, the only place where it is permitted to be produced. In this instance there's a credible claim for the GI, on account of a long history of distilling juniper waters and essential oils in the town. Over 20 distilleries were founded in Steinhägen during the 19th century and two of them still produce Steinhäger gin today: H. W. Schlichte, established in 1766, and Zum Fürstenhof, the latecomer, which was founded in the city of Detmold, in 1902, then moved to Steinhägen in 1955.

The H. W. Schlichte brand markets four types of *Steinhäger* or Juniper Schnapps (as they call it), the most interesting of which is the original Schlichte Steinhäger. Bottled in a genever-style stone crock, this product is not just distilled with juniper berries, but made from spirit that has itself been distilled from 15% ABV fermented juniper berry wine. You don't get much more juniper-y than that!

Finally there is Borovička, which is a Slovakian style of juniper spirit, similar to dry gin. Only Slovakia can produce Borovička and there are various regions and types.

'NEW WESTERN DRY GIN'

New Western is an inexact term championed by some contemporary gin producers, especially in the US. It is not a legally recognized category of gin but more of a distinction between the old boy network of London

Dry Gins – I'm looking at you Tanqueray and Beefeater – and the current set of citrus, spice, herbal and floral-driven gins that flout the law by allowing other botanicals to share centre-stage with juniper.

If a classification such as New Western Dry was to be put in to effect, its benefit would be two-fold. Firstly, it would create a home for the growing number of interesting and – by their very nature – innovative gins that have forgone the traditional approach. And secondly, it would tighten up the London Dry category, providing sanctuary to only those brands that are faithful to the [juniper] cause. Ultimately it would be the consumer that benefits, allowing them to make a more informed brand choice at the point of purchase, which is the whole point of product labelling in the first place, right?

GENEVER

For those that are just beginning to explore the world of Genever (also called Jenever, Geneva, Genebra, Holland(s) Gin, or Dutch Gin), the apparent complexity of the category, as well as potential for pronunciation pitfalls, can make it feel like quite daunting subject matter at first. And truth be told it often is. This is not least down to the fact that there's very little clear-cut law governing how the stuff should be made. In fact, according to the law, Genever need only be produced in either The Netherlands, Belgium, or certain parts of France and Germany – it doesn't even need to be alcoholic!

And that goes for the individual styles of Jonge (young), Oude (old), and Korenwijn (grain wine) too, which are limited only by the location of their production. The manner in which they are made is uniquely constrained by tradition and unwritten law alone, and it's for this reason that I'm using the word 'should' in place of 'must' in the following descriptions. See page 56 for a more detailed look at the production process of Genever.

Jonge Genever, the newer style, is the closest style of genever to London Dry Gin. It is made from neutral spirit and juniper (distilled or otherwise). Other optional flavourings can be added too, it can also contain sugar up to a limit of 10 g (⅓ oz) per litre and it can comprise up to 15% *moutwijn* (malt wine). Since neutral spirit (page 48) can be made from any agricultural source, some products choose to label themselves as *Graanjenever*, indicating that it is made

ABOVE Bols' flagship genever doesn't advertise its style, but a high maltwine content places it in corenwyn territory.

entirely from cereals and not molasses or other sugar products.

Oude genever, the older style, should be made with 15–50% *moutwijn* with the remainder being juniper, other (optional) botanical flavourings, sugar (up to 20 g (⅔ oz.) per litre/¼ US gallon) and neutral spirit. Colourings are also permitted and the product can be matured in oak casks, too, if you like.

Korenwijn, is an even more old-fashioned style of Genever than *Oude* and it is made from 51–70% *moutwijn*. *Korenwijn* is more commonly aged in oak than the other two styles, and its tough flavour profile, which moves closer in style to a whisky than a gin, lends itself well to the softening effects of wood. As with *Oude* Genever, up to 20 g (⅔ oz.) per litre/ ¼ US gallon of sugar is permitted.

THE GIN TOUR

ENGLAND

For a drink whose ingredients are generally sourced from anywhere except England, the inextricable link between gin and England is a strange fit. But gin is, in some respects, the liquid embodiment of a well-travelled empire that colonized large swathes of the world, distilling its flavours along the way. The Queen drinks it. Churchill drank it. And, contrary to what you might have heard, James Bond drank it. In better times and in worse, gin has always remained a quintessentially English product.

If this book had been written 20 years ago it would have been a rather miserable ending to the story of English gin. London had only one distillery at that time (Beefeater) and you could count the others in the country on one hand. At the time of writing, there are around 50 different gin distilleries in England producing 150 unique brands. Most of these distilleries are new, independent, small, and fiercely driven – if you live in England, the chances are you've got one within 50 km (30 miles) of your home, so it's easy to get caught up in the thrill of the gin renaissance.

The only problem with all this is that, as each new distillery opens, the pool from which to choose a unique selling point (USP) from becomes shallower and more muddied. Many new brands are relying on increasingly tenuous tales of family history, priceless botanicals, and artisanal practices to flog bottles. Filtering through the liquor store shelves, one thing does become clear: the older brands, which it has become so easy to be dismissive of are old for a reason. Their spirit has been tested through far greater horrors than a gin renaissance, and when the dust finally settles – and it will – you can rest assured that they will barely have noticed that anything even happened.

That's not to say that some of the new kids on the block are not pulling their weight, though. The freedom that novelty offers has given gin makers the opportunity to survey new realms of gin possibilities. From state of the art flavour extraction technology, to innovative means of large-scale production, some of the most interesting gins in the world are still being made in England.

BELOW AND RIGHT Every style of gin-making operation can be seen in England today, from the industrial contract distiller through to the boutique, backyard scientists. The question is: how do they differ in the bottle?

ADNAM'S

Adnam's is a respected name in brewing, as well as in their capacity as operators of a (sadly declining) number of pubs, off-licenses and one or two hotels and guest houses. Founded in 1872 in the now highly-desirable seaside town of Southwold in Suffolk, the brewery produces around 90,000 barrels of beer a year. In 2010, their 'Copper House' distillery (named after the copper brewing kettles that were once housed there) was fitted and in only a few short years they have topped the 100,000 bottles mark.

There's no doubt that Head Distiller John McCarthy is a large part of their success story. On first appearances John looks every bit the distillery engineer: strong back, loud voice, big hands, no nonsense. But scratch the surface a little and you'll find the inner geek who, like a giddy school kid, has been let loose on an experimental candy shop of his own design. On my most recent visit to the distillery he was fussing over the finer details of a pot of cold-brewed coffee. It reminded me of the first time I met him,

which was at a trade show shortly after the Adnam's distillery opened. On that occasion he had lured me in to a quiet corner then surreptitiously poured a sample of some mystery spirit from a hip flask. It turned out to be absinthe, which was just one of many pet projects he was working on at the time. Some of those 'paths of enquiry' have been confined to the kitchen cupboard (literally) but others are now real bottles and part of the Adnam's range, which currently comprises over a dozen products. Three belong to the gin family – it's a wonder the marketing department can keep up.

Barely able to conceal a devious grin, John bounds around the Copper House like it's his own multimillion-pound playground. But then I suppose it is. He designed it, built it, manages it today, and is chief conspirator when it comes to product development.

BELOW Adnam's 'Copper House' is among the best equipped still rooms in the UK. The steel column still on the left produces all their neutral spirit requirements.

Not bad for a former brewery control systems engineer. It was a combination of John's engineering expertise and a decent measure of blind-ambition that got him the job. Adnam's chairman, Jonathan Adnam, invited John to join him on a distilling course in Michigan, back in 2011. On the return flight Mr. Adnam discussed the possibility of running a distilling project at the brewery. John, knowing nothing about spirits other than that he 'liked them', put himself forward for the job. Four years on and spirits is still a very small section of this brewery's wider business revenue, but it's a section that is growing year on year.

Only a handful of the new wave of distilleries distil their own neutral spirit – the equipment is expensive and the licence is harder to obtain, and ideally you need brewing capabilities – but Adnam's is one of them. For a consumer interested in provenance and authenticity, this is a good thing, and those people can rest easy, knowing that every drop of liquid in an Adnam's bottle has been birthed in Southwold from water, yeast and cereal. As a visitor it makes for an amazing spectacle, being faced with a three-storey column of copper penetrating up through the Copper House, distilling a 7% beer (fermented using Adnam's 70-year-old yeast strain) right up to 96.3% ABV. The resulting spirit is then cut down for Adnam's vodka range, or redistilled in to one of their gin of flavoured spirit products.

Speaking of gin, the distillery makes two London Dry gins and a sloe gin. Both gins are distilled in a 1,000-litre (264-US gallon) copper pot still.

'First Rate', as the name suggests, is the more premium of the classic gins, bottled at 48% ABV. It finds its roots in Adnam's Long Shore vodka, which is based on oats and barley, but the gin is intended to be a classic London Dry through and through. The recipe calls for 13 different botanicals, so it more or less exhausts the conventional range of flavourings, adding thyme and fennel seed (two personal favourites of mine) into the mix.

But the headline act is the ingeniously named 'Copper House' Dry Gin. It accounts for roughly 80% of Adnam's gin sales, and about 75% of their total spirit sales. Built on a base of barley vodka, it features only six botanicals and has won enough industry 'Best New Product Awards' to be a genuinely credible modern classic. Hibiscus is the stand out of these flavours, but John tells me that the only reason Copper House uses

ABOVE The 'Copper House' from the outside, which overlooks the East Anglian coastline and the Southwold Lighthouse. It's well worth a visit.

hibiscus flowers is that John was once served cold hibiscus tea on a diving holiday and decided that he wanted to maintain a constant supply of the stuff at work. Of course, John appears relatively unfazed by the praise and attention his products have received. The man possesses a refreshing and endearing combination of child-like curiosity and ability to make things happen. And if the hibiscus flower is anything to go by, I'd venture that 'luck' might be the final botanical in this recipe for success.

COPPER HOUSE (40% ABV)

Cooked coriander seed, lemon balm, and only a light pine-y note. Sweeter than most on the palate, with some subtle cooked cherry, raspberry, and plum notes that seem to be whispering 'hibiscus' to me. Citrus comes through in the finish.

Throw it in a Bramble cocktail, or in French 75 garnished with a preserved hibiscus flower.

FIRST RATE (48% ABV)

Spice-drawer dust and a brooding kind of dark vanilla hits you on the nose. This quickly gives way to florals, citrus, fennel, and a touch of soapy coriander, which all adds up to freshly pressed sheets in a tree-house. On the palate it is floral, spicy, and zippy. The juniper not as explosive as it could be.

ATOM

These are strange times we're seeing in the world of gin making. Who would have thought that a mail order retailer of malt whisky, established in the 1980s, would one day become one of the most important and most prevalent innovators in the today's gin market. Atom, who are based in Kent, employ around 80 people; roughly 12 of them are dedicated to making and selling gin. Today, they manufacture around 17 different gin expressions, but the brands have no website of their own, and their distillery – if you can call it that – is still a very long way off from opening its visitor centre. In many ways the products made by Atom are a bit of a mystery: Experimental in their design, innovative in their packaging, and seemingly absent of an originator. Mysteries are, by their very nature, intriguing however, and when you combine that thought with the enormous retail clout of the sister company, Master of Malt, what you're left with is the ultimate clandestine spirits compounder for the 21st century.

Under the Atom umbrella, you will find Master of Malt, an online drinks retail company, Maverick Drinks, a brand agency (which distribute and market for distilleries such as FEW, NY Distilling Co. and St. George) and their very own product development company, Atom Brands. If you think that sounds confusing, it only covers half the pies that these guys have their fists firmly shoved in to. They also produce and distribute a special grade of sealing wax for spirit and liqueur bottles, as well as manufacturing a whole range of alcohol-infused advent calendars. If you fancy tasting 30-or-so gins in the run up to Christmas this year (who doesn't?) you could do a lot worse than buying one of their 'Ginvent' calendars.

Spirits production and brand distribution came a lot later for Atom, who it's fair to say established themselves through drinks retail. Their 'production suite' consists of a bottling line, a centrifuge and a pair of rotary evaporators. Most of the work conducted here is of the mixing kind, as their biggest brand by a long way is Professor Cornelius Ampleforth range which is gin of the compounded order. They also make a specially commissioned gin for *The Times* newspaper and *The Spectator*, as well as 1897 Quinine Gin, Cream Gin, and the Origin range.

As you will soon discover, I have a long and happy history with the gents from Atom and Master of Malt. The team, led by Ben Ellefsen, have found themselves in a highly enviable position, where financial clout meets a culture of vigorous innovation. This has granted them rights to prod and poke at the category through their inventions, often eliciting a cry of 'I wish I thought of that first' from onlookers.

CREAM

I'll begin by mentioning that I had a hand in creating this brand. The product came about when my team and I were developing the cocktail menu for my second bar, The Worship Street Whistling Shop, which opened in 2011. The menu was very much a celebration of forgotten libations realised in a ruthlessly modern fashion. One of the drinks of old that we eyeballed for rejuvenation was 'Cream Gin', formerly a popular moniker for above average quality gin served in the gin palaces of the 19th century. Although there are references to gin being mixed with cream (find me something it wasn't mixed with) during that time, the term was more popularly used in a similar way to the crème in crème de cassis, which implies it is the 'cream of the crop' or 'best of'. We thought it would be amusing and, indeed, challenging to take it literally.

The idea of a gin and cream cocktail was not too appealing though. The Alexander cocktail (gin, cream, crème de cacao) attempted a similar feat, failed, then quietly handed the reigns over to its superior sibling, the Brandy Alexander. We thought about clarifying the cream by using an enzyme to split the emulsion, but eventually landed on the idea of distilling the cream and gin together. This was done in our rotary evaporator at a very low temperature so as not to cook the cream. The resulting distillate is crystal clear and definitively gin, but with an added oily, buttery quality.

ABOVE Cream Gin was originally only made at my London cocktail bar, The Worship Street Whistling Shop. It's good… not that I'm biased.

The drink became very popular and after only six months we had an agreement in place for Atom Brands to produce and bottle Cream Gin on our behalf. These days it is made in exactly the same way, where cream and gin are distilled together, then cut back with more high-strength gin to reach bottling strength. Each bottle contains around 140 ml/¼ pint of cream distillate.

CREAM GIN (43.8% ABV)

London Dry with a twist. Juniper butter and herbal, fatty notes combine with a waft of citrus cheesecake. On the palate, it's thick, wholesome and full of lactic goodness. There's juniper and coriander – in its spiced

lemon form – here too, and earthy spice. The finish as long as the liquid continues to writhe around on the tongue. At Whistling Shop, we serve it in a 4:1 Martini using Gancia Bianco. Garnish with a radish.

ORIGIN

This product almost belongs in the botanicals mini-section of the book, as it is less a brand of gin and more an investigation in to how terroir and origin affect the flavour of the juniper berry. Each expression (there are seven in total) is distilled from English wheat spirit and juniper berries sourced from one location only: Macedonia, Kosovo, Croatia, Albania, Bulgaria, Italy and The Netherlands. No other botanicals are added.

If you're a gin geek (you've got this far already), this presents a fascinating insight in to the many and varied facets of the juniper berry. If you're thinking about starting your own gin brand, it's nigh on a compulsory purchase by my reckoning.

For anyone concerned that they're buying an interesting experiment rather than a bottle of gin, fear not. Also included with every 70 cl/24 fl. oz. bottle is a 10-ml/2-teaspoon vial of cold-distilled botanical tincture. Once you've nosed, tasted and mused over the effects that soil, location and climate have had on the juniper berry in question, you can mix in the other botanicals to complete the gin. Nice.

AREZZO, ITALY (46% ABV)

Juicy blue juniper, oily leather, but still quite light. Medium concentration.

ISTOG, KOSOVO (46% ABV)

Lighter, more ethereal, with green eucalyptus notes, mint and bay. Water settles the liquid in to pine and cardamom. Hotter than most of the palate, but with a linger to match.

MEPPEL, THE NETHERLANDS (46% ABV)

Big leather and spiced tobacco aromas. Sweet on the palate, with more leather, anise, white pepper and salt. Water really sweetens it up.

SKOPJE, MACEDONIA (46% ABV)

Dense pine and violet, gooey and ripe. The leather is softer. Thicker on the palate, like juniper treacle. Peppered through to the finish.

VELIKI PRESLAV, BULGARIA (46% ABV)

Waxy pine, candied violet and some lemon zest. The lightest of the five on palate: vapid and nondescript.

PROFESSOR CORNELIUS AMPLEFORTH

The curiously titled Professor Cornelius Ampleforth is, rather unsurprisingly, a fictitious character. The marketeers have run away with this one though. Packaged – nay clad – in authentic brown paper wrapping, and emblazoned with wonderful typography of the era, Professor Cornelius' range of products (they stretch beyond gin) are a sublimely ironic re-imagination of some of history's lowest drinking moments.

This brand is currently shifting around 35,000 bottles a year, so in spite of the made-it-in-my-basement appearance, it is not a small brand. The 'manufacturing facility' at Atom is not capable of making that much London Dry Gin, so this product is sold unashamedly as a compounded gin. Individual botanicals are infused in to neutral spirit using big muslin/cheesecloth 'tea bags', then the whole lot is mixed together and sent for bottling.

There are now half a dozen gins in the Professor's product portfolio, which includes the aptly named 'Bathtub Gin', a navy strength option, barrel-aged versions of both, an Old Tom and a sloe gin. You'll want to buy them for the look of the bottle alone, but the gin is actually quite good.

BATHTUB GIN (43.3% ABV)

Carrot cake spices: ginger, cinnamon and clove. Florals announce their arrival with hops, elderflower and orange blossom. There's a cider edge to the aroma too, which is quite intense. Water reveals orange soda. Cassia-spiced whipped cream in the mouth eventually gives way to pine-y juniper and orange custard cream. This makes a fantastic White Lady, where the spiced notes of the gin couple nicely with triple sec and lemon juice.

NAVY STRENGTH (57% ABV)

Boozy on the nose. Big alcohol fumes do a good job of masking subtle juniper and a gentle seasoning of spice. The taste is more defined. Juniper dominates. It's dry and tenacious, holding firm for a number of seconds. Cassia and clove edge in towards the finish. But overall the balance is better than the Bathtub. This makes a very good classic dry Martini. I promise.

QUININE 1892

A gin with the tonic already mixed in? Not exactly. The bitter quinine molecule is too large to distil, for the same reason that it's also not possible to smell quinine. What you can distil however, is some of the aromatics from cinchona tree bark, which in this instance has been mixed with a separate, low-pressure, distillate of pink and white grapefruit, orange peel and lemon peel. Those two components are then diluted into a classic London Dry gin comprising coriander, nutmeg, cassia, cinnamon, orris, liquorice/licorice, angelica and, of course, juniper.

It was launched on 20th August 2015, the same day in 1897 that the Indian-born British doctor Sir Ronald Ross discovered how malaria is transmitted. After infecting eight mosquitos using the blood of malarial patient Husein Khan in Secunderabad, India, Ross dissected the insects and was able to identify the malarial parasite inside its gut. Ross later won a Nobel Prize for his pioneering work.

So no, it doesn't taste like a gin and tonic, but it will leave a pleasant taste in your mouth. That's because £5 from every bottle sold goes to support the Malaria No More UK charity. This is enough to buy, deliver and hang a mosquito net for a family living at risk from malaria in Africa. Buy a bottle now.

QUININE 1897 GIN (45.8% ABV)

Classic London Dry on the nose. Solid juniper and parma violet (tablet-sized violet-scented British confectionery classic). Water reveals grapefruit and orange cordial. Taste-wise it's quite classic too. Nice balance of peppery juniper and cool spice. Some bitterness through the mid-palate, before coriander and liquorice/licorice kick in, adding a warmth and dryness which lingers through to the finish. Drink it in a gin and tonic. Duh!

BEEFEATER

With a name like Beefeater, it's tough to imagine how this classic London gin could have taken the world by storm. Beefeater is, along with Bombay Sapphire, Gordon's, Seagram's and Tanqueray a member of the elite 1 million+ case club. And it is with the latter of those brands that Beefeater competes for the London Dry Gin crown. Truth be told, they are very similar liquids, but Beefeater has one distinct advantage: it's made in London.

The Beefeater story begins with James Burrough who was born in Devon in 1835. Burrough trained as a pharmacist, a job that took him all the way to Canada and back again, before eventually deciding to apply his alchemical know-how to more pleasurable uses. His time as a pharmacist must have paid well, as at the ripe old age of 28, he bought the Cale Street Distillery in Chelsea. The year was 1863, London's gin palaces were doing a roaring trade and the Industrial Revolution was in full swing. The Cale Street Distillery was founded in 1820 and would have been one of over 40 distilleries in Greater London. Not much is known about Burrough's early forays into the spirits market, but stock lists from 1876 show a range of gin products, including 'Ye Old Chelsea' and 'James Borough London Dry', as well as Old Tom styles.

The oldest reference to Burrough's 'Beefeater' brand (named after the floridly attired Yeoman Warders that guard the Tower of London) dates back to 1895. The recipe is apparently unchanged, including the same nine botanicals that are used today: juniper, angelica root, angelica seed, coriander seed, liquorice/licorice root, orris root, orange peel and lemon peel – London Dry flavours for sure.

Burrough died in 1897 and, seven years later, the Cale Street Distillery moved to the London Borough of Lambeth. The new distillery was next-door to the famous Royal Doulton pottery and tableware manufacturer. The two companies collaborated around that time, with Burrough releasing some whiskies and gins in Royal Doulton carafes and decanters.

After over 40 years of making gin at Plymouth and Beefeater, master distiller Desmond Payne is the human embodiment of the 'old guard' of gin distillers. He's a well-cultivated, debonair gent, who's vehemently driven when it comes to gin. On one occasion Desmond was conducting some small-scale distillation training with Beefeater's global ambassador, Tim Stones, when he asked him to measure a small quantity of orris root. Tim weighed it, but the measurement was out by $\frac{1}{200}$th of a gram. When Tim asked Desmond what he thought, the distiller responded: 'I'd say you have a fairly cavalier attitude towards making good gin'.

In the next two years, 60 million bottles of Beefeater will be consumed. The botanical cellars at the distillery stock an enormous volume of ingredients – around 100 tons (112 US tons). Each distillation batch uses up to half a ton of botanicals, all of which is still loaded in by hand and macerated for 24 hours prior to distillation. It's a multi-shot gin, so will be cut back after distillation with neutral spirit. Five stills (with a combined capacity of 22,000 litres/5,800 US gallons) are dedicated to producing Beefeater and Beefeater 24.

The copper-fest does not end there though. Five huge pot stills with rectifying columns stand like enormous bronzed sentinels, overseeing activity on the distillery floor. They have been dormant for over 30 years, and their size and number mean it's entirely possible that the Beefeater

LEFT The Beefeater brand is perhaps not the most elegant, but fortunately it's fantastic gin, so t doesn't matter.

Distillery is home to the largest mass of idle spirit-making equipment in the world.

The classic London Dry bottling accounts for over 99% of production at the Lambeth distillery, but it was Beefeater 24 that was being made on my recent visit – an event that takes place only twice a year. On the much smaller end of the scale, there's Burrough's Reserve – the company's first gin designed to be sipped neat. Beefeater have pumped out many special releases in recent times but Burrough's Reserve is a different kettle (or barrel) of gin all together. It's made to the standard Beefeater recipe, but distilled in a tiny 268-litre (59-US gallon) pot still complete with a whisky-esque 'worm tub' condenser. It's the oldest still in the distillery, dating back to the 1870s. After distillation Burrough's namesake gin is then matured in Jean de Lillet oak casks.

ABOVE TOP Rectifying stills once used to purify Beefeater's bought-in neutral sprit now just sit idly by.

ABOVE Master distiller Desmond Payne has access to notes and recipes dating back to the time of James Burrough.

BEEFEATER LONDON DRY [40% ABV]

Lemon sherbet, orange sherbet and green juniper flare up at first. Earthy angelica root is cooled by lemon verbena, then juniper sinks in to the mix, with an oily and dry feel. The taste is as classic as they come: dry and not overly intense: Hot juniper and citrus notes lead the charge, giving way to anise and pepper through to the finish.

BEEFEATER 24 [45% ABV]

Juniper and citrus are again the dominant force here, but there's a soft green note protruding through as well. It's matcha, nettle and moss, but there's also a steeped tea note, roasted and nutty. Extra alcohol carries the flavour nicely, but it's surpassingly light. Hold it in your mouth and the nuances become clearer: lime oil and grapefruit pith.

BOMBAY SAPPHIRE

I first became formally addicted to the G&T when I was about 19, working as a chef in a local pub in Cornwall. The bar only stocked Gordon's, however, which, for me, might as well have been the only gin in the world at that time. But when my birthday came around, the landlord of the pub handed me a square, vaguely bottle-shaped package. That package held a gift so wondrous that it would rock me to my very core. Glacier-blue glass, cut with the precision of a jeweller, emblazoned with lustrous gold leaf and featuring none other than the face of Queen Victoria herself as guarantor. This was a bottle of Bombay Sapphire gin. Things would never be the same again. I'm certainly not the only gin drinker who has Bombay Sapphire to thank for kindling some curiosity in the category. It would be no exaggeration to suggest that Bombay Sapphire was and, to some extent, remains today, the driving force in the gin revival story.

It was in 1959 that Allan Subin, a New York-based lawyer turned spirits importer, conceived and launched Bombay Dry Gin. Subin's wife was British and Subin was a bit of an Anglophile himself, so they decided to distil the product in England, at G&J Greenall (see pages 92–96) using their vapour-infused 'Carterhead' Stills. The recipe was based on a 1761 offering from the founder of G&J Greenall, Thomas Dakin, although it's certain that Dakin never made a spirit quite like Bombay Dry, as he died in 1821, over a decade before vapour-infused gin became a reality.

It wasn't until the mid-1980s, in the midst of gin's dark ages, that Bombay struck gold… or sapphire as it turned out to be. Credit for this must go to the spirits visionary, Michel Roux, who was largely responsible for the recent success of Absolut Vodka. When he turned his attention to gin, working with G&J Greenall in Warrington, he conjured up a new realization of the category. With previously unheard of botanicals, and a name and packaging that somehow managed to not

only exonerate, but glamorize the British Raj, Bombay Sapphire was launched in 1987. It was based on Bombay Original, with a couple of appendages in the form of cubeb berries and grains of paradise, both spices related to peppercorns.

The Bombay Spirits Company is today owned by Bacardi Global Brands, the largest family-owned drinks company in the world. And it's the Bacardi coffers that have been raided to fund the three-year migration of Bombay production to a shiny new distillery at Laverstoke Mill, on the outskirts of the North Wessex Downs. There has been a mill on the Laverstoke site since the 10th century and it's mentioned in the Domesday Book of 1086. In 1719, the mill was converted in to a paper press by Henry de Portal. Laverstoke Paper Mill manufactured paper for the Bank of England up until 1968, and Portal's company was responsible for developing and introducing the watermark to English banknotes. All that history was too tantalizing a proposition for a brand with very little history of its own, so the decision was made to buy it.

The team broke ground in 2012, installed stills in July 2013, and opened to the public in Autumn 2014. It's with no degree of exaggeration when I say that it is the most spectacular gin distillery that I have ever visited. The extraordinary botanical greenhouses, designed by Thomas Heatherwick, function as ecosystems-in-miniature, inhabited by 120 species of plant, including every one of the 10 botanicals used to make Bombay Sapphire. Impressive in itself, but even

RIGHT One of the most recognised names in premium gin, Bombay Sapphire ticks all the right boxes when it comes to authenticity.

more so when you consider that they are warmed using the excess heat from the still house and every pane of glass is both unique and structural. Take a few panes out and the whole thing is at risk of tumbling down. Impressed? Well, there's more. Laverstoke Mill houses a cocktail-training academy, a museum dedicated to the martini glass, a botanical sensory experience, as well as offices for staff and distillery workers. The 7,500 visitors who walk through the door every month are given a 'personal interactive guide', which is embedded with a microchip that triggers audio descriptions at various locations around the distillery's grounds.

And as if the Hampshire countryside weren't green enough, the distillery is as environmentally 'green' as they come, too. Approximately half of all the energy used on site is recycled from either their 900°C (1,650°F) biomass boiler, or the sophisticated heat-recovery systems that work in tandem with the stills. Once the River Test, the purest chalk stream in the UK, which flows through the site, rises a little, their water turbine will go on-line too, generating a further 10% of the distillery's energy requirements.

When presented with such a plethora of show-stopping feats and achievements, it's easy to forget that Laverstoke Mill is primarily a gin distillery, and a very good one at that. Half a million litres (130,000 US gallons) of high strength grain-neutral spirit is stored on site at any one time, enough to service operations for a mere ten days. The spirit is delivered on 30,000 litre (7,925 US gallon) tankers, which can fully jettison their cargo in under two hours – five times the speed of your local petrol/gas pump.

You might be wondering how a distillery like this can be even imagined, let alone built and operated on a daily basis. Well, for that we have to turn to Nik Fordham: distillery builder, operations manager, master distiller and Laverstoke evangelist. Sporting a combined Honours Degree in Biology and Chemistry, Nik went on to train as a research and development scientist. Later, he got into spirits manufacturing, and while working as distillery manager at Beefeater, he completed a three-year brewing and distilling diploma in just two years, bagging the Gin & Vodka Association Award and the Worshipful Company of Distillers Scholarship in the process.

Wandering the grounds of the distillery, his conversation skips effortlessly, from the implications of the project to local wildlife — Laverstoke is denominated as a Site of Special Scientific Interest (SSSI) – to the feedback loop he has installed in the stills that automatically adjusts the steam pressure based on the distillate temperature. When Nik told his previous employer he was leaving to make Bombay Sapphire, they asked him what it would take to make him stay. He said 'build me a distillery'; they declined. Their loss.

BOMBAY ORIGINAL (37.5% ABV)

Fizzy citrus on the nose, sherbet lemon and sizzling coriander seed. Roots come through next, soft, nutty and medicinal. Juniper envelopes the other aromas. Taste is more earthy and supple than Sapphire. Residual and groggy, juniper loiters around through the finish. A perfect G&T gin. Garnish with a strip of lemon or yellow grapefruit peel.

BOMBAY SAPPHIRE (40% ABV)

Clean, green, citrus gives an initial blast of freshness, quickly followed up by vibrant pink peppercorn, punchy coriander seed, then slower, drier spices. It's light, but there's intensity and depth there too. The palate offers up juniper, dried peels, and plenty of aromatic pepper effects. For me, this gin has always performed well in a White Lady or an Aviation.

BOMBAY EAST (42% ABV)

There is certainly an Eastern theme. It's aromatic with grassy lime and lemon notes, which are pervasive, but not overwhelming. There's a sweetness there too, like soft brown sugar in Thai curry. Taste steers towards juniper, but ethereal; citrus notes kick in, drying the mid-palate like yellow paint on a stiff brush. Black pepper tingles on the lips. Try it in a Gin-Gin Mule – top up with ginger beer, a squeeze of lime and a splash of sugar syrup.

STAR OF BOMBAY (47.5% ABV)

Unparalleled intensity for a vapour-infused gin. Bergamot comes through thick and fast, bright, but also soft and musty. Heat on the palate carries peppered juniper to the forefront, but drip feeds citrus as the spice really kicks in. This gin remains balanced while taking fascinating developmental turns all the time. This has to go in a Martini. Keep it as dry as you can. It needs only a tiny strip of grapefruit or bergamot peel.

ABOVE The striking botanical biomes at Laverstoke Mill, (which are part of the visitor's tour), emerge, as if aromatically from the wall of the still house.

BELOW Laverstoke Mill was once a paper mill that printed English and Commonwealth bank notes. It was also, briefly, a training ground for police dogs.

CHASE

Chase was the UK's first independent craft white spirits distillery for over a century and in my humble opinion, the model for many others that followed. There was no formula to work from when construction began in 2007, and I suspect there were some doubts about whether or not it would be a success. Either way, the decision was made to go the 'whole hog' and fit a full-size rectification column, capable of producing spirit at over 96% ABV. These things don't come cheap and it was a brave, but necessary one, and Chase remains one of the few gin distilleries in the UK that has one. But to call Chase a 'distillery' wouldn't be a fair assessment. Chase is really a working farm, a place where people walk around in wellies and where tractors are casually parked here and there Once a year the farm holds a booze-industry music festival, called 'Rock The Farm', where the family invites bartenders to camp in the field and drink in the barn. Honesty and integrity have been a consistent theme with matters concerning this distillery from day one, which is one of the reasons that I admire the brand and the family so much.

The story starts with William Chase, a potato farmer from the county of Herefordshire. Will set up a highly successful crisp (potato chip) business in 2002 called Tyrrell's. If you live in the UK you will no doubt be familiar with the brand. They are delicious 'skin-on' crisps (potato chips), and so they should be at over £1 (US $1.50) for a bag of fried potato. Setting up and running a potato chip factory isn't easy you know, so

Will brought in help from an engineer called Jamie Baxter, a man who would one-day go on to set up Will's distillery and many other distilleries besides.

It later transpired that small potatoes aren't suitable for crisp (potato chip) making. In 2004, Will got the idea of distilling his surplus stock into vodka when he encountered a small distillery in the US doing exactly that. 'Build me a distillery' was the instruction Will gave to Jamie Baxter, and Jamie happily obliged. Fortunately there were funds available for this endeavour, as Will was in the process of selling the Tyrell's brand (for a reported £30 million/US $46 million).

The focus at Chase is very much on provenance. They are farmers when it comes down to it, and their neutral spirit is still made entirely from apples and potatoes grown on the farm in Herefordshire. There's no money-saving mentality to distilling their own spirit – a litre of potato or apple spirit costs around five times the price of bought in grain spirit. They do it this way because they think it makes a better product.

I got my foot in the door very early indeed when it came to Chase, having met the guys at a Christmas food fair only six months after the first distillery run in 2007. That early on, the brand (which then consisted only of vodka and some fruit liqueurs) was still called Tyrell's, but it didn't take long to change. Then came more products, including 'Williams Gin'. This was conceptualized quite early on and I was lucky enough to get a sample from Will's son, James (who heads up the brand) while it was still in its developmental stages. The product used an apple base, brewed from Chase's cider apple orchard. It's distilled in perhaps the most aptly named gin still of all time, 'Ginny', and included hops, elderflower and apples amongst the botanicals. For me, the early edition was too floral and hoppy. James, Jamie, and Will must have thought the same. It was dialled back a touch in the final bottling.

After that, everything went crazy. Numerous other liquids were added to the portfolio, which includes

RIGHT The Williams Chase Distillery epitomizes the grain to glass approach to distilling, only it's not grain they use here, but apples and potatoes.

ABOVE Attention to detail in their products and an affinity to the surrounding countryside is what makes Chase tick.

RIGHT Good liquid, a nice bottle and a free bow-tie with every bottle – you can't say fairer than that.

Williams Gin, Williams GB Gin, Williams Seville Orange Gin, Chase Eureka Citrus Gin, William's Sloe & Mulberry Gin and Chase Fruit Cup.

WILLIAMS ELEGANCE 'CRISP' (48% ABV)

Fermented fruit, apple crumble, hops and carrot cake (complete with cinnamon spiced cream cheese icing/frosting) fill the very intense nose on this punchy gin. Clean and (yes) crisp on the palate; soft vegetal notes wax and wane, as cassia, dried basil and elderflower make repeated counter-strikes. Big, complex and not at all hot. Here's a gin that plays nicely with fruit juice. Apple, being the most obvious choice.

WILLIAMS GREAT BRITISH 'EXTRA DRY' (40% ABV)

Concentrated. Big blast of fruit salad on the nose then custard tart and juniper. Juniper is heavily pronounced on the palate, accompanied by dry, nutty spices and soft herbal notes. It's full and fruity, yet dry, right through to the finish. A winner in a gin and tonic.

CHASE EUREKA CITRUS GIN (40% ABV)

The nose is lemon bonbons and candied lemon peel, rather than the intensely fresh kind. The taste is lemon pith crescendoing in to bright lemon juice. The finish is long and steady, with black pepper and citrus rinds slowly tailing off. If you like your lemons lemony, look no further and mix it with bitter lemon.

EAST LONDON LIQUOR COMPANY

It's all well and good turning out a 'hand-crafted' bottle of gin. But whether it's made from alpaca-foraged Himalayan mangoes or bottled in mouth-blown Murano glass, it won't matter much if you can't sell the damn thing. At the premium end of the wedge the price of gin continues to rise, and if it's not the price going up, it's the bottle getting smaller. For a distillery to be sustainable beyond the next five years, it has to progress past the high-price 'novelty' purchase from the farmer's market stall and secure some repeat trade. The most effective way to bring about repeat purchases is to get the product listed in a bar.

East London Liquor Company (ELLC) will not have this problem. The ambition of its founder, Alex Wolpert, is plain to see, not only in the investment that has clearly been pumped into this former glue factory in East London's Bow Wharf, but also in their considered approach to the marketing and pricing of their product. In short, the plan here is not to sell everyone a bottle, but to sell lots of people a case. And then some more cases after that. This kind of approach isn't all that surprising when you consider Alex's background working for London-based Barworks operators, a company with their hands in pies such as Camden Brewery, The Diner chain of restaurants, and The Hoxton Hotel to name but a few. Barworks are backing this project too, which in my mind is the first of its kind: a small independent distillery bringing craft spirits to the masses.

Distiller-for-hire, Jamie Baxter (see page 88), was brought in to help with recipe development and distillery amenities, and has since been supplanted by

BELOW With gin, whisky, vodka and rum on the cards, the East London Liquor Company will soon be the most sustainable bar operation in the UK.

biochemist Tom Hills. The complex is all rough wood, exposed steel and warehouse glass, and home to a pair of stunning (650-litre/172-US gallon and 450-litre/119-US gallon) Arnold Holstein stills, which produce three expressions of gin, a vodka, and in the not too distant future, whisky. ELLC also import their own label of rum and rye whiskey from America and stock all this stuff, as well as other brands, in their distillery cocktail bar and shop. Throw in a fully functioning kitchen, a maturation warehouse in the cellar as well as parking for up to 50 cars, and an evening at the ELLC is rather like a day out at a booze-themed shopping mall.

Everything except the neutral spirit is produced and bottled on site. Their standard London Dry is housed in a cheap, clear wine bottle, but the quirky upside-down horse label – a fiendish reference to the historical 'usefulness' of old horses to the glue manufacturing industry – gives the whole thing a light-hearted, hipster edge. Cutting down the bottle cost is one of the measures the team have taken to keep the wholesale price of the product down too. You can pick up a 70 cl (24 fl. oz.) bottle of this gin for under £20 (US $30). A cocktail bar might be able to buy one for under £15 (US $23), before tax, which makes ELLC's London Dry astonishingly affordable and a genuine consideration for a house-pour gin. The distillery bar uses it in this way, but add in the dozens of outlets that Barworks operates and there's probably a maintainable business model in that alone. Not that they'll need to rely on that. Since distribution began in October 2014 they have already exported product to Singapore, Japan, South Africa and most of Europe.

Two 'special release' gins complement the London Dry, and I suspect we will see further releases in the future. Batch No. 1 toys with the idea of Darjeeling tea as a botanical, and comes in at a slightly higher strength of 45% ABV. Batch No. 2 is stronger still, at 47% ABV, and is one of the most herbaceous gins I've tried.

The bar (and the parking) make ELLC one of the best distillery visits you could make. Drink and eat to your heart's content while spectating over the distillery goings-on behind the huge glass-walled backbar.

LONDON DRY GIN (40% ABV)

Spices are the name of the game here, with ground ginger and cardamom. Some citrus comes through too, but juniper again takes a back seat. Water reveals coriander and tonic water amplifies it even further. On

ABOVE An independent gin produced in its own distillery for under £20 a bottle? Yes.

the palate it's light, tight and dry. Works nicely with tonic, and even better with bitter lemon.

BATCH NO. 1 (45% ABV)

Initially, there's a warming lavender and rosemary note that gives way almost immediately to familiar, plump juniper berries. Racy grapefruit soap reveals itself once water is added, but the overall impression is dryness. The palate is, as expected, very dry indeed. Juniper plays only a brief appearance as the finish drifts into the cubeb berry and other peppery things. If you like your Martinis dry, this gin is for you.

BATCH NO. 2 (47% ABV)

Cool, cooked cucumber and fresh mint give this a gin a beautiful tzatziki nose at first. This drifts in to a more musty, oak moss effect, but the overall impression is still an unnerving, cooling, sensation. Very herbal on the palate, with dried basil, dried savoury and dried violet flowers. Herbs take the finish away. This makes a good herbal Martini, but also plays nicely with the mint and lime of a Southside (a gin-based Mojito).

G&J DISTILLERS

The town of Warrington in Cheshire stands on the banks of the River Mersey, still undecided whether it's a suburb of Liverpool or Manchester. Or neither. At first glance, Warrington seems an unlikely place for a gin distillery, especially the oldest continually operating gin distillery in the UK, but there's a lot of history here, and plenty of gin brands to boot.

In the 18th century, Warrington was in the midst of significant expansion, riding the tidal wave that was the Industrial Revolution. The Mersey became a navigable river during that time and the UK's first canal networks connected nearby Liverpool to London. Manufacturing boomed and along with fishing, wire making, soap boiling, glass blowing and textiles, brewing was one of the principal trades of the town. And where there was brewing, distilling was never far behind. This was true in the quite literal sense where the history of G&J Distillers is concerned.

In February 1760 an ambitious young businessman from Warrington called Thomas Dakin bought a strip of land on the West side of Bridge Street from a wealthy old spinster. He paid £816 (US $1,240) or roughly £150,000 (US $228,000) by today's standards. The plan was to open a gin distillery, which at the time would have seemed a wholly mad idea.

British distilling was stagnant thanks to a three-year long outright ban on distilling, due to poor grain harvests that required all cereal stocks be reserved for bread making. And gin's reputation remained rock bottom, having been dealt a near fatal blow thanks to thirty years of 'craze'. Somewhere amidst all the gloom Dakin found an opportunity however, and by the end of the century the Bridge Street Distillery was a thriving family business, consisting of a manufacturing floor, warehouse space, a shop and accommodation. The business also traded in other alcoholic commodities; porter, sherry, ale, rum and brandy.

In 1790 operations were passed on to Dakin's son, Edward. But it was Edwards's wife, Margaret Stanton who handled most of the distillery's operating stresses. It was not unusual for enterprising women to handle brewing and distilling operations during these times, and in one 1809 directory Margaret was listed as the 'Rectifier of Bridge Street Distillery'. That job title wasn't earned without significant suffering and loss mind you, Edward died suddenly in 1802 and in 1815 their eldest son, Edward Stanton Dakin died, too. One might think that the highly capable Thomas Dakin (now in his 79th year) might have stepped back in and help out, but Margaret pushed on single handedly.

By the 1860s it would seem that the Dakin's passion for gin making was waning, and the distillery was being leased to the Greenall family, who were a dynasty of brewers who had established themselves in nearby St Helens at around the same time that Thomas Dakin had first setup shop. In 1870 the Greenalls finally bought the Bridge Street Distillery, along with all of Thomas Dakin's recipes, for £3,500 (US $5,300). In 1926, the distillery moved to a new location in Loushers Lane and the company continued to grow through the 20th century, thanks mostly to the Vladivar Vodka brand.

Disaster struck in 2005, when a fire broke out on the bottling line. The vast lakes of spirit stored on site fuelled the flames and it grew to become the largest fire in Cheshire since World War II. Save for the company offices, everything was destroyed. Amazingly,

LEFT The Carterhead Still (on the left) and converted pot still (in the middle) were used to make Bombay Sapphire until quite recently.

Greenall's master distiller, Joanne Moore, was able to recommence production a mere ten days after the fire had started. It was only a temporary measure of course, and one that was necessary to fulfil production quotas for third parties. A new distillery was built on an industrial estate just on the western outskirts of Warrington and production shifted over in 2007.

Today, the Greenall's distillery, now known as G&J Distillers, is the biggest white spirit producer in the UK. Approximately 60% of all British gins pass through their doors, totalling 20% of the entire world's supply. Quintessential Brands, who own the distillery, produce five of their own brand name products there: Greenall's, Bloom, Berkeley Square, Opihr and Thomas Dakin. They also distil Langtons, Brockmans, Boodles (all omitting the apostrophe), Boë, and Bulldog gin brands – which along with Berkeley Square and Bloom makes for six gins beginning with the letter 'b'. All of the British supermarket brands are manufactured here, and up until quite recently a seventh 'b', Bombay Sapphire (see pages 85–87), was also distilled at G&J. It's still bottled there today.

The distillery has two nearly identical still houses – a contingency plan after the lessons learned in 2005 – each containing a Carterhead Still (formerly used to make Bombay Sapphire and still the property of Bacardi), a John Dore pot still and a second pot still converted to use a vapour infusion chamber. One of the still houses also has a bulbous No. 8 still, which at a comparatively small (at 500 litres/132 US gallons) is used to make the new range of gins. All of the gins made at G&J are of the multi-shot persuasion, all except for Thomas Dakin.

The bottling line at G&J is reminiscent of the robot factory from the *Terminator* movies, where

ABOVE LEFT In spite of the size of the G&J operation, gas and steam pressure is still carefully monitored by hand and eye…

ABOVE Bottling, on the other hand, is a highly automated process.

lasers, pressure sensitive plates, infra red scanners, and £10,000 (US $15,000)-a-pop filling nozzles manoeuvre up to 300 bottles a minute. It usually takes less than five minutes for any one of 40 different bottle shapes to be de-palletized, cleaned, filled, capped, labelled, boxed and loaded onto the next palate ready for shipment. All under the watchful eyes of barely half a dozen human beings.

BERKELEY SQUARE

If feels as though G&J's master distiller, Joanne Moore, is, with great dexterity, mapping out the extremities of the gin universe with this range of releases from Quintessential Brands. I say 'new', but both Bloom and Berkeley Square were launched in 2008, which by current standards means they have are entering their twilight years. Where with Bloom we see an emphasis on florals and Opihr on spice, Berkeley Square is all about the herbs. Basil, lavender, kaffir lime leaves and 'hand-rubbed sage' (don't go there) are used to great effect in this altogether *green* tasting gin. Care has been taken not to drown the juniper, however, so this product sits in what I call the 'highly stylized' London Dry category.

The production process calls for the basil, sage and lavender to be secured in a muslin/cheesecloth bag for a 24 hour maceration in high-strength alcohol – like dropping a *bouquet garni* in your *bourguignon* – before distillation commences. The muslin/cheesecloth bag was found to be a necessary component, after early trials of Berkeley Square found a green tinge in the spirit, presumably because some of the chlorophyll from the herbs had precipitated over. The more traditional botanicals, along with the lime leaves, undergo a 48-hour maceration, indicated by the number 48 on the label of the bottle. According to Berkeley Square, 'the still runs at a very *slow rate* to simmer all the ingredients *gently*' – I struggle to digest statements like this, since, regardless of how the still is run, the botanicals have to be cooked in upwards of 80°C (176°F) spirit.

Being from the Quintessential stock, the marketing of the brand is of the more colourful kind. I've heard it remarked that this is the *yin* to Bloom's *yang*, making this a male-orientated gin. The packaging is fairly masculine I suppose, and it's true that Quintessential Brands promote the product as a 'single malt of the gin world', but despite the solemn, savoury edge that the sage and basil provide, I don't see why this gin can't be enjoyed by everyone and in a number of different ways.

BERKELEY SQUARE (40% ABV)

Sage is very apparent, accompanied by anise – like Peking duck. Sage persists with a nice mossy, green note, then dried basil filters in slowly. The palate is intensely herbal, but more dry and woodsy, rather than fresh and vibrant. Dried basil occupies the linger. Try it neat, with ice. But also try it in a gin and tonic garnished with cucumber and mint.

BLOOM

Not that I'm a cynic, but the flowery bottle, use of chamomile and honeysuckle in the recipe, and of course the name itself, leads me to think that this gin might be ever-so-subtly engineered towards the female market. Of course, if I make that connection I am in grave danger of perpetuating a feminine cliché that is more than a little patronising to all the discerning lady drinkers out there. I would also be at risk of alienating male drinkers from Bloom Gin, because men don't like flowers, right? The only solution is to accept that this is an unequivocally unisex product, that just so happens to have flavour and packaging that leans towards the floral side of things. If you like flowers and flowery flavours – be you a man or a woman – you should try this gin.

In all seriousness though, Joanne Moore has created a product of great interest here, where the limits of London Dry are poked and prodded. Through the use of floral and citrus notes, provided by chamomile, honeysuckle and pomelo, we have a fresh and fragrant

BELOW LEFT This image captures perhaps 20% of the huge bottling and packaging operation that happens at G&J.

BELOW Almost all the own-label gin and vodka in British supermarkets is made and bottled here.

gin that doesn't fall into the usual trap of 'stewing' the delicate ingredients and, crucially, doesn't altogether forgo the juniper that we expect to find in a London Dry gin.

BLOOM (40% ABV)

Delicately floral. Pomelo and honeysuckle are the two most prominent aromas, but it's subtle to say the least. On the palate it's still an achingly soft affair. There is structure, and finesse, but besides an initial hit of sweetness and a soft citrus element through the finish, the particulars are indistinct. Good in a floral-themed Martini for those who might normally choose vodka, or ice cold with just a splash of rose lemonade.

GREENALL'S

A few years ago, Greenall's Original London Dry was dead in the water. But in 2013 the brand was tactically repositioned, with a 2.5% drop in alcohol and an even bigger drop in price, thus placing it well within the realms of the low-budget purchase. Even though this brand takes its name from the longest established gin distillery in the world it now walks a lonely path through the valley of gin. Somewhere beneath the trusted names of Tanqueray and Beefeater and just above the own-brand labels.

With premium products like Opihr and Bloom included among the Quintessential range, it's understandable that one brand must take one for the team and assume the role of the undersold, low-budget offering. Quintessential may have demeaned their brand – denatured their own DNA you might say – but in the short term at least, the move has clearly paid off; 1.3 million bottles were sold in the UK alone during 2014, almost double the volume shifted in 2011. For the Original London Dry, the gin uses eight modest botanicals: juniper, coriander, lemon peel, angelica root, orris root, liquorice root, cassia bark and bitter almond. Add to that 'Sloe' and 'Wild Berry' renditions, along with a selection of canned and carbonated Greenall's based 'cocktails', and the range is complete (and all dignity lost).

But putting price and packaging to one side, this is still good gin. Yes, it might be only 37.5% ABV in the UK (look out for the 48% ABV export strength that's quite popular in Germany) but at under £12 (US $17.50) a bottle it's difficult to grumble. Greenall's is one of those paradoxical situations where it would be easy to channel more enthusiasm towards the product if its packaging were more 'authentic' and its price 20% higher. It's covertness coupled with its quality and low cost does make it an excellent impulse buy for some spontaneous afternoon gin and tonics though!

GREENALL'S ORIGINAL LONDON DRY (37.5% ABV)

Very light and spirituous on the nose at first; juniper makes a fleeting appearance and is followed up by lime cordial and old spice (not the aftershave). Water brings out violet notes. The palate is light, but inoffensive. Juniper kicks in quickly and lingers for some time. The finish drifts off in to spirit heat. I don't imagine anyone will be doing anything other than mixing this with tonic.

OPIHR

I'll confess that I did waste 10 minutes of my life punching 'opihr' in to Google Translate in an attempt to understand what it actually means. It turns out that it's not a valid word in any language, or at least the ones that google is aware of. But switch the letters around slightly and you have 'Ophir', a Biblical nation, possibly located in southern Arabia or the eastern coast of Africa, from which gold, silver, sandalwood, precious stones, apes and peacocks were brought for King Solomon. Interestingly, the website for Opihr gin makes some reference to this mythical land of plenty, leading me to think that someone, somewhere along the way made a bit of a typo.

Spelling pedantry aside, in the today's crowded swimming pool of gin this is one brand that has its head clearly above the water. In fact, the IWSR (International Wine & Spirits Research) recently named it the fastest growing super-premium gin in the world, with volumes increasing by 277% between 2013 and 2014.

Much of this success has to be credited to the presentation of Opihr 'Oriental Spiced' gin, which is strikingly simple and devilishly effective. Reds, blues and golds evoke a colonial feel, which the elaborate elephant decals back up. The squat, solid, bottle (I'm told that the shape is known as 'sumo' in the bottle business) gives the impression of something rare, precious and well travelled. There's even a free piece of

LEFT Each of the distillery's two still-houses contains a 1960s pot still that has been specially converted to make vapour-infused gin.

Sapphire and Greenall's Original London Dry are both based on recipes originally penned by Dakin in the 18th century, but in a curious turn of events, this new gin from Quintessential Brands is not.

Master Distiller Joanne Moore has developed an entirely new concept for this, her fourth release, and brought about an unfamiliar botanical too – horseradish. In the 18th century, horseradish was known as 'red cole' in the north of England, and was habitually eaten as an accompaniment to a meal. It was also used in the manufacture of flavoursome liqueurs, wines and cordials, and crops up in numerous historical medicinal distillates too, often accompanied by orange peel. During their research, the team at G&J discovered an old recipe for a red cole and orange cordial, which was sometimes used as a pick-me-up for folk travelling between London and the north. The story seemed to click in place after that, with red cole deftly traversing the bounds of historical plausibility while appearing to be original at the same time. There are 10 other botanicals in this gin: juniper, coriander seed, angelica root, orange peel, grapefruit peel, cubeb berries, liquorice/licorice, plus a further three that are undisclosed.

The Thomas Dakin bottle is one of my favourites right now. The label looks like it belongs on a Bourbon bottle, rather than one containing gin, but that's all part of the charm. As rich on information as it is on typefaces, the bottle offers a concise backstory about Thomas Dakin, along with details on some of the botanicals and a nice illustration of Pot Still No. 8, the tiny still used to distil Thomas Dakin Gin. Thomas Dakin is the only single-shot gin produced at G&J.

THOMAS DAKIN (42% ABV)

The nose is sweet and pungent, like a permanent marker pen, and petrol/gasoline, developing in to cedar, soft ripe juniper, and a touch of soapy coriander seed. Water reveals ethereal notes, along with Juicy Fruit chewing gum. Coriander features more heavily on the palate, which is peppered with cubeb throughout. It's intended for Martinis, but works a lot better with longer cocktails and with citrus juices.

red and gold tassel cord tied around the neck of the bottle. But in all seriousness, this is an excellent piece of branding and highly reflective of the liquid that it contains.

Which brings us on to the liquid. Ah yes, the liquid. I really like the idea of a gin that traces the spice routes. All the way from the East Indies through to India, Africa's Eastern Coast and up in to Europe. The various Asian and African spices used to make the gin tell a story of gin's history, and the efforts taken to transport these precious commodities to European distillers. Cubeb pepper from Malacca on the Malay peninsular, cassia from China, Tellicherry black peppercorns (a larger, more aromatic black pepper) and cardamom, both from Malabar on the southwest coast of India, cumin from Turkey, coriander from Morocco and so on… if this is all sounding a bit like a recipe for a curry to you, you might not be surprised to find that this gin tastes a bit like curry too.

OPIHR (40% ABV)

This gin smells of cumin. After that, expect to find turmeric and curry leaf notes too, maybe even some fresh naan bread. The palate is soft, the pepper interacting well with the curry house of aromatics that presents itself. It really isn't a gin at all, but it is a nice spirit. It forms the basis of a good twist on a Negroni.

THOMAS DAKIN

When one considers the entrepreneurial heroics of Thomas Dakin (G&J Distillers' founding father) as well as the legacy of gin recipes he left behind, there's no question that a gin that touts his name on the bottle had better be something very special indeed. Bombay

HALF HITCH

Bloomsbury, Clerkenwell, Chelsea and Bayswater – all London boroughs synonymous with gin distilling during the 19th century. But Camden, with its canals, stables and rail network, rivalled them all. Not because there were a lot of distilleries there, but because there was one: Gilbeys.

W&A Gilbey was formed in 1857 as importers of wine from South Africa, moving to the Camden Goods Depot on 24th September 1869. Over the years that followed, Gilbeys transformed an 8 hectare (20 acre) chunk of land around the Grand Union Canal and Chalk Farm Road – an area today occupied by the sprawling Camden Market – into space for whisky and gin production, bottle processing, storage and transportation. Vast underground vaults were filled with industry, serviced by a maze of horse tunnels used to transport stock in and out. Sir Walter Gilbey, the founder, was a keen horse breeder, and there was even a horse hospital on site. Camden's famous Roundhouse, now a music venue, was one of three bonded spirits warehouses. Rail tracks within the Roundhouse were later replaced, in favour of wooden tracks for barrels of booze to roll down. If there was a ground zero to the whole thing it had to be Dead Dog Basin, an enormous subterranean amphitheatre where barges could float in and transfer goods onto trains. A 5-m (16-ft) high, unscalable wall was erected around Camden Goods Depot to stop people from stealing alcohol from the stores. Parts of what was dubbed the 'Great Wall of Camden' still remain to this day. Street names including Gilbey's Yard and Juniper Crescent are throwbacks to the days when distilling and shifting gin was Camden's main industry.

If it all sounds rather awe-inspiring to you, you're not alone. Native Camdenite Mark Holdsworth thought the same thing when his daughter was tasked with producing homework about the history of the area. Mark used to work in research and development,

RIGHT Half Hitch is a one-man historical crusade that seeks to recapture the forgotten history of gin making in London's Camden.

as well as marketing for Bacardi. During his time there, Mark was heavily involved in the launch of Oxley Gin (see pages 124–125) and Martini vermouth.

Spirit was, up until quite recently, being bought in from Langley Distillery (see pages 108–111), but Mark has now installed a 250-litre (66 US gallon) copper pot still in to the modest premises. The distillery is a tiny space, right in the heart of Camden Market, in a building that was formerly a blacksmiths servicing the Gilbey's operation. Mark starts with a London Dry formula, then adds hay distillate, English wood tincture, black pepper tincture and bergamot tincture, giving the gin a straw-coloured hue.

And the name? It comes from the knot. A round turn and two half-hitches were used to moor barges along the canal. Back then the ropes were made of cotton rather than hemp, which wore away at the iron mooring posts. If you're around Camden Market, you can still find evidence of mooring points where the post has been rubbed down in the shape of the knot.

HALF HITCH (40% ABV)

On the nose this is an intensely citric gin; warm bergamot and coriander seed dominates, but it's backed up by lemongrass and green lime leaf, too. The palate is soft, but citrus-y, starting with coriander and drifting in to lemon bon bons/lemon drops. The linger is like sucking on lemon peel. The obvious choice would be a White Lady, but this gin gets lost in there. Match it with bergamot (or grapefruit) peel in a citrus-led gin and tonic instead.

HAYMAN'S

When Christopher Hayman's Beefeater distillery was sold to Whitbread PLC in 1987, it could have spelled the end of over 100 years of family distilling. At that time Christopher was the operations director for the business, which was originally started by his great-grandfather, James Burrough (see page 83), in 1863. But an opportunity to buy back the 'James Burrough's Fine Alcohols Division' part of the business, which had moved to Essex in the 1970s, meant that Christopher could keep his foot in the distillery door. From his base in Essex, Hayman dealt in industrial alcohol for the spirits and cosmetics world, ran bottling services for brands such as Plymouth Gin, and generally bided his time. In 1996 he invested in Thames Distillery (see pages 124–130) in South London and, after a series of product launches in the US and Asian markets, decided to bottle and market a gin brand under his own name.

That was 12 years ago, and since then Hayman's have released a further five products and more recently, in 2013, moved liquid production from Thames Distillery to their own manufacturing plant in Essex. The still itself is a German design, named 'Marjorie' after Christopher's mother, Marjorie Burrough. Now, with a top directorial team comprising a pair of Hayman offspring, in the form of James and Miranda, sales director Lewis Johnstone (a grizzled veteran of the Beefeater days) and last but not least, master distiller, Lizzie Bailey (who has a Herriot Watt brewing and distilling diploma under her belt as well as prestigious names like Sipsmith and Chase on her CV), it's very clear indeed that this operation is no vanity project.

The whole Hayman's line up of products screams tradition. The six expressions present a consistent narrative between them, as their individual styles neatly plot the history of gin in all its forms (leaving out the dark days of turpentine, of course). The packaging is authentic, the bottle shapes refreshingly original, but for me the botanicals are the main point of interest. Every expression uses the exact same 10 botanicals: juniper, coriander, angelica, liquorice/licorice, lemon peel, orange peel, cinnamon, cassia, orris root and nutmeg. Only the formula for each gin changes. This means that Hayman's offers a fascinating insight into how botanical ratios can have a serious impact on the flavour of a gin.

Lizzie Bailey described to me how the London Dry, for example, uses more citrus peel and undergoes a 24-hour maceration at 60°C (140°F). Hayman's Old Tom has a higher concentration of botanicals, but also higher amounts of liquorice/licorice. Lizzie also explores different particle sizes in some ingredients, like angelica. She explained that 'a fine or coarse grind can help us highlight strong top and bottom notes from the root.' She, like me, prizes coriander above other botanicals, but is quick to add that juniper is the star of the show. Lizzie sees the other botanicals as accents, used to gently tweak the prevailing flavour of juniper in their products.

By defining boundaries within the product range, the Hayman family have actually given themselves more room to explore, drilling down in to the 'DNA' of each botanical and selectively bringing its merits to the forefront based on the requirements of each product. Of course some expressions are sweetened, matured, flavoured or just bottled at a higher strength, but it remains a neat way of doing things, and a refreshing change from all the crazy ingredients that are being bandied about in other distilleries.

LEFT Even today, the Hayman family still bottle and distribute a range of gin brands besides their own.

ABOVE When recreating 19th century gin cocktails, you could do a lot worse than Hayman's Old Tom as the base.

RIGHT The 450-litre (120-US gallon) still is named Marjorie after Christopher Hayman's mum, Marjorie Burrough, the great-granddaughter of Beefeater's James Burrough.

HAYMAN'S LONDON DRY GIN (40% ABV)

Steely dry juniper does brisk battle with citrus on the nose of this gin. Spices make their presence known too. In aroma, at least, this is a very carefully balanced product. The palate is as London Dry as they come, grippy, full and dry. Not overwhelmingly juniper-y, but it's there. The finish is spice and dry roots in equal measure. Nice. Versatility is the name of this game here. Gin Fizz or G&T, it's your choice.

HAYMAN'S ROYAL DOCK (57% ABV)

Concentrated spice and heady alcohol fumes fill the nose. The palate is all hot juniper oils and heavy root spice. Juniper comes through assertively on the second sip, bold and beautiful. Juniper continues into the finish, drying off to violets and root spice, before

begging for another sip! This robust liquid stands up well to the demands of a wet Martini; try it 3:1 in favour of the gin.

HAYMAN'S OLD TOM (40% ABV)

The nose is all limeade and sherbet; generally very citric. The palate focuses more on the roots: nutty, spiced and aromatic. Sweetness is subtle, but it structures and holds the ensemble, which is concentrated and rich right through to the finish. Sip it, or put it in a Martinez.

HAYMAN'S SLOE GIN (26% ABV)

Super-dry smelling, featuring redcurrants, soft liquorice/licorice, ginger and menthol. Taste is thinner than expected, not too sweet. There's cinnamon, clove, bramble, soft cherries, marzipan and Vimto.

JENSEN'S

I first met Christian Jensen at a trade show in 2007 where he was proudly touting his gin to an industry that was only just becoming aware of the impending gin boom. Christian's background was not one of distilling, running bars or working for one of the big drinks companies, but in I.T. (which I am told he is really rather good at) which still remains his day job. His I.T. origins were impressively well reflected in the unfussy – dare I say – basic packaging design, featuring every computer geek's favourite typeface: Courier. But once you get past the fact that it probably took an hour's work on MS Paint to hash the label together there's a nice surprise waiting for you: Christian was bottling two gins; a London Dry and an Old Tom.

It's important to remember that 2007 was a time where Old Tom was still the stuff of myths and legends. Bartenders who had done their research were aware of its status in classic cocktails (see pages 188–215) but the gin-buying public would never have heard of the stuff (many still haven't). Christian's Old Tom was based on an 1840s recipe that was entirely unsweetened. I distinctly remember my first encounter with Christian because it resulted in a rather heated debate over whether Old Tom should be sweetened or not. We didn't speak again for a few years. But let's go back a few years to understand how Jensen's gin came to be.

On a fateful trip to Tokyo in 2001 a Japanese bartender, Oda-san, introduced Christian to some vintage gin. Christian knocked back a few Martinis made with the gin and deemed it superior to any gin available at the time. Once he returned to London (with the last bottle), he set about tracking down more vintage bottles, marking the beginnings of a collection that would eventually top 900 gins. To say he became obsessed would probably be underselling it. Evenings turned into research sessions as Christian immersed himself in old public records of distilleries that had long been forgotten. This led him to a number of old distillery handbooks and collections of gin recipes, including one recipe, allegedly, to make the old gin he had been served in Japan.

Christian had no idea how to distil gin and no equipment either, so recipe in hand, he approached Charles Maxwell at Thames Distillery (see pages 124–130) and they worked together on the liquid. Once the recipe had been finalised, Christian ordered a couple of cases, at which point Charles dropped the bombshell that the minimum order would be 1,500 bottles. In for a penny, in for a pound, Christian placed the order and from that day on was the proud owner of his own gin brand.

The product that Thames Distillers bottled became Jensen's London Dry Gin. It grew organically in London, popping up in cocktail bars and at wine merchants' shops. Satisfied that the market was there for his brand, Christian turned to another old recipe dating back to the 1840s, this time for an Old Tom Gin. We have come to expect Old Tom recipes to be quite sweet, a necessity of the time to mask the inferior spirits used to make them, but this recipe called for no

LEFT The Bermondsey Distillery is becoming a popular weekend destination and is a nice place to enjoy an afternoon G&T.

ABOVE Jensen's brand ambassador, Hannah Lanfear, shows off her elegant bartending style

TOP RIGHT If you're drinking Old Tom, there's no better place for it than in a Martinez.

RIGHT Who knows what experiments are going on here... they wouldn't tell me!

sugar. Christian believes that in the mid 1800s the sweetness was achieved by a more intense, sweeter, botanical formula, not by the prohibitively expensive addition of sugar. The result is a spicy, highly aromatic product, with just a hint of extra sweetness in the fold.

After nearly 10 years of production at Thames, Jensen's now has its own Bermondsey Distillery, under one of the Maltby Street railway arches in south London. I'm pleased to see that the packaging has been nicely updated too. The distillery is fitted out with a sought-after John Dore still, a near replica of Thames's 'Tom Thumb' still. Dr. Anne Brock, who studied organic chemistry at Oxford, has taken on the role of Master Distiller and has already made quite a stir in the gin world through her explorations in to multi-shot and single-shot distillations (see pages 54–55). Jensen's, like Thames, uses the former, and when Anne recently and quite famously conducted a blind-tasting comparison of the two methods, she successfully made fools out of a panel of gin experts.

JENSEN'S BERMONDSEY DRY GIN (43% ABV)

Juicy juniper and soft green curried notes. Lime peel and delicate florals are also there in force, but it's the juniper that defines this gin. On the palate it's a slow start, like a near silent whisper evolving into expressive song. Botanicals have been well drilled here, marching in order and delivering a classic London Dry with great poise. Highly mixable. Serve it in a G&T and garnish with a lime wedge. Or go for a Martini and serve with lime zest.

JENSEN'S OLD TOM (43% ABV)

More of that curry spice on the nose, with curry leaf, tamarind and turmeric notes. Lemon fizzes through on the second sniff, with vanilla shoving it in to confectionery, like yellow bon-bons. Makes a belter of a G&T and stands up well in a Gin Fizz, too.

THE LAKES

These are exciting times in the world of spirits. Super premium brands are growing, the calibre of product is the best it's ever been, and new distilleries are popping up every other week. That said, it's a sad and inevitable truth that not all of the new distilleries in this book will survive to see their tenth birthday, and if you will allow me to play the role of 'prophet of doom' for a moment, my prediction is that there might be good trade in second-hand copper a few years from now.

One distillery that you can probably count on though, is The Lakes Distillery in Cumbria's Lake District National Park. This £7 million (US $10 million) project is built to last and I'd wager that, barring Prohibition or zombie apocalypse (the latter being the more preferable), if The Lakes makes it to 50 years, it'll make it to 100 years, too.

There are a number of reasons I believe this to be true. Firstly, an astonishing 15 million people visit the Lake District every year, which makes it second only to London on the British tourism rankings. A distillery with visitors is a happy distillery and at only 18 months old, that makes The Lakes Distillery very happy indeed.

The site was formerly a collection of 150-year-old derelict farm buildings on the edge of Bassenthwaite Lake, but since opening, it has already become very popular among visitors to the area and spirits geeks alike. There's a rather nice bistro in the distillery, a 30-seat boardroom for private dining events (and board meetings, presumably). The interactive tour is fantastic, and a shop kitted out with all manner of The Lakes Distillery merchandise, as well as a tasting suite. And just when you thought it couldn't get any better, there's even a field full of alpacas to keep the children entertained. Gin has never been so family friendly before.

It's not surprising to learn that the man behind The Lakes has done this sort of thing before. Managing Director Paul Currie set up the Arran Distillery on the Isle of Arran back in 1995, correctly identifying the malt whisky boom that followed. Now he has his eye fixed on whisky making away from the traditional

BELOW The Lakes Distillery looks directly over the River Derwent. If the distillery is capturing this kind of terroir in its products, it can only be a good thing.

whisky regions. On this mission, he's started with Cumbria, and specifically with gin.

The only thing is that the Lake District is not as non-traditional as you might think. The northern tip is only 40 minutes from the Scottish border, and the whole area is full to the brim with old tales of smuggling contraband liquor up the 105-km (66-mile) span of the River Derwent. The banks of the river (such as the one on which The Lakes Distillery sits) was once overrun with countless smuggling 'stashes' where mule and boat were said to meet. Trading was fiercely territorial and violent disputes were endemic to the area. It's a bit more peaceful there these days.

When it was time to order the gin still, unlike most distillers, Paul Currie did not pick up the phone to Christian Carl, Arnold Holstein or any one of the other German still manufacturers who are currently rubbing their hands together as they churn out still after still. The gin still at The Lakes was manufactured by Edinburgh-based McMillan coppersmiths, who have made bulbous copper objects for nearly 150 years, and it's really just a smaller version of the whisky stills that it sits next to. I say smaller, but at 1,200 litres (315 US gallons), 'Chemmy' is probably the largest gin still to be installed in any new distillery over the past 10 years. If any evidence of ambition at The Lakes is required, let it be Chemmy's generous midriff.

Distillers from Langley (see pages 108–109) helped develop the recipe – a classic formula of 10 botanicals,

embellished with bonus, locally sourced ingredients in the form of bilberry (a wild blueberry), heather, meadowsweet, and a small amount of (wait for it…) juniper. The water is, of course, locally sourced too. Drawn directly from the Derwent, it runs along a thick blue pipe that the alpacas carefully step over as they head towards their troughs, which are filled with spent cereals from the whisky-making process.

It's hard to pick fault with this distillery. The gin is great, the setting incredible, the carbon footprint minimal and the attention to detail almost painful. Perhaps its biggest fault is that there is no fault at all. As you wander the manicured pathways, you find yourself irresistibly searching for evidence of chemical waste dumping, or listening for a muted cry as a member of security personnel drags away a visitor who doesn't meet the distillery's strict demographic guidelines. Incidents like these do not happen though. Or if they do, they are very carefully handled. Just like everything else at The Lakes Distillery.

THE LAKES GIN [43.7% ABV]

The aroma is altogether blue. Whether it's just the juniper, or the influence of the bilberries, it's bright, focused and ripe as hell. It's gooey, peppery and very dry in the mouth. The finish is spicy and bone-dry; lemon rears up and lingers with a splash of juicy blue fruit. The juniper intensity means this gin will lap up tonic water (in a G&T) or vermouth (in a Martini).

LEFT Nobody puts 'Chemmy' in the corner! Well, in this instance they had to because the whisky stills are even bigger than the gin stills, and this still house is jammed to the rafters.

RACHEL

CHEMMY

LANGLEY

The Langley Distillery's official name is the amusingly straightforward Alcohols Ltd. Langley is every bit the alcohol factory, and I'm not just talking about the drinkable stuff. Everything from rocket fuel propellants to solvents used in hairspray is made here.

Named for the Langley suburb of Oldbury, on the outskirts of Birmingham, the distillery encompasses a vast block of land. Three spring-fed underground rivers service the area, cooling water for the distillery's condensers. It's the availability of water that likely prompted Walter Showell to set up the Crosswell's Brewery on the site in 1886. Six years later, a syndicate of local pub owners pooled their resources and built a distillery at Crosswell's, and gin production soon began in earnest. The current owners, W. H. Palmer, purchased the distillery in 1955 and added chemical manufacture to Langley's list of capabilities.

A fire in 2009 decimated almost all of the original brewing buildings, including the malting houses. All that's left now is a kind of Western movie-style facade of red brick Victorian buildings. Today, the vacant window orifices frame the large distillery and yard, which is filled with all manner of gruesome looking silos and stacks of blue barrels brandishing chemical symbols.

The distillery itself is a much fairer prospect and currently a refuge for a mismatched family of six stills. Only three are used for gin production at present, the first (perhaps quite literally) being the 3,000-litre (660-US gallon) 'Angela', which was commissioned in 1903. There are another two 3,000-litre (660-US gallon) stills, but only one, 'Constance', is currently in use – and it's this still that is charged with manufacturing the smaller-scale brands. High-volume products are made in the newest still, 'Jenny', which has a capacity of 10,000 litres (2,200 US gallons), making it one of the biggest gin stills in use today. Jenny is so big in fact that the distillery's roof was removed to fit her in!

At the time of writing, Langley produce 11 different gin recipes. Despite Langley being a contract distiller, they do produce one brand of their own.

Palmer's is a London Dry gin, owned and made by the W. H. Palmer Group. The gin is based on a recipe that is allegedly 350 years old. That takes us back to the mid 1600s, so it would certainly be closer to Dutch genever in style, but adapted to be more gin-ny.

Some Langley recipes are proprietary to the brand, produced for no other. Others recipes are more generic and may go on to be blended and appear under a range of different own-brand labels – the 'Cream Gin' brand that I launched in 2011 for example, starts its life at Langley before being re-distilled and bottled in Kent by Master of Malt. In total, Langley Distillery produces spirit for over 100 brands. It's the male escort of the gin world. You give them your requirements (or pick a model from the brochure) and await delivery of a massive plastic container filled with un-cut gin. All that remains after that is to pick up the bill.

The following gins are a selection of some of the better products distilled at Langley.

BROKER'S

Broker's gin, with its cheerful bowler hat lid, always reminded me of a slightly questionable Tequila brand that dishonourably sported a sombrero on top of the bottle. My instinct was to assume that, like the Tequila, Broker's was a product trying all too hard to make up for a liquid deficient in character and quality. That isn't the case however. This is good gin and the 47% ABV export strength is even better, kicking hard and ticking all the boxes for intensity and depth.

Not only that, but this is an old brand now. It was first distilled at Langley in 1998 under orders from brothers Andy and Martin Dawson, which means it's nearly 20 years old! The recipe is adapted from a 200-year-old formula and uses 10 classic botanicals.

BROKER'S (47% ABV)

Rooty-tooty! Massive root influence gives the gin a savoury, wholesome edge. Big with the juniper too. Nice and dry on the palate, erring on the dry nuttiness rather than citrus. The finish is complex, as citrus begins to shine before being muscled out by pine and pepper. Juniper shines through nicely in a G&T.

FINSBURY

Finsbury Gin is a very old brand, surpassing Gordon's, Plymouth and Beefeater, The Finsbury Distillery was established in – yes, you guessed it – Finsbury, London, in 1740, about the same time that Booth's first began distilling gin. The founder was a man named Joseph Bishop, the great, great, great, great, great, grand-father of Charles Maxwell (Bishop was his mother's maiden name), the current owner of Thames Distillery. The gin runs strong in Bishop veins it seems. However, it's not Thames that make Finsbury Gin today, but Langley! I thought this a bit odd, like when a teacher sends their children to the school they don't teach at. But it turns out that Finsbury is no longer owned by Charles' family, and actually belongs to Borco, a German-based spirits company.

Today it is one of the leading gin brands in Germany, but has little momentum across the rest of Europe. The product itself is fairly unremarkable, but that's not to say it isn't quaffable.

FINSBURY PLATINUM (47% ABV)

Vibrant 'yellow' aromatics on this gin: lemon peel and chamomile. Dry spice of the coriander persists and, at first, almost overwhelms the juniper element. Coriander is awkward on the palate too. Persistent soapiness balanced by a level helping of juniper vigour works to dry everything out. The dryness of this gin makes it a highly versatile option for mixing with.

GERANIUM

I always find myself getting in a tangle pronouncing the name of this gin. My brain automatically attempts to place the word 'gin' in to 'geranium'. The result is a noise that sounds something like 'gerani-gin'. With all that out of the way, let's move on to the gin, which was created by a Danish father-and-son team, Hudi and Henrik Hammer. Hudi (Hammer senior) was pivotal in the development process thanks to a career working with essential oils for flavourings, but he sadly passed away before the gin was released in 2009. Now, still working under the Hammer & Son banner, Henrik

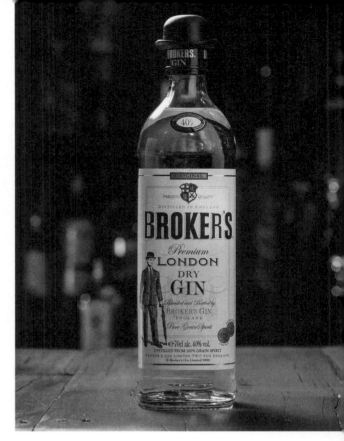

ABOVE Broker's is a bit of a dark horse in my eyes, and probably the best gin to come out of Langley.

also owns the Old English Gin brand (see page 106).

The unique botanical in this product is (unsurprisingly) geranium. Geranium leaves were chosen because they have similar chemical properties to other common gin botanicals like coriander, where geranyl acetate can be found, and orris root, with which it shares many floral attributes. An ingredient like geranium can act as a bridge between botanicals, helping to meld them together into a unified flavour profile. Geranium has been used therapeutically, so fits the bill quite nicely when it comes to gin.

Once development had been completed by the Hammer family, they turned to Langley to take care of large-scale production. The product is popular in Denmark, and shifts around 50,000 bottles a year.

GERANIUM (44% ABV)

Clean, light and elegant on the palate, tethered down by a cool breeze of juniper. The taste is dry and crisp, but underpinned by a cooked green note that attaches itself to the otherwise classic juniper-forward flavour. Finish remains dry, with a bitter green tea finish. This is designed for tonic water, so use it that way.

LANGLEY'S NO. 8

Confusingly, this brand is not owned by Langley and is unashamedly aimed at the male market. Do men need a gin of their very own? Probably not, and even despite ladies having a couple to choose from (I'm looking at you Bloom and Pinkster), there are more than enough 'unisex' gins in the marketplace in my mind.

The product is made from eight 'secret' botanicals, and according to Langley's website, is produced 'in the smallest pot still we could possibly use.' This seems a slightly odd concept to me, since I know of no reason why a smaller still should produce a better gin, but it's an even stranger claim to make when you consider that the smallest pot still at Langley distillery is a whopping 3,000 litres (660 US gallons), making it one of the largest stills of any gin in this book.

LANGLEY'S NO. 8 (41.7% ABV)

Warm and masculine. The nutmeg on the aroma provides a slightly savoury pumpkin pie element to the drink. There's pepper there too. Juniper plays second, or perhaps fifth fiddle, but there's enough to promote muscularity of the gin. On the palate it's dryer than the nose suggests. Citrus finally emerges at the back end, leaving a lingering dryness. Makes a tasty Negroni. Try it 2:1:1 in favour of the gin.

MARTIN MILLER'S

Martin Miller's Gin was one of the only gin brands to predict the impending gin boom when they launched in 1999. With top-draw liquid, quality packaging, a 'secret' ingredient (which later turned out to be cucumber) and one of the world's foremost authorities on antiques on the label, the late Martin Miller, you have a recipe for success. As if all that wasn't enough, Miller's was one of the earliest independent brands to recognise the importance of engaging with the bar community in the UK, meaning that Miller's cocktails featured on the lists of many of the country's top bars.

There are 10 botanicals used in the recipe: juniper, coriander, angelica root, liquorice/licorice, nutmeg, orris, cassia, cinnamon and orange peel. Not forgetting the aforementioned 'secret' botanical, cucumber. The cucumber is a blunt and watery thorn in the side of Miller's in truth. With the benefit of hindsight it would have been a better approach to champion the cucumber element rather than leveraging the 'mystery' angle. That way Miller's might have gained ownership of the stupendously popular cucumber-garnished G&T before Hendrick's came along and snapped it up. Worse still, because the cucumber compound is added to the gin after distillation, Miller's were forced to omit their London Dry classification from the label in 2010.

MARTIN MILLER'S (40% ABV)

A citrus-forward gin, starting with lime oils and orange pith. Lemon arrives later to the party, with clean and vibrant coriander spices in tow. Juniper well presented but relegated to the corner (nobody puts juniper in the corner!). The taste is thicker and more unctuous than expected, which provides the perfect medium for juniper to sing on. Texture is resiny and waxy through the long finish. If you like your G&Ts fresh, or even bracing, this gin is for you. No garnish necessary.

MARTIN MILLER'S WESTBOURNE STRENGTH (45.2% ABV)

Citrus is less pronounced here, as the higher strength (and perhaps a different ratio of botanicals) allows the juniper and angelica to shout louder. Although polished, the aroma is dark, earthy and foreboding, translating in to a spiced, slightly stewed, vegetal character on the palate. Works well in a 2:1 Martini, garnished with an olive.

OLD ENGLISH GIN

I first encountered this brand in quaint old pub near Henley-on-Thames. I was enjoying a Sunday roast with my family and had just approached the bar to order another pint of whatever warm, flat, ale was currently on tap. You couldn't have scripted a more quintessentially English storyline. That was, until I spotted the chunky green glass bottle on the back bar, emblazoned with English lions, shields and archetypal insignia, and the label reading 'Old English Gin'.

Of course I ordered a glass to try, and was quite excited to find that it was a sweetened gin, and every bit an Old Tom in both its outward appearance and flavour profile. When the Old Tom-style first came

RIGHT Three quite different brands, all made under the same roof. From the steely citrus notes in Martin Miller's through to the intensely juniper Old English and gently spiced Whitley Neill.

about, in the early 1800s, gin was packaged in whatever vessel the customer could lay their hands on, but folk would often recycle empty wine bottles. Old English Gin comes in a Champagne-style bottle to reflect this (England was a big importer of Champagne around the turn of the 19th century) and is dipped in black wax, making it one of the most striking gin products on the market today. The bottle even has a driven cork, so just like a wine bottle it requires a corkscrew to take it off and a strong hand to unceremoniously force it back in-between drams.

Despite being distilled and bottled in England, Old English is somewhat ironically the creation of Henrik Hammer, a Dane, who also produces the Geranium Gin brand. The recipe apparently heralds from 1783, although how faithfully the recipe has been followed I wouldn't know – not too much, I hope.

I personally applaud loyalty to the cause like this. Old English is unlikely to become a speed-rail product anytime soon, but an authentic recipe coupled with cripplingly authentic packaging gets an ever-so-slightly hesitant thumbs-up from me.

OLD ENGLISH GIN (44% ABV)

Sappy, slick and intense on the nose. Serious juniper concentration, backed up by a healthy lick of rooty angelica and a prickling of spice. Sweetness is almost imperceivable, but serves to accentuate the oiliness of the juniper, backed up by candied angelica and sherbet lemon bon bons. Gentle undulations of liquorice, cardamom and orris carry through to the finish. Great with lemon juice. Owns it in a Gin Fizz and delivers well in a White Lady.

WHITLEY NEILL

At over 10 years old, Whitley Neill could be considered long in the tooth. There's no Navy Strength bottling, no 'Summer edition', in fact no deviation at all from the standard liquid. Here is a product capable of weathering the gin bubble bursting, even more so now that the brand has undergone a major (and most welcome) packaging re-design, making its presence known in an uber-stylish matte black container with golden flourishes – like Hendrick's though it does keep you guessing how much gin is left in the bottle.

The one consistency between the old bottle and the new (besides the name) is the preservation of the tangled baobab tree insignia on the front. This gin is inspired by Africa and features both baobab fruit and cape gooseberries (physalis) amongst an otherwise standard issue range of nine botanicals. One notable, non-cosmetic alteration between old and new is the dropping of the 'London Dry' designation. I'm not entirely sure whether this is down to a legal issue or an effort at market repositioning.

WHITLEY NEILL (42% ABV)

This gin reminds me of a freshly tested Martini. It's gin, but with racey citrus zests and pithy appeal. Coriander is perhaps the dominant botanical, in both its lemon and gingerbread form. There are distant florals too and a backbone that has a weight of its own. The palate has a well-defined piquancy, with sweetness (baobab?) and bitterness in gentle balance. Another highly mixable gin from Langley. Worthy of a Martini, but bright and fruity in a G&T too.

MOORLAND SPIRIT CO. (HEPPLE)

What do you get if you take one of the most celebrated figures in the global bar industry, a televangelical food guru, two of Britain's brightest brains in distillation and flavour extraction, a super-critical carbon dioxide (CO_2) extractor, and an English baronet with 2,450 hectares (6,000 acres) of wild Northumberland moorland? You get the Moorland Spirit Company, and Hepple Gin.

'We didn't want to just buy a copper still, call it Matilda, and make a London Dry gin', Nick Strangeway tells me. Nick has been at the forefront of the UK cocktail scene for over two decades now. He's opened, managed and consulted on some of the best and most influential venues the world over, and now, along with TV cook Valentine Warner, he's turned his hand to making gin. But to describe what is happening in the Northumberland National Park as simply 'making gin' would be doing Hepple a great disservice.

Sir Walter Riddell is the patriarch behind all of this. His baronetcy dates back to the 17th century and the farm at Hepple Whitefield has been the family home since Victorian times. Back then entire hillsides were covered in juniper bushes, but all that remains today are gnarly old ladies, huddled together in gravity-stricken clusters, some of them almost as ancient as Walter's family tree. Walter and wife, Lucy (a trained horticulturist) feel a burden of responsibility to the land. Wellington boots and trowels will be their tools, rejuvenation and conservation of juniper across the landscape of the moor, their legacy.

It's early days still, but it's working. Walter has identified the first few naturally propagated trees on the moor (an immaculate conception if you like) and fenced it off to protect it from hungry sheep. They are saplings, so a couple of years away from fruiting. Meanwhile, Lucy is busy germinating new seedlings which will, after around five years of careful parenting, be planted in the wild. Each cone has three seeds, which Lucy picks apart by hand on the kitchen table. Each tree is individually named, usually after distant family relatives, like Dorothy, an old aunt who was rumoured to have had an affair with the gamekeeper.

All purple (ripe) berries are carefully processed in this manner, none are used for making gin because the quality can't yet compete with imported juniper. But the team are also foraging green (unripe) berries, and they are being used to flavour their spirit. Collected in August, at the perfect time of the season, their flavour is preserved by low-pressure, low-temperature distillation in neutral spirit through one of the largest rotary evaporators (see pages 48–49) I have laid eyes on. The flavour is undeniably juniper-y, but greener, more crisp, fresh. It was news to me that green juniper berries are a popular condiment in Nordic cuisine. Nick first got

BELOW A hi-tech production suite would normally be more than enough to get me excited, but this distillery has much more going on. There's the wild juniper bushes that cling on to the wild Northumberland moorland, the juniper conservation program and of course the skilled individuals behind it all.

the idea for using them from the chefs at Copenhagen's Noma restaurant, who would pickle or brine the berries and serve them like olives or capers.

It's not just the juniper that the Hepple boys are interested in. The moorland is a treasure trove of other forageable matter, from catkins through to blayberries. Douglas fir (also known as Oregon pine) was the first botanical guineapig, but this was later joined by bog myrtle, then blackcurrant leaf and lovage from Lucy's venerable vegetable garden. These ingredients are treated with the care and attention of a palaeontologist obsessing over a dinosaur fossil, their processing methods refined, their captured flavour nuanced.

The Douglas fir distillate is sensational in its complexity: sweet, ginger-like and curried. Bog myrtle tastes warm, like bay leaf, with green eucalyptus notes. The lovage is an epiphany, rich with cardamom and florals. Blackcurrant leaf is vibrant, fruity, creamy, yet green. There's absolutely no question that these individual distillates could all be bottled as products in their own right, but in this instance they are A-list actors playing supporting roles. That can only be good for the finished gin.

The gin is a complex composite of ingredients, starting with a traditional (steep and boil) pot-still distillate. The botanicals include the usual suspects of juniper (Macedonian and Bosnian), angelica, orris, English coriander seed, fennel seed and liquorice/licorice, joined by fresh lemon, dried Douglas fir needles, Hepple blackcurrants (fruit and leaves) and Hepple bog myrtle. This flavours a base spirit that ticks all the boxes as a standalone gin. The four rotary evaporator liquids mentioned previously are then blended with this along with a cold distillation of Amalfi lemon to make the final product.

But there's one more thing… in the corner of the barn there's a big, unassuming, beige box. It looks like a supercomputer from 1970. Open the case up and there's not much to see inside, a couple of pipes and a cylinder. It's a supercritical CO_2 extractor, capable of turning gases into supercritical fluids – just about the most efficient way of extracting flavour from a product that there is. Chris Garden, former Head Distiller of Sipsmith (see pages 1116–117) uses the machine to convert 1 kg (2¼ lbs.) of juniper berries in to a meagre 10 ml (⅓ fl. oz.) of absurdly concentrated juniper extract, leaving only spent husks of barren juniper ash. The concentrate is diluted into ethanol, and a tiny amount added to complete Hepple Gin. It's potent enough that a single 10 ml (⅓ fl. oz.) extract is enough to impact 720 bottles of Hepple gin.

Nick tells me that the super-critical CO_2 extract makes the gin bulletproof; it doesn't matter how you mix it, it'll stand up to the stresses of bad garnishing or poor-quality tonic. That's not to say you should test it in that way, but I can testify to the persistence of the juniper flavour in this gin. High definition is perhaps the best way to describe it; a celebration of the juniper berry in liquid form.

So there you have it. Probably the most important gin distillery to open in this decade. Like the iPhone reshaped mobile communication, Hepple is a grand coalition of highly desirable factors, somehow crammed into a single bottle.

HEPPLE GIN (45% ABV)

Ripe, oily, juniper; pine and moss, fading to spice: cardamom and curry. Green citrus too. There's just a touch of blackcurrant there, but the juniper is the star of the show. No change on the palate: grippy, slightly tannic juniper hits in waves, leaping to the forefront off the flavour profile. It's supported by freshness from the lemon, but the green juniper notes power through, too. The finish is dry spice and an oily, resinous, but clean feel. Benchmark stuff. Good for anything you can throw at it, but accomplishing the most in a G&T.

PLYMOUTH GIN

When it comes to history, there's scarcely a gin maker in the world that can challenge the Black Friars Distillery in Plymouth, and the tale of Coates & Co., the operators of Black Friars Distillery and originators of the Plymouth gin brand, is already a very well documented one. Once a Dominican monastery and later a house that gave shelter to the Pilgrim Fathers before they set sail on the Mayflower, Black Friars has boasted the title of 'oldest working gin distillery', 'oldest gin still', and up until quite recently even had its own geographical indication (see pages 74–77). But many of the existing accounts of Black Friars are nothing more than recycled myths and legends that were propagated by Coates & Co. in the early 20th century and again in a 1980 pamphlet entitled *The History of Plymouth Gin*. The good news though, is that the true story of Plymouth Gin is no less fascinating than the fiction.

The oldest part of the building, where the distillery shop and refectory bar are located, is a heritage gem, dating back to the 1560s. It has served many uses, most famously as lodgings for Mayflower Pilgrims before they departed for Virginia. An image of the Mayflower forms the central part of Plymouth Gin's logo even today. In the mid–1600s, it was the Marshalsea jail, and in the 1660s, the building was turned into a secret meeting place for French Huguenot refugees, before becoming a church for nonconformists.

The building was first named Black Friars in 1706, in reference to the Dominican monastery that had apparently occupied the site in the 15th century. From the late 1800s up until 2008, Plymouth Gin's branding leaned heavily on the friary connection, depicting a smiling monk on the bottle. The upstairs cocktail bar is still called 'the refectory' in homage to the distillery's Dominican roots. The problem is that the Black Friars building is not old enough to have housed a friary, and there is no record of a Dominican (black) friary ever existing in Plymouth. Where exactly the confusion came from is uncertain, but it's possible that when the building was constructed in the 1560s, stones were salvaged from Plymouth's former Franciscan (grey) friary, on New Street, which was demolished during King Henry VIII's Dissolution of the Monasteries.

Alcohol-based activities started in the 18th century, when various parts of the current building – then, separate buildings – were used for brewing and malting. Black Friars was home to the Webb's Brewery, the Hoegate Brewery and eventually, in 1807, the King's Brewery. By 1817 (but not before 1812), King's had licensed themselves as distillers, but deaths in the family meant it was time to lease the rectifying part of the business to a third party. Enter Thomas Coates, James Fox and John Williams, in 1821. It was under the supervision of these three men that gin production began in earnest at Black Friars. The 1793 founding date claimed by Plymouth Gin is a difficult one to fathom. It's possible that Coates was distilling elsewhere prior to taking over the King's Distillery, but he is not listed in the earliest Plymouth directories as a distiller. In 1812 he was a 'merchant' in Finewell Street.

In 1828, James Fox left the partnership and shortly after that, in 1831, Thomas Coates died, leaving Coates, Williams, & Co. in the hands of John Williams, and newcomer, Mark Stephens Grigg (Fox's brother-in-law). In 1842 the last of the original partners, John Williams, left the operation too and, in time, the distillery became known simply known as Coates & Co., It was over the next 100 years that Plymouth Gin really established itself, mostly under the management of three generations of the Freeman family. Coates & Co. acquired properties on both sides of Southside Street and Blackfriars Lane, contributing to an operation far larger than the present day setup. During this boom time, Plymouth became known for its superior, dryer style of gin, where little or no sugar was added to the recipe. Spices arrived at New Quay docks, which was just a stone's throw away, and the docks also brought in Royal Navy sailors who soon developed a taste for Plymouth Gin. The docks also helped shift the product from Plymouth to London and abroad. There are plenty of independent references from the era that back up the advertised quality of the brand, but none advocate its use as much as the recipe for a 'Marguerite' – a Dry Martini in all but name – which was published in Stuart's *Fancy Drinks and How to Mix Them* (1904). It was Plymouth Gin that was specifically called for.

Plymouth Gin's popularity swelled to such an extent, in fact, that it became a regular target for counterfeiters, or at least that's what Coates & Co. would have had you believe. There are no shortage of references to bogus bottles of 'Westcountry' and 'Plymouth Gin' in the late 19th century, and by 1930, Plymouth Gin labels were making reference to court injunctions that were granted against counterfeiters in 1881 and 1884. Actual records of these civil cases, either involving Plymouth Gin or Coates & Co., remain elusive, however. What is known is that in 1898 Coates & Co. won a case against Alexander M. Finlayson, who were distilling gin in America and passing it off as Plymouth Gin. The case is still cited as establishing a principle in the protection of trademarks incorporating geographical names.

The distillery was damaged during World War II, during which time the town of Plymouth, a strategic naval base for allied forces, was targeted in over 50 air raids. Fortunately the oldest parts of the distillery escaped the bombings relatively unscathed. The Freeman family didn't do so well, however. Harry Freeman (2nd generation) resigned in 1957 and his son, Robert Freeman, shot himself the following year. So ended 87 years of Freeman involvement in Coates & Co.

The distillery changed hands half a dozen times over the next 50 years, maintaining good sales up until the 1970s, but dropping off a metaphorical cliff through the 1980s and 1990s, despite the diligence of legendary distiller Desmond Payne. On-site bottling stopped, and moved to Hayman's in Essex. Salvation came in 1996 when the entire operation was bought by private investors led by Charles Rolls, who would later go on to set up Fever Tree mixers. Many measures were taken to improve the product's image and its quality. Sugar beet natural spirit was switched for cereal-based spirit, and the distillation returned to a one-shot process. The packaging changed to a more streamlined 'Art Deco' piece. It wasn't a popular change, and the bottle changed again in 2012, shortly after the current owners, Pernod Ricard, purchased the

ABOVE These bottles were recovered from a private residence in Boston, Massachusetts, USA, where they had been hidden during Prohibition.

brand. The current bottle speaks more of the seafaring origins of the brand. I like it.

The distillery's oldest still, No. 3, is sometimes credited as the oldest working gin still in the UK. Built by Bennet, Sons & Shears Ltd., it was almost certainly manufactured between 1895 and 1906, placing it in the same ballpark as Hendrick's Bennett Still, but not quite as old as Beefeater's 268-litre (70-US gallon) pot, or Tanqueray's No. 4 still. There are two further stills, a rectifying still that was also built by Bennett's and installed at Black Friars at some time in the 1950s, and a Carterhead Still, which was built in 1952 and installed in the 1960s, but has never even been plumbed in!

PLYMOUTH (41.2% ABV)

Soft spearmint and clean citrus washes through the aroma of Plymouth. Juniper is wild a prickly, but softer than anticipated on the palate. The method turns more violet-like on the palate, where the nostalgia of the candy shop continues, with lemon pastilles, orange soda and mint gum. Plymouth is a solid companion to vermouth in a Martini, but be sure to keep it nice and dry lest the gin get swallowed up.

SACRED

As the number of 'craft' gin distillers nears breaking point, it's becoming easy to be dismissive of quaint marketing back-stories and inventive USPs. These are designed to trigger an emotional response, with the product portrayed as something we can identify and empathize with, and as something novel and exciting. But the story and, more importantly, the reality of Sacred Gin is so exquisitely unorthodox that it bypasses the empathy pre-requisites altogether, leaving you dumbstruck at the innovation and genius of the whole thing. 'Artisan', 'craft' and 'handmade' are all terms that are misused and misconstrued, but if any distillery in the land deserves those three labels, it has to be Sacred.

The setting for this extraordinary distillery is Highgate village, one of the most desirable suburbs of North London; I should know – I used to live and pay rent there. With idyllic leafy streets and tall Victorian townhouses, Highgate is a middle-class utopia where miniature dog breeds graze manicured lawns and skinny lattes flow like wine. In Ian and Hilary Hart's house, however, there's a far more interesting liquid flowing.

On the face of it, Ian is an unassuming, softly spoken guy. At one time he was a Wall Street trader and then ran his own mobile/cell phone business, which went bust in 1999. Fortunately, when things turned sour, Ian had his Natural Sciences degree from Cambridge to fall back on. He set up the distillery in 2009, and was a regular (as was

his gin) at my first cocktail bar, Purl, which also opened in 2009. In 2014, Ian sold 34,000 bottles of gin across 17 countries, which seems like an impossible quantity to produce in one's living room. What makes Sacred such an interesting operation for the gin lover is Ian's unique approach to producing gin. Restricted by the size of his living room/distillery, Ian's solution was to make flavour concentrates, where each botanical is macerated (for up to a year), distilled separately then sent away to be blended into neutral spirit and bottled as a finished product. Put simply, the flavours are made in Highgate, but most of the liquid never enters Ian's house. If we're being honest and impassive about it, this is cold-compounding (see pages 54–55). But remove the stigma associated with the term and what you have is a highly resourceful approach to gin making.

The living room is full of glass. Bulbous vessels are interconnected by plastic pipes, and blue valves control, permit or prohibit the flow of liquid. This is low-pressure distillation and most of the apparatus is under a near vacuum, dramatically lowering the boiling point of the

BELOW LEFT This is what it looks like when gin takes over your life.

BELOW With most of the house busy with gin-making activities, Ian Hart is lucky that his wife, Hilary, likes his gin.

ABOVE A bottled isolation of eugenol, an aromatic that is typically found in clove, cinnamon and bay leaf.

RIGHT Sacred also sell blending kits, which allow you to blend individual botanical distillates to your own formula.

distillate, meaning that little heat is required to evaporate it. The advantage of this, in Ian's eyes, is a more faithful reproduction of the raw botanical. Ian gives me a traditional (hot) distillate sample of coriander seed to compare with his low-pressure offering and I have to concede that his one is a lot better; less soapy, cleaner, fresher and more vibrant.

The 'still' is a double-skinned glass flagon. The outer skin has warm water circulated through it from a sous-vide bath. Some botanicals are distilled up to five times, often with a water-based distillate at the end, which is blended with the previous spirit distillations to finish the concentrate. His condenser has very cold water pumped through from a -34°C (-29°F) chest freezer. Meanwhile, a noisy vacuum pump, which lives in his summer house, provides the horse power to make the madness work. Also in the garden is Ian's stock portfolio. Stacked high in the garden shed, dozens of 20-litre (5-US gallon) drums are filled with macerations, distillates and other experiments at varying stages of completion. Coded notes are scrawled on the lids. If Ian hired an apprentice, he or she would need years to work everything out.

The methods applied at the Sacred Distillery have been refined over a number of years' scrutiny that have sought to extract the best possible flavour from the botanicals. Here is a man who truly lives up to the title of Master Distiller, unafraid of experimenting with new approaches along the way.

I'll leave you with a story: a few years ago, Ian sent me an email to see if I wanted 10 kg (22 lbs.) of stoned/pitted apricots to use in my restaurant down the road. Of course I accepted them with thanks, no questions asked. Three years later, I'm at his house and he offers me a taste of his apricot stone/pit distillate. Now, any good chemist knows that apricot stones/pits, cherry stones/pits, apple pips and bitter almond kernels can contain varying amounts of cyanide. So, while sipping on this delicious apricot kernel spirit, I asked Ian if he had run any tests. He told me he had: 'I caught some wasps in a plastic cup then injected the distillate in to see how they would get on… they died'.

SACRED (40% ABV)

Calm and collected. The nose is soft, but well-prepared: grapefruit peel and soft orange notes are most apparent, leading to a touch of juniper then warm and heady spiced accents from frankincense and nutmeg give a gentle hug. The taste is light, but resolute, building upon each sip. It's best preserved in a Martini – try it 8:1.

SILENT POOL

With so many new distilleries opening up, it was really difficult to pick the best of them to showcase in this book. Some are interesting because of their staunchly traditional approach, others for their modernity. Some however, are interesting because they do things differently, and that was the vibe I got from my friend Simon 'Ginge' Warneford, brand ambassador at Silent Pool, when he first told me about the place.

The Silent Pool is an actual pool of water, or to be more precise, it's a tiny spring-fed chalk lake near Guildford in Surrey. As the name suggests, the pool is eerily still, there's no pond life and no movement, save from the gently bubbling spring that feeds it at a rate of up to 10,000 litres (2,650 US gallons) per day. The pool has been a point of interest for at least the last 1,000 years, having been mentioned in the Domesday Book and still to this day being popular site for Druidic activities. Oh, and it's haunted.

Local folklore tells of an incident involving a woodcutter's daughter. As the maiden bathed in the lake one day, she was disturbed by the sound of a horse and rider approaching. With no time to dress, she waded towards the deepest part of the lake. The stranger on the horse approached the edge of the lake, and seeing the unclothed woman, attempted to lure her out. The woodcutter's daughter swam deeper into the lake and found herself in a spot of trouble. The rider wasn't put-off so easily however, and coaxed his horse to the edge of the lake in an effort to snatch her up. At this point the maiden's brother appeared having heard the screams of his drowning sister. But tragedy befell them, and in attempting to save his sister, both siblings drowned. The horseman, who arguably caused all the mess in the first instance, trotted off and went about his business. The legend states that the horseman was in fact 'Evil' King John of Robin Hood fame. Apparently if you visit the silent pool at midnight, you might catch sight of a ghostly presence hovering over the lake accompanied by the whispered screams of a drowning maiden.

With a backstory like that, the cynic in me would assume that a distillery on the banks of the silent pool,

BELOW The famous silent pool itself, looking… well, silent.

BELOW LEFT The relaxed exterior belies the passion and dynamism going on inside at Silent Pool.

RIGHT The Silent Pool pot still with maceration vats visible on the right of the image.

BELOW RIGHT 'The Major' is a wood-burning steam boiler that generates all the heat required to power the still.

naming their product after it, and even depicting drowning maidens on their bottle, might be guilty of placing too much faith in their marketing strategy and not enough in their gin.

But the reality of the Silent Pool Distillery is a family of young (mostly!), impassioned distillers producing good-quality liquids. Ambition and curiosity are well represented, but this is balanced with a seemingly relaxed approach to things. The still room has music playing, which is a surprisingly rare find in this industry. Dogs potter about the yard and a barbecue/outdoor grill is fired up for lunch.

When the team discovered that mains electrical power was insufficient to heat their still, they turned to a wood-burning steam boiler affectionately known as 'The Major'. The still itself is a modified 350-litre (90-US-gallon) Arnold Holstein, sporting a column that allows one of the (two) MSc-graduate distillers to tweak the body and brightness in the finished product. Maceration vats surround the wall space and there's no shortage of botanicals to fill them – 22 ingredients in total, although some are repetitions of the same. Two types of juniper (Bosnian and Macedonian) top the botanical list, and you only need to smell them both to understand how different they are, which bodes the question: why is juniper blending not a common practice? Ginge likens them to opposing but complementary musical instruments, 'Bosnian is the bass guitar; Macedonian is the banjo'.

With a great number of botanicals comes a great degree of methodology, or so it would seem. Seeds, roots, dried peels and Bosnian juniper are macerated and distilled in the traditional manner. Lavender flowers, fresh peels, fresh pear and Macedonian juniper are vapour-infused, and some floral ingredients (kaffir lime leaf, chamomile, rose, elderflower and linden) are brewed like a tea, in high-strength spirit, then filtered out before that spirit is re-distilled, thus avoiding cooked notes in the finished product. It's a complex process, but a logical one when you consider the diversity of the botanicals. The guys are using local honey too, but the plan is to go even more local and install their own hives near the pool.

Besides the 'Silent Pool' bottling, there are special releases already in the marketplace. Experiments with wood are taking place, too. Oak, acacia and mulberry – the latter of which which I'm told tastes terrible – are all under observation, but by far the most exciting and head-slappingly obvious type of wood under trial is juniper. I got to try a 12-day-old sample, which had been the first fill of a 7-litre (2-US gallon) cask. It was slightly overdone, its nuances muddied by woody notes, but I'm told that the fifth fill is tasting very good.

SILENT POOL (43% ABV)

Coiled tight with floral and ethereal notes, which relax in to woodsy, nutty spice. Then comes the juniper (which you realise was there all along), which is both bright and earthy at once. Water reveals meadowsweet and perhaps a touch of that honey. The taste is viscous and sweet, with peculiar notes of vanilla and condensed milk to accompany the medley of botanicals. Sip it.

SIPSMITH

If you're talking about contemporary British gin distillers, it'll only be a matter of time before the subject of Sipsmith crops up. This is the gin brand, beyond all others, that has spearheaded the gin renaissance in the UK. Now a staple back-bar product, as well as in the liquor cabinet of any credible gin aficionado, it's really quite hard to believe that Sipsmith has only been with us for seven years.

With humble beginnings, the original Sipsmith Distillery was set in what can only be described as a 'lock-up' in West London's Hammersmith district. That lock-up was not without pedigree, mind, having been previously home to a micro-brewery, and before that a tasting room for the late, great, spirits' writer, Michael Jackson. Founders Sam Galsworthy and Fairfax Hall both sold their houses to fund the endeavour, then set about opening London's first copper pot distillery for nearly 150 years – yes, that's right, the previous licence before Sipsmith was granted to James Burrough (of Beefeater fame) in 1863!

When in need of expertise they called on one Jared Brown, cocktail historian and master distiller extraordinaire. Jared, who externally resembles a kind of bon vivant messiah, and internally is an encyclopaedia of drunken stories (both those of others and his own) began his distilling career at the tender age of 10 years old, when he attempted to distil cider in his backyard. A long career spent researching and writing books awarded him no shortage of reference material when developing the Sipsmith recipe. So, with a copy of Ambrose Cooper's 1757 book *The Complete Distiller* as the starting point, Jared trawled through various 19th century texts until he landed on the right formula. A Christian Carl Still was ordered up, and the first spirit runs took place in March 2009.

There are now three stills – 'Constance', 'Prudence' and 'Patience' – at Sipsmith's new distillery in London's posh suburb of Chiswick. Between them, they produce 14 times the output of seven years' ago. Constance (1,500 litres/400 US gallons) is in charge of producing London Dry, Prudence (300 litres/80 US gallons) re-distils neutral spirit in to Sipsmith Vodka, and Patience (also 300 litres/80 gallons) makes their latest release, VJOP, which we'll come back to later.

Back in the old distillery, the London Dry was distilled in Prudence, so when the move took place and Constance arrived, it was a bit of a challenge to upscale the recipe and keep the liquid consistent. Jared tells me it took 15 runs (and a lot of wasted spirit) before he was happy that the flavour was exactly the same.

And speaking of the flavour, well, it's delicious. London Dry through and through. In Jared's own words, 'London Dry is not a category that needs reinvention or expansion. This is a place for traditionalists.' And I tend to agree. There is nothing exceptional about the 10 botanicals that make up the Sipsmith recipe, other than the fact that the result is perfectly balanced and fully primed for mixing with tonic water or in a Martini. Can't ask for more than that, can you?

Which brings me neatly on to the subject of VJOP (Very Juniper-y Over-Proof), its name cleverly corrupted from the VSOP Cognac classification. Jared describes this special release product, which was over three years in the making, as his 'masters thesis'. This product literally takes balls to produce. A pair (why two, I'm not sure) of perforated spheres are suspended above the boiling spirit and the additional juniper contained within is vapour-infused in this manner. In addition to this, two sets of juniper are added to the macerate at different times (one for 48 hours, the other just prior to

LEFT In the space of 10 years, this distinctive bottle has become a familiar sight on the UK's backbars.

distillation) to extract different properties from the berry. Borrowing an analogy from musical theatre, Jared compares the juniper to three violins, which at first are dissonant, but through gentle manipulation, harmony and intensity prevail. The overall effect is not the slap in the face that one might expect, but an aromatic exploration of juniper in all its diverse glory.

Sloe gin, damson gin, and a summer cup (see pages 214–215) complete the portfolio, but there's still more to come from Sipsmith. A comparatively small 20-litre (5-US gallon) still called 'Signet' now occupies their R&D space. While at the distillery recently I tried a cherry wood-smoked gin, which had been infused next to a haunch of venison in a Weber barbecue/outdoor grill – it was the most delicious smoked spirit I've tasted outside of Scotland. I expect the venison tasted good too.

SIPSMITH LONDON DRY GIN (41.6% ABV)

Everything as it should be. Pine and hard leather are tempered by gentle lemon curd and soft, sweet spices.

ABOVE The new Sipsmith Distillery is something of a museum of copper, which includes three production stills with a combined capacity of 2,100 litres (554 US gallons).

The palate is reflective of the aroma, but in this instance botanicals are not kept in too close a check, and given freedom to wander, wax and wane. A careful, thoughtful gin that also doesn't take itself too seriously. Capable of standing up to the Negroni, but not too overwhelming for a G&T either.

VJOP (57% ABV)

She's a boozy one. Juniper is certainly present – fresh, leathery, pine-y, and earthy. The alcohol holds back the finer details. On the palate it's a different story. Juniper ebbs and flows over the length of the flavour and the spice punches juniper with the force of a boxer, but the poise of a ballerina. It can only be a Martini (but it's damn fine with tonic water too).

SOUTHWESTERN DISTILLERY

The Southwestern Distillery is a small business unit, on a twisty country road, only a few miles away from the town where I grew up, in Cornwall, England. The county of Cornwall is a very popular tourist destination for Brits and foreigners alike, which has given rise to quite a lucrative market for locally produced, Cornish-branded goods… sometimes of questionable quality. Looking at the rise of craft gin distilling in the UK over the past 10 years, it was only a matter of time until someone came up with the idea of making gin in Cornwall. In fact, it was a complete inevitability, which is why I was skeptical to say the least when two distilleries opened their doors at the same time. 'Tarquin's Gin', made at the Southwestern Distillery, appeased my fears however. And before you protest at the silly name, you should know that it is a real name, belonging to Tarquin Leadbetter, the distillery's founder and master distiller of the gin in question – so I suppose it's, quite literally, Tarquin's gin.

The story begins like so many others. Tired and disillusioned with his desk job in London, Tarquin dreamed of a better life where he was his own boss, making gin by night, and surfing the Cornish coastline by day. In 2012, he bought a 15-litre (4-US gallon) alembic still off an internet website and spent the next year trawling through the American distilling forums

and following 'how-to' guides on homedistiller.org – quite possibly the most comprehensive resource of up-to-date distilling know-how out there. In early 2013, he was granted a licence to distil in a tiny lockup not far from the fishing village of Padstow. A dumpy 220-litre (58-US gallon) alembic copper still, of Portuguese origins, became the workhorse behind the distillery and in Autumn 2013 they launched their first two products: a pastis (a French, anise-flavoured spirit) named 'Cornish Pastis' – a delicious pun on the Cornish Pasty, which, for the uninitiated, is a legendary crimped meat pie – and the first Cornish gin for over 100 years.

Tarquin's Gin was an immediate hit with with the tourists, but also with the capricious Cornish populace, and quickly became a must-stock item in tourist hotspots and local pubs alike. I cite two main reasons for this success. The first is the packaging, which nimbly traverses the precipices of luxury and authenticity, with a Burgundy-style bottle adorned with a silver and matte black label, topped with a splurge of vivid blue wax seemingly dripping down from the neck. It's instantly recognisable and somehow highly reflective of the liquid it embraces. And that, by the way, is their second strength – really decent gin.

On the face of it, the attitude at the Southwestern distillery appears to be typically Cornish. Tarquin's has his entire family hard at work wax-dipping and labelling by hand, while the alarm on his phone tells him it's time to attend to the latest spirit run. To an outsider, the setup could come across as makeshift and messy. But Tarquin wears his skills lightly, and behind the self-deprecating humour, there's a very well-versed young distiller, who by his own admission is making better-quality gin every day.

Tarquin uses juniper, angelica root, coriander seed, fresh orange, lemon and grapefruit peels, orris root and

LEFT A sea change from his 9–5 life in London, Tarquin Leadbetter now gets to surf and make gin. And he's not too shabby at either.

violet leaves, the latter being sourced from his family's garden. The botanicals are steeped overnight before distillation takes place.

Tarquin's is a one-shot gin, and each batch makes a paltry 300 bottles. Now with bigger premises around the corner and a pair of alembic stills, both fired by direct gas flames held together by uncooperative lumps of wax resin, the Southwestern Distillery is producing five days a week and approaching capacity. Lucky then, that Tarquin has just taken delivery of a 500-litre (130–US gallon) still from Andrea Macchia's Green Engineering, the Italian firm of still manufacturers that worked on the Bombay Sapphire stills at Laverstoke Mill. It should be operational in Spring 2016.

BELOW When you can see the fingerprints on the resin used to hold the still together, you can rest assured that it's truly a hand-made product you're drinking.

Some limited edition releases are hitting the market at the time of writing, but it's possible and indeed quite probable that they will have sold out by the time you read this. They are: a Navy strength, which given Cornwall's connections with pirates and naval men, is both an obvious move and a welcome one; a 'Hedgerow' gin that uses foraged honeysuckle, apple, sloe and alexander seeds; and 'Electric Daisies', which sees the tongue-tingling central florets of the daisy flower macerated into gin after distillation.

TARQUIN'S DRY GIN (42% ABV)

Leafy green and nicely juniper-scented on the nose. Coriander is softly spoken, and it's a floral, grapefruit note that emerges after a few moments' sniffing. The taste builds gently, then pepper and root notes kick in. The finish is crisp and clean. A second sip builds on the juniper side of things.

Great in a G&T, and easily the match for a Martini. Garnish with grapefruit in both instances.

THAMES

So, you want to start your own gin brand? Firstly you're going to need somewhere to make it. Then you'll need to buy a still to make it in and get a licence to make the whole thing legal. You'll need to source and store your botanicals, buy lots of large containers to hold the distillate, install some kind of bottling line, pay someone to stick on labels, and allocate a decent chunk of space to store your freshly bottled product. Then, finally, you'll need to get your product out to market. Sounds like a lot of work, right? Well, there is an easier route that removes nearly all of the headaches listed above: go to a contract distiller, like Thames.

If you have the money to spend, Thames will help you develop your very own product, distil it for you, hook you up with designers to assist with brand design and packaging, bottle and box it up, then send it on to the wholesaler for distribution. You need never even lift a single juniper berry. It might sound like a detached way of doing things, but it needn't be. Some of the distillery's residents are very hands-on indeed, closely monitoring the methods of the Thames workforce and delivering their own botanicals by hand. Others, like London No. 1, are hard-hitting mainstream products (at least in Spain), and rely on Thames to get the job done autonomously. Around 40% of the product made at Thames is bottled by Thames too; the rest is shipped to Greenall's, Hayman's or abroad to be dealt with. Other gins arrive already made, and Thames quietly assume the role of bottler.

Around 60 unique recipes are produced at Thames today, making approximately 70 different brands of gin – although even Charles Maxwell, Thames' head honcho, seems uncertain of the exact number. Amazingly, all the brands produced here share only two 500-litre (130-US gallon) stills between them; Tom Thumb and Thumbelina, both of which look like a witches hat perched on top of a dustbin (sorry Charles). Tom was built in 1982 by the legendary still manufacture John Dore, Thumbelina joined him at a later date. All of the gins made at Thames are of the multi-shot persuasion, typically at a ratio of 20:1 in favour of neutral spirit.

The director's office at Thames resembles something of a gin grotto. At least 200 bottles line the shelves, desk, and even the floor. Sitting in the middle of it all is Charles Maxwell, 8th-generation distiller, and Thames' very own Santa Claus (only it's Christmas every day and these gifts are not suitable for children). It's quite possible that there's not a human on the planet who has developed more gin recipes .than Charles Maxwell, which is kind of fitting given his bloodline. Charles was born in to the London's

BELOW LEFT Charles Maxwell describes how the incredible Oxley still works its magic.

BELOW At Thames, it's bottles, bottles everywhere and many a drop to drink.

Finsbury Distillery dynasty and worked there until his late thirties, right up until it was sold to the drinks wholesaler Matthew Clarke. Charles pottered around for a few years, then heard that the Old Chelsea Distillers Co. in south London had closed down and, as part of a consortium that included another one of gin's landed gentry, Christopher Hayman, they decided to buy it. At that time, Thames was the only other distillery in London besides Beefeater.

With somewhere in the region of 70 brands, you could write an entire book on Thames' products only, and it simply isn't feasible to include all of them in this book. I've featured eight brands from the collection, but I hasten to add that there are many others, and many of them are good juice too.

DARNLEY'S VIEW

Darnley's View was launched in 2010 by the Wemyss (pronounced 'weems') family, who are based in Fife, Scotland. The family ties to the region go back a long way and their connection with whisky is about as concrete as they come. In 1824 The Wemyss family leased a piece of land to the Haig family, which they used to open the Cameron Bridge distillery (see pages 144–147), which today produces the Tanqueray and Gordon's Gin brands among others.

Darnley's view is distilled at Thames, but the family have recently built an impressive whisky distillery of their own, Kingsbarns, not far from St Andrew's golf course, so I suppose there is potential to move gin production there in the future if they wish.

The name is taken from a family connection with Mary Queen of Scots (I told you they went back a few

ABOVE The stills at Thames see a lot of action. Tom Thumb (in the foreground of the image on the left) handles most of the throughput, which makes it among the hardest-working gin stills in the UK.

years). The story goes that, in 1565, Mary spied her future husband, Lord Darnley, through the courtyard window of Wemyss Castle. The pair got married and their son, James, successfully united the thrones of England and Scotland, becoming James VI of England and James I of Scotland. So I suppose it was Mary's view of Darnley rather than the other way round, but hey – you get the point.

The gin combines juniper, coriander seed, angelica root, lemon peel, orris root and elderflower.

DARNLEY'S VIEW (40% ABV)

Plump florals, elderflower and chamomile are first to touch base. Soft red fruit, especially redcurrant and cranberry, hit next, along with sweet cinnamon and clove. Spicy and sweet on the palate too, curiously taut and stiff, like the liquid is nervous to give too much away. Cassia lingers in the finish. Bold enough for cocktails – excellent in a Clover Club.

FIFTY POUNDS

Remember the Gin Acts? Of course you do. The 1736 Act, the government's second attempt to curtail gin production and consumption during London's gin craze, was perhaps the most ridiculous of all the six acts. It asked that gin compounders apply for a £50 (US $75) annual licence, (nearly £5,000/US $7,500) in today's money). Most of London's gin compounders were not wealthy people, which was the very reason they ended up flogging nasty gin in the first place. Well and truly priced out of the game, only two licence applications were made in the three years that followed. All the other gin compounders disregarded the law and gin making became a much more underhand and underground kind of game.

Fifty Pounds Gin, which is distilled at Thames in south London, gets its name from the cost of a compounding licensed in 1736. The brand was only launched in 2010, but I award lots of kudos points for the notion that Fifty Pounds might just have been one of the two lonely licensed payers from the era. Whoever the two compounders who did fork out for a licence were, it's quite likely, given their strong moral sensibilities and deep pockets, that they were manufacturing a gin of superior quality. That's not to say it would have been great, just that it would have been better. Maybe it's the belief in 'better' that drives the makers of Fifty Pounds? Or have I just done the marketing job for them?!

Fifty Pounds uses 11 botanicals in total: juniper, coriander, angelica root, liquorice/licorice root, grains of paradise, orange peel, lemon peel and a further three botanicals that are undisclosed.

I've always found myself drawn to the brand, in part because of the historical tips of the hat, but also in the bottle, which is very much in the style of the broad shouldered glass bottles that early Holland's gin was packaged in. It's a beauty and the gin is tasty too.

FIFTY POUNDS (43.5% ABV)

A cleanly citric, but savoury gin on the nose. On the palate it's herbal and nutty, where the herbal notes bring a warmth and breadth to the taste, but avoid becoming flabby or cooked-tasting. The texture is viscous, which gives the impression of sweetness to balance all that lemon meringue pie and nutmeg. This is benchmark Gin Fizz material.

FORD'S

Launching a new spirits brand is no easy thing, but launching products in four separate spirit categories at the same time is the stuff of madness. The New York-based 86 Co. have gone and done it though, and thanks to their team – which includes bar legends like Simon Ford, Dushan Zaric, Dan Warner and Jason

Cosmos – as well the quality of their products, Ford's Gin, Aylesbury Duck Vodka, Cana Brava Rum, and Tequila Cabeza, are quickly becoming the first products a bartender reaches for once the bar's 'speed rail' brands have been exhausted.

Simon Ford, the smiling face of 86 Co., was formerly the US Ambassador for Beefeater and Plymouth Gins, and during his tenure there became one of the most popular figures in the bar industry. Simon is a friend of mine, and I can tell you that he is as gentlemanly and honest as they come (I couldn't find any dirt on him) and so is his gin.

Ford's gin has been ruthlessly designed with ease of use and the bartender in mind. The bottle is ingeniously imagined. Ridges on the neck and an embossed band around the waist make it super easy to latch on to, even when you're on your fifth Negroni. It's weighty enough to be substantial, but not impractically so. The label is chock full of useful information in the style of passport stamps, like someone got carried away with the 'vintage design elements' clip art pack – you could spend 10 minutes examining and still not be finished.

Ford's Gin is, as far as I am aware, the only gin in the world whose recipe is publicly available online and the whole production process stripped bare. The formula comprises (by weight) 49.5% juniper, 30.5% coriander seed, 3.2% lemon peel, 3.2% orange peel, 3.2% grapefruit peel, 3.2% angelica root, 2.1% cassia, 3.2% jasmine flowers and 2.1% orris root. It apparently took 80 iterations of the product before this recipe was settled on, where each new sample was sent out to top New York bartenders for testing in cocktails. It's thanks to that obsessive developmental process that the recipe has been refined in such a way that the gin plays nicely with a variety of mixed drinks. Cassia for the Negroni; grapefruit plays nicely with citrus-based drinks; jasmine to work in honey cocktails like the Bee's Knees.

After distillation the high strength gin concentrate is shipped to the Chambray distillery in California, where it is cut with spirit and water then bottled. The alternative would be to get Thames to do the bottling, but that would of course result in significant shipping costs, not to mention a sizeable carbon footprint as the product is hauled over to the US. The US remains the biggest market for this gin by far, which, at only three years old, is already shifting 180,000 bottles a year.

FORD'S GIN (45% ABV)

Juniper forward on the nose, but there's a nice summer meadow note to it: cut grass, sun baked bark, honey, and jasmine. Clean and gritty on the palate, tight citrus, leading in to soft spices and a dry juniper finish. Designed to be good in everything, so test it for yourself! (I like it in a Gin Fizz).

GILPIN'S

According to Gilpin's website, 'our goal [was] to create the world's best-tasting (and best-looking) gin.'

Under normal circumstances I'm the first to scoff at such wildly ambitious claims, but in fairness to Gilpin's, they were awarded 'World's Best Gin' at the 2014 World Gin Awards, so I guess you could say that Gilpin's have achieved what they set out to do.

The brand was founded by Matthew Gilpin and is inspired by two legendary Gilpins who are, presumably, his distant ancestors. The first was Sir Richard 'The Rider' Gilpin, a man who earned his notoriety for slaying a troublesome wild boar that was causing no end of havoc to communities in Westmorland during the 13th century. The wild boar later became the symbol of the Gilpin family and you'll find it proudly placed on the label of Gilpin's gin today. The second legendary Gilpin was George Gilpin, who, on instruction from Queen Elizabeth I, served as ambassador to the Low Countries when the 6,000 men were deployed to fight the Spanish Armada

BELOW Spent botanicals at Thames, but for which of the 60-or-so recipes were they used?

BELOW RIGHT This chart lists every botanical that Thames uses, with a separate column for the organics.

Gilpin's is made from eight botanicals, and manages to play with safe flavours while simultaneously exploring unconventional ingredients. Juniper, angelica root, coriander seed, orange peel and lemon peel are joined by dried borage flowers, dried sage leaves and lime peel. It's strange that lime peel isn't a more widely used in gin making given its popularity as a garnish to the G&T. Likewise with borage flowers, which in their fresh form offer a similar flavour to cucumber.

GILPIN'S WESTMORLAND EXTRA DRY GIN (47% ABV)

Green things. Definitely sage, which is of the dry and old persuasion, along with dried basil and pressed flowers. There's an antiseptic cassia note to it too, which in combination with the herbs gives it quite a nice medicinal quality. The taste is spicy, with more pine to it, rich and woody. Great with tonic water, garnish with a stick of liquorice/licorice.

JUNIPER GREEN

Proudly declaring itself 'The world's first organic London Dry Gin', Juniper Green was also the first brand to roll off the Thames Distillery production line in the late 1990s.

Making an organic gin is not easy however, and certainly deserves some small applause. Sourcing organic botanicals is of course the first step, and in this case they are juniper, coriander seed, angelica root, and savory. But remember that it's not just the botanicals that need to be organic, but the neutral spirit too. That means tracking down a spirit made from organic barley, wheat, or corn from a distillery that is committed to producing it.

Being an organic product and getting in to the craft gin game so early on should have given Juniper Green a significant advantage over competitors. Add to that a Royal Warrant granted by HRH The Prince of Wales, and that you can sometimes find bottles of Juniper Green for as little as £15 (US $23) on supermarket shelves, and it's a complete mystery to me as to why this product isn't everywhere.

Like many of the brands launched in the late 1990s and early 2000s, which were arguably ahead of the time, growth seems to have plateaued, rather than… grown, and empty bottles on the backbar have been supplanted by youthful new entries in the category. The packaging of Juniper Green probably hasn't helped matters. Taking 'no-frills' to the next level, the typefaces and layout are so outdated that the bottle is almost on the verge of becoming achingly cool.

JUNIPER GREEN (37.5% ABV)

Sweet, light juniper sits nicely on the nose, with a herbal fuzz of savoury lingering around in the wings. On the palate the lack of alcohol is reflected in the drink. A little too watery, flat through to the finish, and crying out for a kick up the backside. A shame. It'll survive a G&T as long as you go easy on the tonic.

OXLEY

All gins are unique, but some are more unique than others. That makes no sense at all, of course, but in the case of Oxley it might just be true. Cast your eyes over the bizarre piece of distillation machinery that is used exclusively in the production of Oxley, and it's difficult to work out what's going on. It's a vacuum still in principle, but looks more like a frozen-up U-bend. No doubt the still's designer, Les Farl, wouldn't be happy to read that, and it's fair to say I'm doing the engineering an injustice. After all, this still is capable of boiling spirit at -6°C (21°F). That's about the same temperature as a good Martini, and under normal circumstances, it's 85°C (185°F) too cold to make gin. But a rather temperamental vacuum pump and some chunky pieces of steel arranged in the correct manner means that this still operates under a very low pressure indeed – very nearly a complete vacuum.

LEFT A triumph in packaging design, Oxley stands out from a mile off. Thanks to its unique distillation process, the flavour is pretty distinctive too.

Thames Distillery is responsible for making it and the process is fairly unconventional too. Around 1 kg (2.2 lbs.) of botanicals are loaded in to the still from two mystery bags that are supplied to Thames by Bacardi, the brand owner. The bags of botanicals that make up the mysterious-sounding 'Recipe 38' are prepared back at Bacardi HQ in such a way that the person responsible for compiling the ingredients for 'Bag A' is in the dark as to what goes in to 'Bag B' and vice versa. There are 14 botanicals in total, three of them I would eyeball as being unusual: vanilla, cocoa, and meadowsweet, but the end product leans more towards the clean, crisp, citrus botanicals.

After a 15-hour maceration, the distillation is quick, taking only a couple of hours. Spirit cuts are unnecessary here, because the low temperature run makes for a consistent extraction of flavour from start to finish. In goes 25 litres (6½ US gallons) and out comes 23 litres (6 US gallons). The missing liquid is absorbed by the botanicals.

There's an amusing story associated with the Oxley still. As the brand was readying to launch in 2009 the Bacardi group were busy preparing patent applications to ensure that the technical details of the still and distillation procedure remained their personal property. No expense had been spared on patent lawyers. Unfortunately, the marketing team got a bit carried away and inadvertently spilled most, if not all, of the beans to the media during the launch. A rather bewildered patent lawyer picked up the phone and politely informed them of how much money they had wasted over the seven years of development.

At the time of launch Oxley was the most expensive gin on the market, costing around £50 (US $75) for a 1-litre (33-fl. oz) bottle. Nowadays the gin shelves are rammed full of new brands charging upwards of £30 (US $45) for a 70-cl (24-fl. oz) bottle, so when one considers the quality of Oxley, not to mention the effort that goes in to making it, it becomes quite an attractive proposition.

OXLEY (47% ABV)

Complex, but delicate. This is a veritable fruit salad on the nose: Sweet Seville orange, grapefruit, bubblegum, pineapple and ginger. Under the layers of fruit you'll find a gentle stream of glossy pine, cream soda and then more citrus. The taste errs on the bittersweet side of things as florals and vanilla do battle with citrus piths

and festive cacao. A nice contemporary Martini or a citrus-fuelled G&T.

PORTOBELLO ROAD

*"Portobello road, Portobello road
Street where the riches of ages are stowed.
Anything and everything a chap can unload
Is sold off the barrow in Portobello road.
You'll find what you want in the Portobello road."*

'Portobello Road' was written in the 1970s for the movie *Bedknobs and Broomsticks*, which was set in 1940s' London. The sentiment of the piece was the drudgery of a hard day's work in the smog-filled streets of wartime London. But even today, this Notting Hill destination is a sure bet if you're looking to 'find what you want' – it's positively littered with antique dealers and curio vendors, fuelled by overpriced eateries and lubricated by a blizzard of frozen yogurt. But one thing the writers of 'Portobello Road' wouldn't have found on Portobello Road was the 'Ginstitute' – a distillery, training academy and a museum of gin.

The Ginstitute was formerly an apartment above the Portobello Star, a cocktail bar convincingly posing as a pub, owned and run by Ged Feltham and Jake Burger – the latter being an international libator of great repute and a known accomplice of mine. Jake used to live in the apartment, but after five years, the novelty of living above a bar wore off and he moved out.

The first idea was to build a museum of alcohol, which would have been perfect fit, not only with the antiquarians on Portobello Road, but also with London's historical susceptibility for a drink or five. After further scheming though, it became clear that gin would be the star of the show, 'You can't tell the story of London without telling the story of gin, and you can't tell the story of gin without telling the story of London,' as Jake puts it. The team installed a tiny 30-litre (8-US gallon) Portuguese alembic still in the space too, so when the doors finally opened on the Ginstitute, in 2013, Jake was able to educate 'ginterns' on gin history and cocktails, as well as walk them though a gin distillation run.

From there the Portobello Gin brand evolved naturally from the activities at the Ginstitute. It became clear quite early on that manufacturing would need be ramped up substantially for the brand to support itself in the crowded market place. They approached Charles Maxwell at Thames, who helped to tweak the recipe. Nine out of the original ten botanicals made the cut: juniper, coriander seed, angelica root, orris root, orange peel, lemon peel, liquorice/licorice, cassia bark and nutmeg. Cardamom didn't make it. The product was field-tested in Martinis, Negronis, G&Ts and of course on its own. Test subjects included Portobello Star regulars and a handful of other industry 'known offenders'.

Since its launch, Portobello Road London Dry has seen incredible success in the UK and abroad, and in the next 12 months Thames will produce 200,000 bottles' worth. There's a number of factors that can be attributed to this, not least of all the fact that it's tasty juice. It's also priced competitively and the branding is genius – beautiful, authentic, witty, transportive… need I go on? Interestingly, and unlike most brands, it wasn't designed by a packaging designer per se, but by a typographer. It's for that reason that most of the type on the Portobello Road bottles is hand-drawn.

Portobello Road recently launched a 'Director's Cut' expression of PB, which they see as a chance to flex their creative muscles. Distilled at the Ginstitute, and released every year on 'Founder's Day' (Ged Feltham's birthday), the 2015 expression featured asparagus as a botanical. It should have been a one of a kind, and it is unquestionably the first London Dry Gin to use asparagus, but it transpires that San Francisco's Folsom Asparagus Gin Co. (aka FAG-CO) got there first back in 1916. It wasn't much of a hit, as the company was wound up in 1918. As for future Director's Cut releases, who knows? Portobello Mushroom ought to be high on the list, I suppose.

PORTOBELLO ROAD NO. 171 (42% ABV)

Classic stuff on the nose, bright and sappy, but not without florals and spice. Dry and gritty on the palate, this gin latches on to your tongue like glue. Juniper is there in full force, leathery and potent, but citrus keeps things active and spices (ginger, cinnamon, nutmeg) broaden the taste profile and carry the peppered finish. The dryness of this gin makes for a bangin' Martini.

RIGHT There's a healthy measure of Portobello Road Gin in this glass, which is exactly how Jake Burger suggests it should be consumed.

THE LONDON DISTILLERY COMPANY (DODD'S)

If you've read *The Curious Bartender: An Odyssey of Malt, Bourbon & Rye Whiskies*, you'll be familiar with London's first whisky distillery for 100 years. But what I neglected to mention is that this little distillery, formerly on Battersea's Ransom Dock, is already doing a roaring trade in a gin brand called Dodd's.

Ralph Dodd was an 18th century civil engineer, portrait painter and wannabe distiller, who hatched various crazy schemes through a colourful lifetime, most of which were never seen through to fruition, such as a proposal to build the first tunnel under the River Thames. What Dodd's life lacked in accredited achievement however, it made up for in ambition and legacy. One example being his attempt, in 1807, to raise £100,000 (US $150,000) through the sale of public shares to open a distillery. The Intended London Distillery Company, such as it was called, was never to see the light of day, however. Insufficient funding and a legal row meant Dodd was forced to back out.

What better backstory to a distillery could you wish for than the tragic story of a Georgian engineer attempting to make his way in the world? That's what Darren Rook and his partners thought, and in true Ralph Dodd style they made the dream a reality, using investment partly drawn from an online crowd-funding website to finance the start up.

After barely two years of production, The London Distillery Company (LDC) are also distilling gin for prestigious store Fortnum & Mason and Kew Gardens. As we go to print, operations have moved to a larger distillery in Bermondsey. The original Battersea distillery, formerly a Victorian dairy warehouse, was demolished in early 2016, but it was clear that the distillery was outgrowing it long before that. With further rounds of crowd-funding, the plan, in late 2016, is to move all gin

distilling over to the re-developed Battersea Power Station, where there will be four gin stills, a lab, microbrewery, gin library and the capacity to turn out 300,000 litres (80,000 US gallons) of gin per year.

When it comes to liquid provenance there is no other distillery that I know of which can profess such an acute heedfulness of the finer details. Nothing is left to chance here; everything has been thought through, and there is no question that remains unanswered. Quite literally in fact. LDC, it seems, has nothing to hide. Besides certain specifics of the recipe I left furnished with nearly everything that would be required to accurately recreate Dodd's gin. But of course it would be a lost cause, it is their gin, it has gone through their painfully rigorous development procedure and resides in their gloriously imagined bottles, which might just be the best around. And since I've sidetracked myself by mere mention of the bottle, let's take a look at it. The label and name is based on George Dodd. Besides being a feat of design in itself, the label is printed on a one of a kind Heidelberg print press in Wales. The paper stock is entirely carbon neutral. No varnishes are used. It's a work of art.

Dodd's Gin is distilled from an entirely organic range of botanicals in a 140-litre (37-US gallon) pot still called Christina. One unusual point of interest (amongst many) is the exclusion of coriander seed from the recipe, but lime peel features in its place. Just over 500 g (1 lb.) of London honey is distilled in each batch, and since the honey is sourced from various hives all across the capital if you search on the back of the bottle you can find out which postcode the bees live at! Exactly 1 litre (34 fl. oz.) of the distilled product is set aside and macerated with bay leaves, green and black cardamom, and raspberry leaves, then redistilled in a rotary evaporator.

The result is a soft, but spicy concentrate that is mixed back in with the rest of the spirit run and left to mingle for four weeks before bottling, by hand, at the distillery.

DODD'S (49.9% ABV)

Juniper. If you haven't ever squeezed a juniper berry, smell this gin for a good idea of what the aroma is like: sweet and juicy, with just a hint of eucalyptus coming through from the bay and cardamom. The taste follows through nicely too. A bright spectrum of juniper flavours, from pine and citrus through to more earthy qualities and a minty-fresh finish to, well, finish. Do it justice and put it in a Martini.

FORTNUM & MASON LONDON DRY (47.1% ABV)

Tea tree oil, geranium and eucalyptol notes make you shiver on first inspection. Juniper sits somewhere under the surface, but this is a green and clean gin if ever there was one. The palate is more interesting: concentrated, peppered juicy and packing a juniper punch to fend off the eucalyptus. It works well in a super-dry ice-cold Martini. Just watch out for the hypothermia.

RIGHT You could spend hours studying the intimate details of the Dodd's bottle. Or just drink it instead…

BELOW A whole library of botanical samples and corresponding distillates line the walls at LDC.

BELOW RIGHT Everything has its place and function at LDC. This care and precision extends to the product itself.

WARNER EDWARDS

Sion Edwards and Tom Warner are both farmers. Born in to farming families, and growing up on farms, the two met in agricultural college in 1997. From the early days of their friendship the boys had always planned on starting a business together. The scheme was to grow flowers and herbs that could be converted in to essential oils, but the pair soon realised that gin making involved similar processes and expertise and that it would be far better to have a product they could enjoy recreationally than one that simply smelled nice.

The kitchen table was the staging ground for the operation, a location that was returned to frequently when important decisions needed hammering out. The first of those being where to set up the distillery. Fortunately, they weren't short of options. Sion's farm, Bryngwyn Mawr, in North Wales, was living up to the Welsh cliché and doing a roaring trade in daffodils at the time, but the opportunity to make Welsh gin was a tantalizing prospect. Tom's arable farm, Falls, in the village of Harrington, presented a centralized location for trading from, as well as a reliable source of water. Harrington is said to be built on 'rock and water', and while most of the rock seems to be covered in lush grass and highly desirable English cottages, the village's ancient monastic aquifer – which is mentioned in the Domesday book – certainly ticks off the water part of the claim. Tom's farm was chosen, and the kitchen table vacated.

A 200-year-old stone barn, opposite the farm cottage where Tom's mum and dad still live, was the ideal building to set up the distillery. It had, at one time, housed a big copper basin and served as the wash room

for the farm. Tom's father used it as a hospital for sick animals, decreeing 'if it won't live in there, it won't live anywhere'. Tom has hazy memories of his sixteenth birthday party taking place in the barn too, its old walls softly shaking as they bore witness to Tom's first wobbly steps in to the world of alcohol.

Once the roof was re-tiled and the innards all fixed up, the boys took delivery of the UK's first Holstein Still in 2012. But with little understanding of how to use it and no recipe, it was back to the kitchen table for a brainstorming session. A friend donated a range of botanicals and experimentation ensued using a loaned micro-still. It's the hands-on approach and can-do attitude that resonates here, but hey, they're farmers. Now they are assisted by Olly who, thanks to a degree in medical sciences, has introduced a certain degree of methodology. Tom confesses that 'until Olly turned up we were like, "yeh this tastes good, let's go with it."

The products themselves have clearly been well considered. Botanicals are all safe bets; juniper, angelica, coriander, cardamom, cinnamon, black pepper and a 'secret' botanical. Labelled as 'Harrington Dry' the core product is joined by a sloe gin, an elderflower gin and a rhubarb gin. The elderflowers are sourced from Sion's farm in Wales and from the farm in Harrington. Their 'Victoria's Rhubarb Gin' contains rhubarb of remarkable pedigree – the plants they use arguably trace back to Queen Victoria's rhubarb collection.

BELOW The 200-year-old barn has served many purposes over the years, but none better than as a distillery.

ABOVE The still fits so snugly you could be forgiven for thinking that the barn was built around it.

ABOVE RIGHT Perhaps thistles are the 'secret' botanical in Warner Edwards' recipe?

RIGHT Warner Edwards Distillery features a highly polished example of the popular Arnold Holstein Still.

HARRINGTON DRY (44% ABV)

Floral and green at first; fresh gooseberries and honeysuckle; sauvignon blanc. There's a good whiff of cardamom too, followed up by freshly grated nutmeg. Thick and unctuous on the palate, with an initial honeyed eucalyptus hit followed up by plenty of oily, dry spice. Bittersweet finish, lingering with green cardamom. It's crying out for tonic water.

ELDERFLOWER GIN (40% ABV)

Suspiciously restrained on the nose, giving just a subtle hint of the same sauvignon blanc as the HD and that same green, cardamom note. Sweet and herbal on the palate, though not as elderflower-y as one might hope for. Water reveals a glimmer of florals, but cardamom still dominates. The sweetness makes this a good sipping gin option (with a little ice).

VICTORIA'S RHUBARB GIN (40% ABV)

Bright and fragrant, there's bags of rhubarb running through this gin. Plum jam, rhubarb compote, clove, oak moss and wicked streak of vibrant green olives. The palate is intense; savoury and sweet – there's red fruit, mulled wine spices, raspberry leaf tea, some tannin and silverskin onion. Spices take the finish away. Use it in a Martinez or a Negroni.

SLOE GIN

Warm cherry pie! There's brown sugar here too, and concentrated, oozing sloes (of course). Waves of hot fruit, mostly cherry, but the tea-like dryness reminds you that this is sloe. Sweetness is perfect, doing battle with the finish right to the bitter end. Drink it. This might be the best sloe gin on the market.

WEST 45 (BURLEIGH'S)

In 2014, 26 new gin distilleries opened in the UK. Of that number, some have been set up by people with no shortage of enthusiasm, but virtually no clue about how to distil gin. Luckily for them, there is a guy you can call to help with that. Jamie Baxter, co-owner and master distiller at West 45 Not only has he written his own job description, but in the process he has also created an entirely new profession – Distillery Consultant. Two out of the 26 new distilleries were set up by Jamie, and he'll have done at least another five by the end of 2016. That makes 14 stills in total, at 10 distilleries. For £125,000 (US $190,000), Jamie will deliver a 450-litre (120-US gallon) Arnold Holstein Still, put the whole thing together, and even teach you how to use it. Not bad, eh?

Having previously run his own breakfast cereal factory, Jamie went on to make potato chips for the Chase family in Herefordshire. William Chase sold the Tyrrell's brand and set up a distillery, with Jamie's help. Having virtually no expertise in spirits whatsoever and little understanding of distillation beyond the basics, Jamie set about teaching himself. By his own admission things were a little 'Heath Robinson' back then, but it's safe to say he's got it down to a fine art now.

The West 45 Distillery is near Nanpantan in England's Midlands. It is a culmination of Jamie's learnings from along the way, so it's no shock to find the space planned out meticulously and the copper polished within a millimetre of its usefulness. The best liquids in the distillery come out of the 450-litre (120-US gallon) Holstein Still, managed by Jamie's fair and capable hands. Distillation is carefully monitored by eye and nose.

Botanicals begin with the classic types, but also include dried elderberry, silver birch sap, and dried dandelion and burdock roots. Silver birch harks back to Jamie's Austrian grandmother, who in Spring would customarily tap her silver birch tree for its fresh, clear sap. It's the whole tree that's used in Burleigh's, contributing green and spicy notes, and something slightly reminiscent of eucalyptus. The elderberry and the dandelion and burdock roots were happened upon when Jamie was walking in the nearby Burleigh woods. And yes, that's where the name comes from.

ABOVE West 45 is home to a gin school where participants can make the most of Jamie Baxter's tutelage.

Looking at the liquids, the London Dry is top stuff, but I love the distiller's cut. The recipe calls for a higher ratio of the soft fragrant botanicals like orange, orris and cassia, giving a more pervasive floral note on the nose.

BURLEIGH'S GIN (40% ABV)

Crystal clear juniper on the nose. Soft leather, fresh pine, and impressively well suppressed alcohol. There's a subtle eucalyptus note too, along with some woodsy, earthy, and ethereal notes. The palate builds slowly, lighter than the aroma suggests, but not wanting for chewy juniper. The second sip builds on the first. Big. The finish is green juniper, warm spice, and cardamom. Enjoy in classics such as a Martinez, or Tom Collins.

BURLEIGH'S DISTILLER'S CUT (47% ABV)

Bright juniper and soft citrus fruits hit at first, giving the gin a kind of fizzy orange Fanta and juniper fusion effect. There's violet and warm spice there too. The taste is a juniper bomb, well structured, with nice bitter earthy notes to complement the floral and citrus extremities of the gin. A belter. Using it anything other than a Martini (or three) would be irresponsible.

SCOTLAND

When we think of Scotland we are naturally drawn to malt whisky. But during the 18th century Edinburgh was home to eight gin distilleries and many more if you count all the illicit operations. Leith was the centre of all things gin, where glassmakers and coopers provided the tools of the industry and the docks supplied botanicals and cereals, as well as means of product distribution. While gin production remained strong through the early years of the 1800s, it began to die off later on, as distillers focused more on the commercial production of neutral spirit (for English gins) or on malt whisky, which had its boom time in the 1880s. When Scotland's last gin distillery, Melrose-Drover, closed, in Leith, in 1974, only one Scottish gin brand remained, Old Raj (see page 146).

These days some of the best known and oldest surviving gin brands in the world are made in Scotland. Thanks mostly to the Cameron Bridge Distillery (see pages 139–143), approximately 60% of the London Dry Gin produced in the UK is made in Scotland. Throw in another 20-or-so new Scottish gin distilleries that have established themselves over the past 15 years, and it's fair to say that Scotland has seen one of the world's biggest turnarounds in gin making.

Of the contemporary gin brands in Scotland, foraging appears to be a consistent theme. Five out the eight distilleries featured in this book have released a gin containing at least one foraged ingredient. The much neglected Blackwood's Gin can take pride in the fact that they probably started this trend, sourcing variable amounts of native Shetland botanicals (water mint, sea pink flowers) for their ever-changing 'Vintage Dry Gin' expression. Other Scottish brands, like Dunnet Bay Distillery's Rock Rose Gin uses foraged rose roots, rowan berries and sea buckthorn for their core expression.

THIS PAGE AND OPPOSITE The old and the new, the wild and the well groomed: Scotland is a hothouse of contemporary gin making, and is representative of every facet of the craft.

CAORUNN

Tucked away on the outskirts of Scotland's famous Speyside whisky-producing region, you'll find the Balmenach distillery, in Cromdale. More traditionally noted for its whisky-producing history, the distillery should be high on any malt-maniacs hit list, as it was previously owned, and originally set up, by the MacGregor family, serving as a playground for a young boy named Robert Bruce Lockhart, whose mother was a MacGregor. That boy would grow to become a journalist, bestselling author, footballer, foreign diplomat and secret agent (the character of James Bond was said to be based on Lockhart). In 1951 Lockhart also happened to pen perhaps the greatest piece of whisky propaganda ever released: *Scotch: the Whisky of Scotland in Fact and Story*.

I digress. The current owners, Inver House Distillers, revived the distillery in 1997 and added gin production to its list of capabilities in 2009. Caorunn ('ka-roon' as the label helpfully informs us) is Gaelic for rowan berry, which is one of five locally sourced botanicals that the team brave hell and high-water to forage for. Led by 'Gin Master', Simon Buley, the Balmenach posse also scavenge for bog myrtle leaf, heather flowers, little-known Coul Blush apples (an old Celtic variety) and dandelion leaf.

Gin distillation is done in a proprietorial manner here. The still itself is a generous 1,000 litres (265 US gallons) and botanical flavour is extracted by means of vapour infusion rather than maceration. Balmenach employ a unique piece of equipment to do this, which was built in the 1920s. They call it a 'berry chamber'. I call it a bit odd. It's a horizontal cylinder, attached to the line arm of the still, that has sliding racks which hold the botanicals. Basically, it's a lot like a classic vapour infusion chamber that has somehow fallen over, but in any case the physicality of the process is exactly the same as using a Carterhead still. So it's not shocking to find that the character of the gin is light and delicate, which is rather at odds with the sulphurous, full-bodied whisky that this distillery produces.

On a final note, it's worth drawing attention to the bottle and branding of this gin, as it is excellent. Reassuringly heavy, and like no other, this bottle really stands out on the shelf. The soft hexagonal shape of the glass, as well as the five-pointed asterisk, pay homage to the five celtic botanicals that go in to the gin.

CAORUNN (41.8% ABV)

There's an unmistakable baked apple note on the nose here, which is sharpened up by a touch of juniper and then delicate florals. Those initially volatile elements quickly dissipate however, leaving a light and elegant spiced base. Being that light, it's not surprising that the gin is sweet and spritely in the mouth, giving a quick flash of sweet florals before blushing and shying away. Caorunn recommend a G&T garnished with an apple slice. I suggest topping it up with still farmhouse cider!

FAR LEFT The Balmenach Distillery emphasizes its surroundings when making Caorunn Gin, including the water, which is drawn from the Burn of Cromdale.

LEFT Botanical drawers at Balmenach have perforated bottoms that allow spirit vapour to pass through.

EDEN MILL

Eden Mill is a member of a very exclusive group of distilleries that make gin, whisky and beer. Adnam's (pages 78–9) is another, so is Anchor in San Francisco. After that I begin to struggle. Unlike Adnam's, Eden Mill have only been around since 2012, but these guys are driven, and they've picked a suitably epic location in the former Curtis Fine paper mill that dominates the shoreline of the Eden estuary, just outside of St. Andrews, to tell the story.

You're never far from a distillery in Scotland, and before the Eden Mill site was a paper mill it was a distillery run by the Haig family, one of Scotch whisky's most legendary bloodlines. The Haigs had ties to the Steins of Kincaple (of column distillation fame) and the Jamesons of… well, Jameson, not to mention Field Marshal Douglas Haig, commander of British forces during World War I, and now David Beckham as the brand ambassador of Haig Club whisky. Eden Mill have none of those things, but what they do have is impressive sales figures, some tasty packaging, bags of enthusiasm, and a captive (and thirsty) audience in the form of St Andrew's University.

Distillation is conducted in one of three 1,000-litre (265-US gallon) pot stills which look to be the kind that comes from Portugal. All of the gins except the Original undergo a post-distillation compounding, maceration or barrel ageing, however. A single batch takes a whopping 17 hours from start to finish, and sees nearly a ton of spirit vapour pass through 4 kg (9 lbs.)

of botanicals. Bottling is done by hand, of which about 1,500 are filled every week. Botanicals are as varied as they come and across the various expressions go from the whacky straits of locally foraged sea buckthorn and lemon balm, in to the bizarre depths of mallow root, goji berry, and even hickory chips obtained from a ground-down golf club…

Some of these 'botanicals' have a richer provenance, however. Eden Mill's immediate neighbour is True Baby, run by Scottish farmer Henry Ackroyd. Henry uses state of the art LED arrays and hydroponics to grow organic micro-herbs and vegetables in an indoor farm. Most of the produce gets sold on to Michelin-star restaurants, but some of the more esoteric options are reserved for special release gins at Eden Mill. Amongst the cornucopia of miniature foodstuffs that I sampled, was fresh liquorice/licorice root, red mustard seed, and a fruit that looked like a physalis but tasted like a tomato (an Inca berry). A gin distillery with this kind of access to obscure botanicals is an exciting thing, and I look forward to seeing the fruits of its…(ahem) fruits, in the future.

My only regret is that I don't love the gin produced at Eden Mill as much as I love the people, their story, their setting, their packaging, and even their beer. With

BELOW A cornucopia of mini vegetables and fruits grow right next door to the Eden Mill brewery and distillery. Some find their way in to the gin.

RIGHT A sound piece of advice, I think, although you should feel free to swap the word 'beer' for 'gin'.

five gin expressions under their belt already, four of which are part of the permanent collection, the operation smells a little of throwing botanicals at the wall to see what sticks. The marketing department are clearly earning their money, mind you, and it feels as though there's a bottling for every possible demographic; Original for the purists, Oak for the boys, Love for the girls, Hop for hipsters, and Golf for the golfers. You get the idea.

I suggested mixing the Hop gin with beer, which they had of course done already (along with anything else they could get their hands on no doubt). It works apparently, like a kind of hope field fortifier for those beers that could do with trying a bit harder. One of the brewers has claimed it as a cocktail, proudly titling the concoction 'Skip & Go Naked' — for a classic approach check out my Purl recipe (pages 200–201).

EDEN MILL ORIGINAL (42% ABV)

Light and bright on the nose, with a slight lactic, burnt milk taint. Sweeter than expected on the palate, but quickly dipping in to bone dry spice drawer astringency, pepper, some anise notes. Juniper brings up the rear end, barely.

The spice in this gin makes it suitable for a punchy White Lady cocktail.

EDEN MILL LOVE GIN (42% ABV)

A big waft of dirty spices, including stewed coriander seed and cooked vegetable matter. The not-so-pleasant initial aroma does give way to some intact florals; a touch of hibiscus and rose notes. Water opens the whole thing up however, revealing pink lemonade,

elderflower, confected aromas. The palate is sweet, a little flat and slightly astringent in the finish.

This gin mixes really well with lemonade. You might as well make it pink lemonade…

EDEN MILL OAK GIN (42% ABV)

Damp spice drawer on the nose, balsa wood, with ethanol and (sadly) not a great deal else. Water reveals some soft stem ginger notes, light citrus and a sparkle of something vaguely juniper-y. Taste is altogether too flat. Dry, softly spiced and a bit lacklustre.

Try it with ginger ale, plenty of ice and a slice of lemon. Also a safe bet for a Negroni.

EDEN MILL HOP GIN (46% ABV)

Hops, obviously, that intensely floral, grimy kind of hops. Citrus, passion fruit and peach yogurt, stinky moss, mushroom and elderflower. No sign of the gin. Palate is decidedly and unapologetically hoppy. If you like hops this is most definitely for you. If you like gin, you might like to look elsewhere. Put a drop in your beer.

EDINBURGH GIN

Edinburgh Gin is a brand coming in to its fifth year now, which places it at the maturer end of this quickly expanding market. The gin was distilled at the Langley Distillery near Birmingham (page 104–7) for the first three years of its life, but recently got promoted to its own purpose-built distillery right on the Royal Mile.

Down a flight of stairs in the pavement you'll find the new home of Edinburgh gin, along with the Heads & Tails cocktail bar, which is hidden amongst the old storage vaults that support the structure of the road overhead. The bar is an intimate space for an evening drink and its expansive gin selection makes it a good spot for anyone wishing to try most (but not all) of the gins in this book. The bar is also a busy training space during the day time, for gin enthusiasts wishing to have a tour and for students of the Brewing and Distilling course at Herriot Watt, who seem to have some vested interest in the distillery, along with supplying the distillery with virtually all its staff members – I suspect even the delivery guy could handle a tails-cut if it came down to it.

And the real showstopper here is of course the gin stills themselves. If it's size you're after you'll be disappointed, however. These tiny 150-litre (40-US gallon) pots – one, 'Caledonia', with a rectification column, one, 'Flora', without – are among the smallest production stills that I've seen. Green lights bounce off the copper and brick giving the stills an eerie and somewhat haunted look about them. But with five separate products and the capacity of a pair of thimbles, it's no wonder they look a bit spooked out – the distillery must be working them quite hard. As to why the stills are so small I could find no solid answer from the staff. The price difference between a 150-litre (40-US gallon) still and a 350-litre (92-US gallon) still is comparatively small once you consider that both need the same electrical, gas, water and waste services, and that the cost of running, maintaining and manning the stills would be similar. Perhaps it's a space thing. I know of only a handful of underground distilleries, because confined spaces are usually a big no-no.

Edinburgh Gin claim they are only selling 12,000 bottles a year at the moment, which is a relatively meagre volume of product when you consider that some new distilleries are approaching 30,000 bottles in their first year. It's a one-shot gin, which by my

BELOW LEFT The 'crock' bottle was going to be used for beer, but it was deemed too costly. So it was used for the gin.

BELOW Tucked away under one of the busiest junctions in the city, Edinburgh Gin is every bit the Speakeasy distillery.

LEFT Where Bauhaus meets William Morris – the Edinburgh Gin bottle is unmistakable.

Cannonball is not only a great name for a Navy Strength gin – and at 57.2% no one could deny them that – but the best gin of the range in my opinion. The additional alcohol really elevates the pepperiness of the botanical spices, and you'd be forgiven for believing there's gunpowder in there too.

My experience at the distillery was unusual. The team are proud of their accomplishments, but that confidence, at times, is in danger of becoming arrogance. Maybe it's because they are not Edinburgh's first gin distillery (in truth Pickering's aren't either) or because the product has been contract distilled in England for so long despite having 'Edinburgh' blazoned across the bottle, which will no doubt have attracted a few comments from residents of the city.

CANONBALL (57% ABV)

As explosive on the nose as it is on the tongue. Here we find a drier, leaner gin than the standard offering. Tight black pepper and frozen lemon peel is lifted by that fast hit of alcohol. The taste is gooey, chewy and big. Heat holds the liquid down and botanicals punch you in the tongue. Lemon sherbet, vanilla, then that spice. Always the spice.

Vermouth tempers the heat, so try it in a Martini… just don't try it too many times.

EDINBURGH GIN (43% ABV)

Fruity and sweet on the nose, juniper is accompanied by coriander and citrus peels that have transfigured to lemon pastilles and ginger bubble gum. Succulent fruits on the palate: candied citrus peels, blackberry and cherry. As fruit subsides it's warm autumnal spices that take over.

A great cocktail gin that plays nicely with citrus – try it in a Clover Club and a Gin Fizz.

SEASIDE GIN (43% ABV)

Fruit is suppressed by a slightly cloying vegetal note in this instance, which adds breadth to the taste, but also masks the now subtle citrus elements. Baked spices and roots emerge in the mouth, but the greener note is the most pervasive. More a wet and windy walk on shingle than a slow bake on the sand. Tonic does this gin a lot of favours, garnish with lemon and a pinch of salt.

reckoning doesn't leave a great deal of room for movement when it comes to production capacity.

There's a dispute going on right now between this distillery and Edinburgh's other gin distillery, Pickering's (see pages 147–148). The owners of Edinburgh Gin have a trademark on their brand name, which prevents other gins from calling themselves an 'Edinburgh Gin'. But Edinburgh's other gin distillery, Pickering's think it's only fair that they advertise themselves as Edinburgh's first gin distillery in 150 years, and a big label on their bottle says exactly that.

Their Seaside gin uses bladderwrack seaweed (the dark one with the oval bits that you pop!), scurvy grass and ground ivy. It was actually a Masters project from a student studying at Herriot Watt that was deemed good enough to be added to the range.

GORDON'S & TANQUERAY

Tanqueray and Gordon's gin are both distilled at the Cameron Bridge Distillery in Scotland. Both brands started life as individual distilleries in London, however. Gordon's was originally established in Bayswater, but swiftly relocated to Goswell Road (then Goswell Street) in Clerkenwell. Tanqueray began life on Vine Street in London, which is now present day Grape Street, just off New Oxford Street. In 1898 Tanqueray joined Gordon's in their Goswell Road distillery, where both brands were produced side by side until the entire operation moved to the Laindon Distillery in Essex. It remained there for only a few years however, closing down in 1998, and the former site of the distillery is now a business park named Juniper Crescent.

From Essex, production moved to Scotland. Located around an hour north of Edinburgh the Tanqueray and Gordon's distillery is in fact a distillery within a larger complex of distilleries at Diageo's enormous Cameron Bridge production complex. The world's biggest premium drinks company distil grain whisky for blending here, as well as grain neutral spirit (GNS) used in white spirits. Some of that spirit is destined to become Smirnoff Vodka, the remainder is re-distilled in to gin. Tanqueray gin, Tanqueray TEN and Gordon's are all distilled in the same room, albeit with a different set of stills and different recipes.

The 'Gin House' at Cameron Bridge is home to three enormous pot-stills, one of which is the famous No. 4 Still, also known as 'Old Tom'. No. 4 has a plaque on the front stating that it has been 'In continuous use since the reign of King George III". George III was King from 1760 - 1820, and if the plaque is to be believed, even at the nearer end of that timeframe No. 4 is comfortably the oldest working gin still in the UK.

No. 4 is used exclusively to make Tanqueray products, but would have originally been a Gordon's gin still from Goswell Road. Tanqueray London Dry is a one-shot gin. The other two stills are used to make

Gordon's, which is a multi-shot gin. The fourth still is Tiny Ten, which is used to make Tanqueray No. TEN.

The first time I visited Cameron Bridge was in 2006, when I was being inducted as a brand ambassador for Tanqueray. Part of that induction was to meet Tanqueray's legendary master distiller, Tom Nichol, who retired in 2015. Tom is Scottish through and through, a passionate gin maker and a perfectionist who despises nothing more than corner-cutting. I can call Tom a good friend now, but upon first encounter his blunt responses and thinking out loud approach to character assessment can feel a bit intimidating. But it was then, and remains still, a refreshing change to the marketeers who populate many of the world's distilleries, whose only wish is to impregnate your mind with a bullet point list of 'key liquid identifiers' or some such rubbish.

GORDON'S

The Gordon's gin story starts in 1769 when, just before his 27th birthday, Alexander Gordon married the love of what had, so far, been a quite a short life, Susannah Osborne. The year of 1769 is also given as the date which Alexander Gordon set up his distillery in South London. The eldest of Gordon's numerous children, was Charles (1774–1849), who would carry on the family business, becoming one of his father's partners in 1799. Around the same time, the distillery moved from its original location in Bermondsey, to 67–68 Goswell Road (then Goswell Street), where it would remain for nearly 200 years.

Charles Gordon had three children, two girls and a boy. The boy, also named Charles, started gin making at an early age, and after his father's death he became the

ABOVE **This Gordon's bottle from the early 20th century is the earliest existing bottle to be made from glass.**

sole partner from 1847 onwards. In 1878 Charles Gordon sold Gordon & Co, then valued at £50,000, to John Currie & Co. John Currie & Co were distillers at Four Mills Distillery, once the most important distilleries in England outside London, where they produced neutral malt spirit for a number of gin distillers and had provided Gordon's with spirit for many years. One of their clan, Arthur Currie, had also helped to set up Charles Tanqueray's distillery in the 1830s.

The grand union of the Tanqueray and Gordon families continued, in 1837, when Susanna Gordon, the sister of Charles Gordon (the younger), married Edward Tanqueray, (Charles Tanqueray's eldest brother and business partner). That made Charles Tanqueray and Charles Gordon brothers-in-law, but only for a short time. Sadly, Edward died the following year.

But ever inseparable, even by death, in 1898 the Tanqueray Gordon Co. Was founded. The merger closed down the old Tanqueray distillery on Vine Street, and production of both Gordon's and Tanqueray took place in Goswell Street where it would remain for the better part of the next century.

Gordon's started to produce their 'ready-to-serve' Shaker Cocktails in 1924, which, looking at the range of bottled cocktails available today, is a trend that seems to have come full circle. Gordon's recognised the potential for this range of cocktails, each in their individual shaker bottle, capturing the spirit of the Jazz Age. The cocktails included the 50/50, Martini, Dry Martini, Perfect and Piccadilly. Following the successful launch of this range Gordon's added the Manhattan, San Martin, Dry San Martin and Bronx.

Most of those product lines were discontinued in the 1980s, and the brand lowered the ABV of Special Dry to 37.5% at around the same time – an act which diminished the credibility of the brand no end. Of course you can still get the Export Strength stuff in Duty Free, which comes in at a healthier 47.3% ABV. New additions include the rather tasty 'Gordon's With a Spot of Elderflower' and the not so original 'Gordon's Crisp Cucumber'. Today, Gordon's is still the best selling London Dry Gin in the world. 12 million bottles of Gordon's Gin will be consumed in the UK alone in 2015, accounting for roughly one-third of the market share.

I have a rare claim to fame when it comes to Gordon's that I have unashamedly boasted about for over eight years now. Indeed, Tom Nichol (Tanqueray

ABOVE This US advertisement from the 1940s shows Gordon's at the peak of its post-Prohibition powers.

and Gordon's retired master distiller) himself still regularly mentions the episode during seminars, which enriches my pride even further. Ready? Here it is: I am the only person outside of distillery staff who has ever made a batch of Gordon's gin.

Using the computer software at Cameron Bridge, the equivalent of 22,000 litres (5,800 US gallons) of Gordon's were ordered up in a matter of seconds. Of course I wasn't made privy to the exact recipe, my role was more akin to a wind-up monkey, inputting a range of numbers in to columns on a computer, blindly filling out a spreadsheet, the true meaning of which would be impossible to decipher. Clearly the numbers corresponded to weights and the columns represented loading silos, but as to which botanicals those silos contained… I would be guessing. Once I pressed 'Enter' on the system, pumps began whirring, gas firing and all manner of other activity. I distantly remember the enormous quantity of juniper that went in there… over five minutes of continuous loading and longer than that of all the other ingredients put together. Gordon's tenth botanical, liquorice/licorice had to be loaded in by hand, presumably because it was such a small quantity that the loading shoots wouldn't be able to process it, but it has since occurred to me that the clingy powder could cause mechanical issues if automated. Then the enormous still was heating up and the spirit flowing over.

GORDON'S SPECIAL DRY (37.5% ABV)

Spirituous and light on the nose, with a gentle lemon ring and ginger tingle from the coriander. Juniper is oily and well represented, but lacks intensity. Orris and angelica offer some structure. The taste is gentle, a touch watery, but undoubtedly juniper forward, soft cinnamon on the finish. The good thing about the lower ABV is it means you can drink more of it - In a G&T, of course.

GORDON'S LONDON DRY (47% ABV)

Vibrant and zingy. The extra 9.5% has woken up lemon and orange peel for an citrus soda effect. Juniper is more sonorous too, greener and offering up some sweet parma-violet and geranium qualities. The taste carries far more weight as alcohol drills home hot juniper oil, brown spices and citric intensity. Tonic water draws out the citrus and coriander in this gin.

TANQUERAY

The original Tanqueray distillery was founded in Bloomsbury by Charles Tanqueray, in 1830. The Tanqueray family were French protestants who emigrated to England in the late 17th century. Thomas Tanqueray (Charles Tanqueray's grandfather) was born in St Martin-in-the-Fields, in 1724, just as the gin craze was really kicking off, so it's understandable that gin would feature quite heavily in the family's future. Clearly the gin craze wasn't for them however, and the family left London in the 1730s, relocating to the quiet Bedfordshire town of Tingrith, where they would spend the next 100 years spawning three generations of clergymen. Charles Tanqueray's generation broke the mould and by 1830 he had established a gin distillery at No. 3 Vine Street. Charles wasn't alone however, his older bother, Edward, was a business partner and his younger brothers, William-Henry and John Samuel Tanqueray, joined him too.

Charles kept a diary with all his gin recipes, but in it he also reveals what a creative he was generally. His diary includes a recipe for 'Polish for Boots', and a spirit called 'White Clove' and reveals his love for horses in his 'Stomach Pills for horses'. But following the same pattern as numerous other family-run spirits businesses of the era, it would be the second generation of the family who would make the largest impact on the business's long-term success. By 1847, Tanqueray was already making inroads among the spice planters and traders of far-away Jamaica, shown by the recovery of a tall ceramic crock discovered in a shipwreck in Kingston, Jamaica, bearing the legend 'Tanqueray Gin'.

In time, Charles Tanqueray moved back to Tingrith, and eventually moved away to Scotland, where he died, in 1865. Unbeknown to him, he was less than forty miles from Cameron Bridge, where the Tanqueray distillery would relocate to in 1999.

Charles' son, Charles Waugh Tanqueray, was apprenticed in 1867 at the age of 19, and later joined his uncle and cousin, William Henry and William Henry jnr., in the running of the distillery on Vine Street. Charles Waugh quickly made inroads in to the lucrative export market and in 1898 signed a merger between Gordon's and Tanqueray, laying the foundations for the growth of both brands in the 20th century. The Tanqueray family remained actively involved through to the next generation too, where Charles Waugh's son, Charles Henry 'Harry' Drought, served as company secretary right up until Tanqueray Gordon Co. was acquired by the Distillers Company in 1922. Even John Tanqueray, Harry's grandson (and Charles Tanqueray's great great grandson) worked for Tanqueray Gordon & Co. until he retired in 1989.

The Tanqueray family crest, which can be seen on every bottle, was granted in 1938 and combines one of fruit's all-time most fashionable fellows along with a pair of crossed battle axes. As far as crests go there's little room for improvement in my eyes. The axes allegedly commemorate the role of the Tanqueray family during the Crusades in the Middle East, which is impressive mostly for the fact that the family can date their ancestry back eight centuries. The pineapple is of course the universal sign of hospitality, but was also drawn from a 1767 coat of arms bestowed on the Willaume family, which was Charles Tanqueray's grandmother's maiden name.

ABOVE LEFT The Goswell Road Distillery, shortly after the Tanqueray/Gordon's merger, in 1901.

ABOVE RIGHT The Tanqueray bottling line at Goswell Road, taken in 1961.

LEFT A 1960s advert, signed (posthumously) by Charles Tanqueray reads: 'If this were an ordinary gin, we would have put it in an ordinary bottle.'

Tanqueray London Dry is produced in two strengths, the regular 43.1%, and the export strength 47.3%. Both are excellent, but in an unprecedented deviation from my usual tastes, I actually prefer the standard strength as an unmixed product. Tanqueray London Dry epitomizes the London Dry style: bone-dry juniper and lip-smacking freshness. For a gin that is made from only four botanicals (juniper, coriander, angelica, liquorice/licorice) it's nothing short of a masterclass in the distiller's art. Comparisons are often, and justly, drawn between Tanqueray and Beefeater, and if we are to find benchmark gins that all others most be judged against, it would surely be those two. To put it simply: If you want to know what gin truly is, look no further.

The second addition, Tanqueray No. TEN, launched in 2000 as a range extension. When I first tasted it, in 2003, I remember describing it as 'Gin 2.0'. That's a claim that I stand by today, it is still a fantastic liquid and one that remains highly capable of holding its own against any of the current new wave products, even despite the crowdedness of the marketplace. Tanqueray No. TEN is produced using a small copper pot dubbed 'Tiny Ten'. The heart of Tanqueray London Dry is redistilled in this pot in the presence of a whole fresh grapefruit – I'm told that only one is required – fresh Mexican limes and chamomile. The resulting distillate is then blended back in to Tanqueray London Dry, redistilled, and T10 is born. I don't pay much attention to spirits awards (perhaps because I'm a judge on some of the panels!) but it's worth taking not of the achievements of Tanqueray No. Ten. In 2003 it won the coveted 'Best White Spirit' award in San Francisco's annual competition for the third time, granting it a place in the hall of fame. It remains the only unaged spirit to have ever achieved such a feat.

Since then we have seen the launch of the highly controversial Tanqueray Rangpur. Flavoured with ginger, bay leaf and rangpur limes (after distillation), it is just about the limiest thing I have ever tasted – more limey, even, than a lime. Handy, if you're making G&T's with no citrus in the house of course.

Then there was the re-launch of Tanqueray Malacca, which was first released in 1997, before being discontinued in 2001 due to lack of popularity. Ironically, bottles of Malacca became very hard to come by in the years that followed, and the product gradually achieved cult status. Then, in 2013, after numerous protests from Tom Nichol categorically stating 'we will never relaunch Tanqueray Malacca' they only went and relaunched Tanqueray Malacca in a 'limited' run of 100,000 bottles.

Malacca has been followed up with a further two launches in the form of Tanqueray Old Tom and Tanqueray Bloomsbury Edition, which takes the total up to seven. The later is a recreation of a handwritten recipe from Charles Tanqueray's notebook for what he called 'Common Gin' and served as the swan song for the retiring master distiller, Tom Nichol (may he retire in peace).

TANQUERAY LONDON DRY (43.1% ABV)

Pine oils and sappy forest roots are in perfect harmony on the nose. There's citrus there too, but spiced with notes of ginger beer, pink peppercorn and sweet roots. On the palate it's dry and grippy, with steely juniper being tempered by just a touch of crystallized angelica and more of that soft lemon and ginger. The finish is clean and gently peppered. As versatile a gin as you're likely to find. Perfect in almost any application.

TANQUERAY LONDON DRY EXPORT STRENGTH (47.3% ABV)

Juniper is perfumed here. Soft pine is softened further by rose, aniseed and just a touch of dried tropical fruit (pineapple?!). On the palate it's intense juniper, relaxing in to some soapy, yellow, coriander notes. Hot pepper rises up and sucks the life out of the finish. Pour 100 ml/3½ oz. out of a fresh bottle then top it back up with dry vermouth. Pop the bottle in the freezer. Et voila! Perfect Martinis on tap!

TANQUERAY NO. TEN (47.3% ABV)

Vibrant grapefruit zest, bubblegum and a decent hit of jasmine tea are the first things that hit you. The nose is intensely citric, but it somehow retains, nay, elevates the juniper berry. It's pure witchcraft. The taste is full of grapefruit too, but it's spritely, rather than cloying. Then London Dry elements kick in, juniper, followed by sweetly spiced and floral finish. This might be the best gin in the world. Treat it with respect and put it in a bone-dry Martini. No garnish required.

RIGHT The Tanqueray TEN (or T10 as it is known among bartenders) bottle recently underwent a fabulous Art-Deco-inspired redesign.

HENDRICK'S

The Hendrick's Distillery is less a distillery in its own right and more a tiny oasis of gin amidst the vast desert of cereal-based spirits that is the Girvan Distillery. Located in southern Ayrshire in Scotland, it's owned by William Grant & Sons, who make and market some of the world's biggest premium brands. Girvan is the workhorse behind the William Grant & Sons portfolio, producing grain whisky for blending. That means Hendrick's of course, although once upon a time, not so long ago, their biggest customer was Beefeater.

At the helm of the Hendrick's wheel is Leslie Gracey, and it's fair to say that she is probably not what most people imagine a master distiller to be. But a word of warning to anyone who thinks that a lady of a certain age and physical stature isn't capable of running a world-class distillery. With a background in chemistry and a long career working for the Grant family, Leslie's nose is now responsible for developing new liquids across every single category of the William Grant & Sons portfolio. Five minutes in her company and the signs begin to show. The wicked grin and ferocious dedication to the distilling art do little to conceal the streak of genius simmering away under the surface of this lady. Flashing looks of admiration from co-workers confirm it.

Leslie has been a part of the Hendrick's journey since its conception back in 1999 when she received the brief for a game-changing gin. Plotting away in a dimly lit think-tank, the marketeers strategized a gin for the 21st century that improved upon the revolutionary work that Bombay Sapphire had pioneered in the 1980s. Light, but spicy. Floral, but green. Definitively English in its flavour and innovative in its packaging.

The distillery already had two stills suitable for making gin: a very old 1,000-litre (265-US gallon) pot-style Bennett Still, and a 1,000-litre (265-US gallon) Carterhead Still with a vapour infusion chamber on the lyne arm. Both were bought in the 1960s from London's closed Taplow Distillery. The Bennett Still is a bit of a mystery. It was probably manufactured between 1895 and 1906, but company records suggest it might be an older still built by the Shear company in the 1860s. It did have a brief spell making the Lichfield's brand and possibly (although no one will confirm it) the elusive Grant's Gin, which appeared in the late 1960s as an export-only product.

Mystery gins notwithstanding, the two gin stills at Girvan sat relatively idle through the 1980s and 1990s and were used for little more than training purposes until Hendrick's came along. Their suitability for the brand was tested when each still was trialled with an 11-botanical recipe, including chamomile, elderflower, cubeb berries, yarrow, lemon and orange. The Bennett Still produced a predictably heavy, juniper-forward liquid, while the Carterhead focused on the lighter, spicier end of the flavour spectrum. While both stills performed well, the eureka moment came when the two distillates were mixed together. This is a unique approach; while some gins like Monkey 47 (see pages 164–165) and Silent Pool (see pages 114–115) combine vapour infusion and maceration in the same still, there are no other brands that combine two individual distillates from two different stills, as far as I know.

But that's not quite the end of the story. The formula made allowances for two key ingredients to be added after distillation. Now, as we know, a gin flavoured after distillation cannot be labelled 'London Dry', so this was a bold move from William Grant & Sons.

But it would be these two classically English ingredients that would not only define the product, but shake up the gin category, and go on to change the way that we drink G&Ts. The first was rose. It's distilled at low temperature from the red petals of Bulgarian roses, and besides adding floral notes, also softens the spirit, adding sweetness and suppressing alcohol burn. It is, for me, the principal character trait of Hendrick's.

LEFT Hendrick's black medicine bottle has become an icon in the drinks world.

The second ingredient, distilled in the same manner, requires no introduction. Cucumber. Over a decade on and it seems so obvious now, doesn't it? Clean, fresh, green and the vegetal embodiment of England – the ones used in Hendrick's are in fact grown in the cucumber cornucopia that is Belgium – they were not the first brand to do it (see Martin Miller's on page 106) but they were the first to shout about it. This viridescent rock-star of the gin drinking world is, in my eyes, worthy of praise equal to any piece of category innovation from the last 20 years. Blue bottles included.

The Hendrick's Distillery is set for some renovation over the coming years, although I'm sworn to secrecy on the finer details of the planned works. Work has started already though. A second identical Bennett Still has been added to the array of stills making three in total, and when I say identical I mean identical, they used an x-ray machine to scan the old one and built the new one in-situ just to make sure. I'd imagine a second Carterhead isn't far behind too. And the Hendrick's 'experience' is in the running for a major overhaul… but wait, I've said too much already.

It turns out that the name 'Hendrick's' was proposed by the late great Janet 'Wee Janie' Sheed Roberts, who before passing away in 2012 (at age 110) was Scotland's oldest living person. She was also the last surviving granddaughter of William Grant and the last living person to have met him. Though not an active employee of the business, Wee Janie was granddaughter, daughter, sister, wife, aunt and great aunt to successive chairmen of the company. In 2000, around the time that Hendrick's was being developed, Wee Janie made mention of a gardener called Hendrick who was at one time employed by the Grant family. Apparently Hendrick was a well-known and popular figure among some of the family members. Gin with cucumber and rose? It had to be called Hendrick's.

HENDRICK'S (41.4% ABV)

Floral and green in almost equal measures – a courgette flower perhaps?! Sweet rose water is dominant, followed by soft dry spices, nutty and crisp. Green and damp, like rushes, or reeds, but behind it there's grape bubblegum and a touch of juniper. Rounded and clean on the palate; well-structured heat combined with florals in pink and purple. Soft and well-mannered through to the finish. Serve in a G&T with cucumber, of course!

ABOVE TOP Hendrick's 'cucumbermobile' is a touch incongruous with the enormous grain silos of Girvan Distillery.

ABOVE The 'Gin Palace' at Girvan houses (from the left) one Carterhead Still, one Bennett Still, and one replica Bennett Still.

RIGHT This might be the only instance of cucumber-based graffiti in the world!

OLD RAJ

· ·

I consider Old Raj to be the 'Caramac' chocolate bar of the gin world. Just like the Caramac, it has a huge cult following, nobody knows when it was invented, where it's made, who makes it, whether you can still find a bottle, and most important of all – why it's yellow!?

Old Raj is owned by WM Cadenhead, Scotland's oldest brand of independent whisky bottlers, founded in 1842. Cadenhead is in fact the retail and independent bottling arm of J & A Mitchell, the family-run business who own and operate the legendary Springbank Distillery in Campbeltown. And it's at Springbank that this gin is made. The Springbank Distillery is the longest continually family-owned distillery in Scotland and every bit the working whisky museum.

The gin, which was introduced in 1972, is made from juniper, coriander seed, angelica root, cassia bark, almond, lemon peel and orange peel. Its soft yellow hue (I have heard it likened to lemon, chamomile tea and other, less desirable, things) is the result of a saffron maceration that occurs after distillation. The saffron adds little to the flavour in my opinion, perhaps a soft savoury edge, but it certainly creates a talking point. At 55%, this gin packs a punch, but it is by no means offensive and wears its alcohol gracefully.

Two strengths of Old Raj are available, the common blue-coloured variety, which is 55% and the lesser seen red label version, which comes in at a positively tame 46%. It also has a sister brand of gin, Cadenhead's Classic, which, at 50% is no shrinking violet either. Cadenhead Classic does surprisingly well in the US. Cadenhead are cagey about revealing the botanicals that go in to Cadenhead's Classic, leading me to suspect that it's the same gin as Old Raj but without the saffron.

OLD RAJ BLUE LABEL (55% ABV)

Punchy and bright on the nose (don't get too close). Clean, green juniper, pine and lemon juice. In the mouth it's a handful: big and boisterous in texture, but

ABOVE Drinking Old Raj neat is a dangerous game. At 55% ABV, it's about 50% stronger than a 37.5% ABV gin, such as Gordon's.

floral, green and delicate in its taste. Juniper is more mossy than ripe, but lip-curlingly dry as citrus powers through. The finish has a lick of apple pip and almond to it.

It's a great choice for a Negroni, as the strength of this gin keeps the herbal winey notes of the vermouth in check, and bolsters citrus aromatics in Campari.

PICKERING'S

As the son of a veterinary surgeon, the smell of iodine and dog sweat is a quite familiar and strangely comforting thing. I like the smell of gin too. So when I visited the Pickering's distillery in Edinburgh's former Royal Dick Veterinary College I felt rather at home.

Of course the boys from Pickering's should feel at home there too, in a past life, before Summerhall (as it is now known) was a veterinary college, it was a brewery that dated back to 1710. Most of the current building was erected between 1916 and 1925 and was home to the The Royal (Dick) School of Veterinary Studies, affectionately known to all as the Dick Vet, until 2011 when the school relocated. The McDowell acquired the building and it's now home to 120 small independent businesses as well as an exhibition and events space as well as its own online TV channel!

Pickering's have found a home for themselves in what used to be the kennels. The 'M' shaped area they have to work with should have been a nightmare to contend with, but thanks to founders Matt Gammel and Marcus Pickering's background in construction and property development, it has been adapted into quite an efficient little space. A 500-litre (132-US gallon) Portuguese still with a 'worm tub' condenser sits pretty on top of a tiled pedestal that might have once been used for showering dogs. The small animal cages will accept cases of gin stacked two high and two wide, and the larger cages – some so large that they could only have housed a bear – act as a bonded warehouse space. Even the bottling space, which so often gets overlooked, has been engineered with productivity in mind by someone who probably colour codes their sock drawer. It features a one-of-a-kind custom-built labelling machine that was put together for Pickering's by one of the neighbouring businesses.

Moving on to the gin, it is based on a hand-written 1947 recipe from Bombay that Marcus Pickering's father acquired. The recipe is only for a tiny quantity of gin, mind you, calling for nine botanicals including a meagre 'Juniper Berry – flat tablespoon' and a rather vague 'Cinnamon stick – ¾ fragment' – but you get the idea. Turned out that the resulting gin (when multiplied up) was a bit too spicy, so they dialled back

BELOW Future plans will see Pickering's 500-litre (132 US-gallon) alembic still joined by an identical twin.

on the clove, cardamom and cassia, and bumped up the juniper. Angelica was missing from the original recipe, but was added to the new formula.

Before I tell you what I thought of the gin please allow me to share some further thoughts on this young distillery. Here is a gin producer that is very business minded. All six employees are cross-trained, capable of handing distillation, bottling and distribution. They have a 'Head of Sales' and weekly planning meetings. They have a second still on order already. As new distilleries step on one another to shout about their product, their botanicals and their various USPs, Pickering's maintain an air of quiet confidence about them. And so they should. Their gin is exceptional and a stand-out example among recent Scottish arrivals.

Pickering's also bottle a Navy Strength version of their gin and more recently have begun bottling the original recipe verbatim, labelled as Pickering's 1947. It's an unbalanced product, very heavy on the cinnamon, but clearly not intended as a day-to-day gin. But it remains an interesting insight in to both the kind of gin that might have appeared in Bombay at the time and also the developmental route that the distillery took to get to their standard mark.

ABOVE AND TOP RIGHT Four separate labels are applied by hand to each bottle of Pickering's Gin.

RIGHT This framed, hand-written note from 1947 is the recipe on which Pickering's Gin is based. Mounted near the entrance, it's a respectful nod to the past.

PICKERING'S (42% ABV)

Glorious juniper hits home, supported by sweet spices, cassia and clove. There's a rotund citrus quality to it as well, limey, but not sharp. Bright and airy on the palate, crisp, firm and in no rush. The finish is long, clean and damn tasty. A reference-quality London Dry.

1947 (42% ABV)

Heavy spice; warm, nutty cinnamon; cloves, cardamom, mulled wine. Hot and heavy on the palate, leaving you literally gasping. Cinnamon tramples its way through the finish too.

THE BOTANIST

As if any further confirmation of premium gin's rise to power were needed, it can be seen in the number of respected whisky distilleries trying their hand at gin making. In fact, seven out of the eight Scottish gin distilleries I've featured also make, or blend, whisky. And there are few places more synonymous with Scotch whisky than the island of Islay of Scotland's western coast. The robust, smoky drams that emanate from the isle seem a far cry from the delicate botanical character of a dry gin. Enter Islay's self-titled 'Progressive Hebridean Distillers', Bruichladdich (brook-laddie to its friends), who, true to form, fancied the challenge.

To get their gin distillation dreams underway, Bruichladdich's long-time master distiller, Jim McEwan, salvaged a very rare Lomond still from the Inverleven Distillery, which was demolished in 2004. Only two distilleries in Scotland have Lomond stills (aside from Loch Lomond which has four) the first being Scapa on Orkney, and the second Bruichladdich on Islay. In an act of barbaric surgery, Bruichladdich melded a vapour infusion chamber on to their still, making it the only Lomond still repurposed for gin. They named it 'Ugly Betty'.

And what a gin it is. Nine classic gin botanicals are joined by a whole host of weird and wonderful ingredients, all sourced and foraged from the peat bogs, rocky shores and the wet and windswept lands of Islay. Some are familiar, like spearmint, lemon balm and sage.

Others sound like something out of *The Lord of the Rings*: mugwort, Lady's Bedstraw, downy birch and bog myrtle. Most interesting of all, perhaps, is the small amount of locally foraged juniper that makes an appearance. There are 22 Islay botanicals, taking the number of botanicals in this gin up to a generous 31 in total.

The bottle underwent a re-design in 2012 and really stands out from the crowd, thanks to the botanic plant names embossed across the front. The effect is a bit of a mess at first glance, but look closely and you can discern each individual name, which is especially handy for recounting all 31 of the botanicals (assuming you can read Latin).

THE BOTANIST (46% ABV)

Fragrant and green, there's a multitude of aromas including dried sage, rosemary, lemon posset, red potpourri and red wine. Floral notes are the most persistent, jasmine, chamomile, and meadowsweet. Taste is light and effeminate. Starting with an ethereal woodsy note, it drops in to rich herbals and eventually a gentle, tingling spice.

It's a versatile gin and great in a G&T. Garnish with non-poisonous greens from your garden!

BELOW It's the combination of rudimentary, hands-on, production techniques and business savvy that makes me admire this distillery. Oh, and the gin tastes good too.

EUROPE

Gin's ancestral roots are bedded in the Low Countries, but England was where gin was really born. The rest of Europe was understandably hesitant about getting in on the action, given gin's troublesome history in London. Spain and France were the first to have a go, the former to meet demand for what is arguably the country's national drink – the Gin & Tonic – the latter for more inauspicious reasons that we will come to later. Then came the Germans, with their know-how from distilling fragile ingredients into fruit brandies. They applied a similar degree of scrutiny to their gins. Nordic countries found a different tack, spurred by the subtle flavours of their cuisine and the use of juniper therein, the gins of Scandinavia are reflective of the clean yet potent flavours of the cuisine. Gin distilleries now pop up far and wide, including Portugal, Switzerland, Austria, Italy, Slovakia, the Czech Republic, Poland and Romania, among others.

But gin was based on genever in the first instance, a spirit which has its roots in the Low Countries. Over the pages that follow we turn our attention to corenwijn (corn wine) and graanjenever (grain genever) in an attempt to trace the missing link between what gin once was and what it is now. What we find is something that is often quite different from gin but offers incredible value for money. And, in an intriguing turn of events, we will discover that some of the more forward-thinking genever distilleries have turned their hand to gin making too – like the return of a prodigal son after a few centuries of 'discovery'.

From some of the oldest to some of the newest spirits producers in the world, the freedom to explore and to place a distillery's identity on a gin is a tantalizing prospect for a distiller and a welcome treat for the consumer. Whether it's a revival of traditional techniques and ingredients, or a homage to the local terroir or cuisine, the gins of Europe are as diverse in taste and character as the nations from which they arise.

THIS PAGE AND OPPOSITE Whether it's gin or genever, Europe has a long and colourful history where the juniper berry is concerned, and distillers both old and new are committed to celebrating it.

CITADELLE

When gin was subject to a period of deep slumber through the 1980s and 1990s, there were only a handful of brands that were brave (or perhaps stupid) enough to dare a launch. While I applaud these products for their courage and their contribution to the category's revival, it's a sad truth that few of them have forged a market for themselves that can be compared to the success stories of the mid-2000s.

Sales figures are for salesmen though, and can easily divert our attention from the stories behind the products and the (often) great quality liquid in the glass. As a teenager, standing at the bar with my mother, Citadelle was one of the first spirit brands that appeared to be out of place to me. Perhaps it was because I had, even at the tender age of 15, already developed a comprehensive mental record of backbar brands, or perhaps it was because this was a gin from France. In the 1990s. Strange as that was, the story of Citadelle gin actually goes back a lot further than the 1990s and gets a whole lot stranger, too.

The year is 1771 and at that time there was a genever distillery in Dunkirk, France. The historical fishing town of Dunekerke had previously fallen under Dutch and English ownership during the 17th century, so was a good place to put a distillery, especially considering it was also an important spice trading port back then. In 1775 the distillery's owners, Carpeau and Stival, were granted a royal charter by France's newly crowned King Louis XVI. A royal charter after only a

few years operation was quite an impressive feat, incredible even. But it turns out that there's more to this tale than meets the eye.

France and England had been at each other throats constantly through the 17th and 18th centuries and things were quickly coming to a head. This was apparent not least of all in France's decision to assist the American colonies in their revolution against their British motherland. So any opportunity to capture land, remove power, or simply humiliate one another was high on the list of priorities (and would remain that way for some time to come). One such opportunity arose in relation to this Dunkirk distillery, where the cunning French hatched a scheme to produce vast quantities of wheat spirit with the sole purpose of smuggling it into the UK and selling it tax-free, destabilizing the economy in the process. The distillery was kitted out with 12 large copper pot stills and the games commenced. Amazingly, they got away with it and the smuggling continued right up to 1810, even through Britain declaring war on France in 1803 and the Napoleonic blockades that followed.

It's an almost unbelievable story, were it not for the fact that it is true. Alexandre Gabriel, owner of Pierre Ferrand Cognac, discovered the tale back in the 1980s when he first planned to add a gin to the company's brandy business. During a bout of intense research in to the long since shutdown Dunkirk operation he unearthed a recipe for Citadelle Gin. The original recipe was adapted and embellished, taking the botanical count up to 19 (there can be little doubt that there were not 19 botanicals in the original) and applying a couple of centuries worth of gained distilling knowledge to the old recipe. Speaking of distillation, Alexander also had to convince the French government that it was acceptable for him to use his Cognac stills to make gin. The stills, which sit idle all summer long (eau de vie for Cognac is legally

LEFT Citadelle's blue 'pillar' of a bottle certainly stands out on a back bar.

permitted to only be distilled in the winter) are of the traditional alembic variety, heated by an open flame. The bureaucracy of the whole thing held him up for some time, so the first run of Citadelle gin didn't materialize until 1995.

Of the 19 botanicals only a handful deviate from the classic array and even they are not what you would call outlandish: star anise, cumin, fennel seed and savoury – that's as exciting as it gets, which is no bad thing. The ingredients are steeped for three days in neutral wheat spirit, then distilled over the course of 12 hours in a 2,000-litre (530-US gallon) Cognac still – the only gin in the world to do so. In 2008 a 'Réserve' variant was introduced. The French are the world leaders in oak-ageing spirits, and this gin reminds us of that fact. Split across three separate cask varieties

BELOW When is a Cognac still not a Cognac still? When it's repurposed to make gin during the summer, of course!

BELOW RIGHT The onion-shaped chauffe-vin on a Cognac still is used to preheat spirit and partially condense spirit vapour.

(American oak; ex-Pineau de Charantes; ex-Cognac) the matured spirits are blended into a 'bottomless' solera vat, which is topped up with more gin as quickly as it is emptied to fill bottles.

CITADELLE (44% ABV)

Delicate and floral at first: Violet flowers, orange blossom and jasmine. Juniper soon rises up however, accompanied by medicinal spices, cassia and cardamom. Taste-wise, it's still floral, but more dirty and green, with herbals coming through. Some greener citric elements, too. Plays nicely with lemon juice, and nowhere better than in an Aviation.

CITADELLE RÉSERVE GIN (44% ABV)

Spearmint and clean cut balsa wood on the nose, which slowly make way for lemon peel and peppered roots. Water reveals more citrus, and the mint turns to pine oil. On the tongue it's juicy and positively oozing juniper. Couple that with the fruit and spice (from the cask) and you get the effect of Christmas tree in your Christmas pudding. Good for general sipping (no ice) but a winner in a 2:1:1 Negroni.

DE KUYPER

What with all the new British distilleries out there that are producing modernist, contemporary gins, it's quite ironic to see that one of the most quintessentially British retailers, whose history can be traced back to 1698, have chosen to make their archetypal London Dry Gin in The Netherlands. Berry Bros. & Rudd is one of Britain's oldest wine merchants, purveyors of top-quality plonk from their store on No. 3 St. James Street for over three hundred years now. Over that time the private, family-owned company, has developed a good working relationship with The Netherland's oldest family-owned distillery, De Kuyper. So when Berry's decided it was high time they launched a premium gin, it was their trusted friends at De Kuyper ('The Cooper') that they turned to for help.

Interestingly, De Kuyper trace their own history back to 1695, a mere three years before Berry's opened their doors. At that time Petrous de Kuyper was an aptly named man, as he was a cooper, or barrel maker, living in the village of Horst in the eastern Limburg province. The family emigrated to Rotterdam in 1728 and started buying up distilleries – two in Rotterdam, The Anchor and The Clover, and one in neighbouring Schiedam.

The business moved down through the generations, and more distilleries were added to the portfolio to keep up with demand for the massive Dutch export trade in genever that had come about. By the end of the 18th century the De Kuyper's had no less than seven distilleries between Rotterdam and Schiedam and a malting house to service them all.

De Kuyper suffered along with the rest of the genever industry during the years of the Napoleonic blockade, and the existing distilleries were dished out to different family members, who then either sold them back to each other, or passed them on to the next generation. By the mid-19th century the sixth

generation of De Kuypers were in charge of what was mostly a Rotterdam-based operation. The US were buying the lion's share of export genever and trade at home was good thanks to taxation on spirits lowering to 15.5%. It was around this time that the company began using the heart and anchor emblem (based on the Clover and Anchor distilleries) on their packaging – and what a lot of packaging it was! By 1894 the company was selling 4 million litres (1.1 million US gallons) of genever a year, and twice that by 1913. De Kuyper moved in to liqueurs a lot later than their rival, Bols. Starting with cherry liqueur in 1911, which was quickly joined by apricot, mint and triple sec flavours.

The company moved headquarters, to their current Schiedam location, in 1911. This was partly due to the closure of a canal in Rotterdam, which was essential for efficient movement of goods. The new site was ideal however, as right next to it was the O–I glass factory, which the De Kuyper family later became stakeholders in.

In 1995 De Kuyper were awarded the title of 'Royal' from Queen Beatrix of the Netherlands, which lead to the company changing their name to De Kuyper Royal Distillers. Now in their 11th generation of family ownership, De Kuyper have become specialists in the field of liqueurs and flavoured spirits. The company motto is 'Can we liquefy it?'

The distillery is run by Master Distiller Myriam Hendrikx and veteran distiller Fretz de Jonge, who has served at De Kuyper since the early 1980s. There are two buildings dedicated to distilling and a third that sits above 300 cubic meters (10,500 cubic feet) of subterranean maceration vats. Strict adherence to

ABOVE During World War II, De Kuyper used recycled beer bottles to package their genever.

traditional methods and a keen understanding of the requirements of each ingredient is the secret to how this place ticks.

No. 3 gin is produced exclusively in a 3,110-litre (820-US gallon) 'No. 1' Ketel still at the distillery in Schiedam – there is a No. 2 still used for distilling mint for liqueurs, but frustratingly, no No. 3 still. Both #1 and #2 are old, harking back to 1911, they're brick-jacketed and fitted with a wood- and coal-burning furnace in the base that was adapted to run on natural gas in the 1960s. 2,000 litres (530 US gallons) of 55% neutral spirit go in to still #1 along with 100 kg (220 lbs.) of botanicals: juniper, coriander seeds, cardamom, angelica root, grapefruit peel and orange peel. These are left to steep overnight and distilling starts in the morning. It takes approximately seven hours before the tails cut is made. The resulting distillate is cut back with neutral spirit and water, where seven litres of distillate is sufficient to make 100 bottles of gin. As it stands No. 3 is only being distilled twice a year, but if my calculations are correct that's still in the region of 40,000 bottles.

De Kuyper have recently acquired another old family-run distillery called Rutte. The Rutte family have been making genever in the port town of Dordrecht since 1872, but the last Rutte to lead the company died in 2003. Under the supervision of De Kuyper the genevers are still made in the family home in Dordrecht, but the Rutte gins that were launched in 2012 (including a celery gin) are made at De Kuyper in Schiedam.

Both No. 3 and the Rutte range are bottled in the familiar broad-shouldered 'Schiedam' bottle. I'm told that these bottles are becoming increasingly difficult to use in automated environments due to their tendency to 'pop out' of production lines when they get pushed.

NO. 3 LONDON DRY GIN (46% ABV)

Candied juniper and sweet spiced lemon on the nose. Great interplay between juniper and coriander. Grapefruit zest stands out after more digging. Cardamom is perfectly subtle. The mouthfeel is thick and lively, more cardamom than expected, followed by squeaky clean citrus. Juniper is more assertive on the second sip. Soft finish; bone dry. At its best in a Martini and, given that it is one of the best, it's a damn good Martini at that.

RUTTE DRY GIN (35% ABV)

Pleasant and altogether classic smelling. Spiced cinnamon, orange and a good blast of juniper. Balances the line between fresh and warming. Texture holds well on the palate, pepper carries the juniper. Ideal for all your gin and tonic needs.

RUTTE CELERY GIN (35% ABV)

Everything green, except the celery. Herbal, cool softmints. Plenty of cardamom, lime, sage and black pepper. Taste is more vegetal than the dry. Some peppered salsa verde on the finish. Red Snapper seems an obvious choice!

RIGHT As it stands today, the De Kuyper Distillery is a curious mix of the old and new, sporting ancient brick-jacketed pots as well as super modern vacuum stills... and everything in-between.

FILLIERS

As Jonas Naessens, Filliers' debonair marketeer, says, 'You could run a diverse bar with the range of products we make.' And with over 50 different products covering gin, genever, flavoured genever, cream genever, advocaat, whisky, vodka and liqueurs, he's not wrong. Fillers was originally a farm, located on the outskirts of the village Bachte-Maria-Leerne, near Deinze, and not far from the city of Ghent in the Belgian province of East Flanders. Founded in 1792, by Karel Lodeijk Filliers, distilling was soon added to the farm's list of capabilities as was common among farmers at the time. Distilling in earnest began in the 1880s, however, when the brand name was registered, and the farm side of things shut down in the 1950s. Today, this distillery, which employs only 25 people, produces more moutwijn (malt wine) than any other genever distillery, which goes on to flavour Filliers' own products as well as other Belgian and Dutch genever brands, including Bols. The distillery is still owned and run by the Filliers family, who are edging towards their 6th generation of distilling in the region.

Fillers call themselves a warm stokerij ('warm distillery') which means they make spirits *van de korrel tot de borrel* ('from the grain to the glass'). I have rarely seen so many pieces of distillation equipment in one distillery, scattered around like porcelain figurines on your granny's mantelpiece. Red brick warehouses play host to the mashing room, fermentation vessels, the still house, ageing warehouse, development lab and bottling hall, as well as a bar and office space. Slender white grain silos mirror the lanky Italian cypress trees that populate the surrounding flat countryside.

Moutwijn is made from a combination of rye and malted barley along with corn or wheat. The exact recipe varies according to whether the spirit will undergo maturation and which brand or bottle it is intended for. After a mashing, and followed by a five-day fermentation period, the 'beer' runs through a column still, which takes its alcohol content up to 60%. It is then distilled again in a pot still, resulting in a distillate of 80% ABV. The sample I tried was nutty, like warm hay and digestive biscuits.

The various moutwijn recipes that Filliers make are the cornerstones of their genever brands and may be used in a number of ways to form a finished product. Some might be put in to cask for a few years as part of an aged genever, or it could be redistilled with juniper berries in the No. 6 still to make a 100% moutwijn genever. It could also be blended with neutral spirit distilled with juniper, to form a jonge genever. The company bottles eight of their own genevers, including the Van Hoorebeke brand, which, dating back to 1740 is the oldest genever brand in Belgium. Also included in the portfolio is Filliers flagship 30% ABV graanjenever, which has a portion of 2-year-old moutwijn in it, as well as five aged genevers at 5, 8, 12, 15 and 18 years old.

It was Firmin Filliers, one of the third generation, who, in 1928 shortly after the end of World War I, created the recipe that inspired the current Filliers 'Dry Gin 28'. The story goes that there were a number of ex-servicemen from Britain that settled down in the area once the war was over, and thirsty for a taste of home, they petitioned Firmin to make them a gin. The original recipe was adapted significantly, taking the botanical count to 28. Additions include Belgian hops, allspice, dandelion flowers, elderflowers and chicory. A selection of fresh fruits are used too, like raspberries, and these are added to the mix in their 'fresh' form.

LEFT A vatting of Oude Graangenever readies itself for bottling at Filliers.

Distillation of the gin is conducted in what the Filliers family call their 'Distillers Playground'. This bright and airy room feels like part farmhouse kitchen and part laboratory. Walls are lined with huge glass and ceramic maceration vessels. A portly old 200-litre (53-US gallon) still clings to one of the walls and there are two 500-litre (132-US gallon) pot stills that do all the heavy lifting. Gin is distilled in four distinct batches, where kindred ingredients are processed together. Obviously Filliers hold their cards close to their chests, but it might be that fruits, roots, spices and herbs/flowers are grouped together and processed in separate distillation runs. These are then blended together to make the finished product. No neutral spirit is added.

Filliers produce five different gins under the '28' label today, having launched the brand in 2011. This includes a classic dry gin, a barrel-aged gin and three flavoured gins: sloe, pine blossom and tangerine.

FILLIERS GRAANGENEVER (30% ABV)

Warm apple strudel with cinnamon and clotted cream. Light on the palate, slightly creamy, vanilla, nutmeg and light spice. Apples and pears come through in the finish. Crisp and gentle, but warming.

VAN HOOREBEKE (30% ABV)

Very light. Anise, plum jam and a touch of cream soda on the nose. There's a slight musty hay-like aroma too. On the palate, there's more character: creamy vanilla, butterscotch and raspberry jam. It's surprisingly sweet.

FILLIERS 5 YEAR OLD GRAANGENEVER (38% ABV)

Light oak, marzipan and oloroso Sherry. Boiled milk and burnt latte. Pepper on the palate, and caramel and vanilla, but it's still dry. It's nutty and fresh through to the finish.

ABOVE Filliers is the most important distillery in the entire genever category because it makes nearly all of the world's maltwine.

FILLIERS 18 YEAR OLD (43% ABV)

More Bourbon than Scotch, there's new oak character doing battle with forest fruits. Polished teak, plum tart, sloes, eventually give way to banana custard. Just a touch of black pepper. On the palate expect to find a dry heat that continues in to luscious woody notes, burnt crème brûlée, and spice. The finish has a touch of astringency, begging for another sip.

FILLIERS DRY GIN 28 (46% ABV)

Light and delicate. Lemon oil comes up first, followed by a soft hint of juniper, and a citric wit bier quality. The palate is assertive juniper. It's sweet (candied?), long and wholesome! The length is impressive, as spices and hops come through towards the finish. Drifting away in to dry old spices and sweet fermented roots. This makes a mind-blowing Gin Fizz.

FILLIERS 28 PINE BLOSSOM (42.6% ABV)

Green juniper is accompanied by various other green things; Christmas tree, cardamom, lime leaf, caper berry, fresh dill and musk. Cool and green on the palate, with Christmas tree, bay leaf, caraway, and green chilli/chile through to the finish. Good for a festive Martini, or as the backbone of a Rickey.

FILLIERS 23 BARREL AGED

Orange marmalade, mace, ginger and clove infiltrate the nostrils on this festive gin. There's some wood on the palate, but it's largely spiced citrus fruit and aromatic spices that draw the finish to a close. Juniper gives an unexpected wave just as things tail off. A good winter-time sipping gin, and an exceptional base for a cup of Purl.

GIN DE MAHÓN

At one time there were five distilleries on the island of Minorca, producing dozens of gin brands. The story begins in the mid 18th century when British and Dutch naval forces used the island as a strategic base. Minorca underwent brief colonial rule, during which time the locals were encouraged to make gin. Gradually the industry died out, coming to a dramatic end when the last distillery burned to the ground in the early 1900s. The master distiller, Miguel Gusto, decided to set up a new distillery on the island, in 1910, which is when the Xoriguer Distillery first began trading. It was furnished with stills salvaged from some of the old operations and recipes to match. Today the Xoriguer Distillery stands as a living testament to the history of gin on the island.

Today the distillery produces a modest 60,000 litres (15,850 US gallons) of Mahón gin every year, along with two budget gins and 11 liqueurs. That's a minute share of the market and disproportionate to the fame of the brand. Even though a great number of international bars keep a bottle, regrettably, it's mostly only a token gesture. The truth is that outside of Minorca it's not commonly drunk at all. It's not a problem, though – Minorca gets through more than enough by itself.

The botanical recipe is what you might call limited. It was allegedly created in 1750, and given the crudeness of the formula, in this instance at least, it's a credible claim. The one and only star of the show, used in the standard 38% bottling, is juniper. The US bottling (sold at 41%) also contains trace amounts of coriander, citrus and angelica. The juniper berries for both bottlings are sourced exclusively from the Pyrenees. It's not an area you would normally associate with juniper growing, but the Xoriguer distillery has been buying juniper from there for nearly 100 years. After screening for debris and leaves (by hand) the berries are rested in 20-kg (44-lb.) plastic hampers for up to two years, to exercise some of the moisture out of the berries and concentrate the oils. When it's time to make gin, they're added to the still and macerated for a couple of hours into neutral grape-based spirit that has been cut back to 52% ABV.

The still house is a relic. Four near-identical alembic copper stills take care of production, one of them purportedly over 200 years old, which is the oldest gin still I've encountered. Each is housed in its own stone box, caked in red Spanish tiles and heated by a wood-burning furnace from below. Minorcan wood is used for the fire, lovingly stoked by a single distiller whose nifty

BELOW LEFT Perched on the harbour front of Mahón, Xoriguer Distillery is a popular tourist stop-off.

BELOW The black vents on the side of the stills are a simple means of controlling temperature.

BELOW RIGHT A modest-looking bottling line at Xoriguer Distillery.

footwork opens and closes the furnace door for inspection. If things get too hot – determined neither by thermometers or pressure gauges – the distiller can slide up one of the iron 'letterbox' hatches on the side of the chamber to ventilate the system. Worm-tub condensers bring the spirit vapour back to aqueous form; the coolant is drawn from the harbour water, just across the road. The spirit is blended with more neutral spirit and water to reach bottling strength, then rested briefly in large, 2,000-litre (528-US gallon) American oak casks. These were spent decades ago, though, so perform the role of inert container more than flavour contributor.

It's difficult to imagine a less sophisticated set up. But the distillery's ignorance to this fact is incredibly endearing. For Xoriguer this is just the way. Methods have been handed down here without questions asked, A distiller here is more like a regent, a keeper of the craft. It's not that they're unwilling to change, it just that it simply never enters their minds. And there's no need anyway. The gin is balanced, nuanced, complex. Mahón is a celebration of the juniper berry and a miraculous conclusion to what seems such a primitive evolutionary process. Straight off the still it is all leather and sweetness, pine and tobacco. Two of Minorca's biggest industries are leather products and ice-cream. I swear that they are both present in its gin.

In Mahón gin we have a legendary product that has perhaps become a victim of its own staunchly traditional approach. This is evident in both the methods that are employed at the distillery and even more so in the packaging of the gin. From the quaintly illustrated yellow label to the daft little handle, it's easy to be dismissive of this gin from Minorca that has somehow and inexplicably landed itself a geographical indication. Don't be though. It's fantastic.

GIN DE MAHÓN (38% ABV)

On the nose, it's big, potent, concentrated, juniper. Sticky pine sap and waxy leather, too. The palate is soft, sweet, and oily. There's no shortage of juniper, but it melds with soft tobacco notes, brine and a tickle of pink pepper through to the finish. Drink it in a 'Pomada', traditionally made from gin mixed with lemon juice.

THIS PAGE Craft spirits don't get any more hand-crafted than Mahón Gin, from the hand-sorting of juniper berries through to the Minorcan wood that's used to fire the stills. These methods have been passed down through the generations and are part of the charm of the characterful Xoriguer Distillery.

GIN MARE

It's fair to say that, out of all the gin brands that have launched over the past 10 years, few have made an impact quite like Gin Mare. In the space of six years this family-owned 'Mediterranean Gin' from Vilanova I la Geltrú, just south of Barcelona, has gone from zero to over 400,000 bottles. It all starts with the Giro family, who are now in their 4th generation of Catalan distilling and trace their roots back to 1836 when they were buying and selling Sherry and wine in the region. By 1900 they had added distillation of brandy and whisky to their repertoire, but it was in 1940 that gin making first got underway. The catalyst for this was the Spanish civil war (1935–1939) which found Manuel Giro senior, the grandfather of the current generation (Mark and Manuel junior) hiding in Spain's northern Pyrenees mountain range. While there, he discovered wild juniper bushes, and once the war ended, he returned to Catalonia, inspired to make Spanish gin. Along with his father, he launched the 'Gin MG' brand, which is still produced and bottled at the distillery in Villanova I la Geltrú today. The gin quickly became one of Spain's bestsellers, and even nowadays the company fill over 800,000 bottles of Gin MG a year, which I'm told sells very well in South Korea and Nigeria.

In the 1960s, the family launched Gin Giró, but father and son parted company shortly after that, feeling that it was best for the two brands if they weren't produced in the same place. Gin Giró relocated to the Basque country and has since been discontinued.

The next generation of the family launched Master's Gin, a gin made to look and taste very much like a classic London Dry. It's packaged in a cobalt blue bottle and would be otherwise unexceptional if it hadn't just grabbed the coveted 'Best Gin' award at the San Francisco Spirits Competition in 2015.

Next came Gin Mare. Development for this 'Sea Gin' started in 2007. Formulated and conceived by Mark and Manuel Giro junior in collaboration with Global Premium Brands, this contemporary gin was intended to be representative of the Mediterranean flavours and the area's ardent gin-drinking culture. One hundred different botanicals were trialled for Gin Mare, each distilled in isolation on a tiny 15-litre (4-US gallon) alembic. They were eventually narrowed down to 11 botanicals: juniper, coriander seed, cardamom, Seville orange, Valencia orange, Lleida lemon, Arbequina olives, dried rosemary, dried thyme, dried basil and dried oregano. The oregano was later removed as it was felt that it made the gin smell like pizza!

The making of Gin Mare takes place inside a tiny chapel on the grounds of Destilerías Miquel Guansé. The chapel was formerly part of a larger monastery on the coast, but was moved, stone by stone, in the late 19th century to make way for the port. Inside the chapel you'll find nothing more than a tiny 250-litre (66-US gallon) pot still and a bunch of macerating botanicals. All the botanicals are macerated separately, in 86% neutral wheat spirit, prior to distillation. The maceration term is

THIS PAGE A gin distillery in a chapel, you say? With the pot still sitting in place of the altar. Blasphemy! It does work, though. It's small but perfectly formed.

dependent on the product, where herbs are only held for a couple of weeks and 'tougher' ingredients much longer. They are distilled separately too, and blended together with neutral spirit and water to a bottling strength of 42.4%. The brand is very open about the fact that the gin is produced in a multi-shot manner, stating that the distilled product is mixed at a ratio of roughly 10:1 with neutral wheat spirit.

I was lucky enough to taste each one of the component distillates prior to blending, which really helps with identifying the various components in the finished product. Rosemary, basil and thyme are all of the dried variety and their flavour, for what it is, is captured perfectly in the distillates. They each have that familiar mossy, herbal note to them, giving the subtle juniper aroma an edge. Olive is the most unusual of the botanicals, where 15 kg (33 lbs.) of tiny Arbequina olives will yield you 100 litres (26 US gallons) of sharp and juicy olive distillate. Once you've tasted the distillate it's a lot easier to pick it out in the final product. Two tons of citrus fruit (oranges from Valencia and Seville; lemons from Lleida) arrive at the distillery each year. They're peeled by hand then macerated together for up to two years.

GIN MARE (42.7% ABV)

Cardamom is the most dominant aroma in this gin, but it's followed up quickly by other green things in this order: dried basil, apple, rosemary, pine and olive.

ABOVE LEFT Arbequina olives undergo pulping before being distilled.

ABOVE TOP Gin Mare's small pot still produces distillates with massively concentrated flavour.

ABOVE Each botanical undergoes a long, isolated maceration process before being distilled.

Cardamom dominates the taste, too – mostly in its green, citrus form. Drifting gently in to herbals, but remaining very much eucalyptus-y in style. Put it in a G&T and load it up with herbs!

G'VINE

Now I know 'G'Vine' sounds less like a gin brand and more like a rapper from the Languedoc, but don't let that put you off.

G'Vine is owned by spirit brand development agency EWG Spirits & Wine, and is headed up by charismatic frontman Jean-Sébastien Robicquet. He is straight out of a James Bond movie: suave, debonair and altogether dangerous. The only question is whether he's more like Bond or the villain. Judging by the size of his fortified manor-house on the outskirts of Cognac, kitted out with nearly a dozen stills and a warehouse full of maturing Cognac, I'm leaning towards the latter. Jean-Sébastien's roots run deep in wine-growing country. His family have brewed grape juice in the Bordeaux region since the 17th century. After acquiring qualifications in law, economics and vineyard management, Jean-Sébastien began a career in wine making, but quickly jumped the fence and set up EWG in 2001.

G'Vine 'Floraison' was launched in 2006 and was followed up by the more classic 'Nouaison' in 2008. The process starts with Ugni Blanc grapes, one of the three varieties that can be used in Cognac production. These are harvested in September, pressed into juice, and fermented into wine. The wine is distilled up to 96.4% in EWG's column still, then cut back with water, ready for re-distillation with botanicals when the time is right. Grape spirit might seem an unconventional base material for a gin, but let's not forget the earliest records of juniper spirits, as well as the earliest record of a recreational 'gin', all used *eau de vie* (grape spirit) as their base.

Both gins comprise the same nine botanicals: juniper, coriander seed, cassia, liquorice/licorice, green cardamom, cubeb berries, nutmeg, lime peel and ginger. Each botanical is macerated in spirit and distilled individually. They are then blended together with a separate maceration of grape vine flowers that must be harvested during a one-week window in June. The macerate, along with the botanical distillates, is then redistilled with more neutral grape spirit – *et voila!* – G'Vine gin.

FLORAISON (40% ABV)

I get a healthy dose of lime on the nose of this gin. This is met with a delicate, fleeting, floral note, and some gentle aromatic spice. If it weren't for the late arrival of juniper and liquorice/licorice, I'd be referencing Thai curry, but better-late-than-never-juniper finally makes an arrival. Floraison's punchy flavour moves quickly between fleshy florals, cinnamon and a pat on the tongue from the liquorice/licorice. Makes a cracker of a French 75, with a touch less sugar and sparkling Mauzac Blanc in place of Champagne.

NOUAISON (43.9% ABV)

The masculine to Floraison's feminine; much drier on the nose and less floral. The strength seems to have elevated the juniper, subduing the lime slightly and warming the whole thing up. On the palate it's a good balance of juniper, lime, cinnamon and ginger. The finish is dressed up nicely too, with subtle coriander and a light prickle of heat from the cubeb. This is a versatile little number that carries itself well in to all kinds of gin inspired applications.

THIS PAGE Young grape buds and grape vine flowers have become the trademark flavour of G'Vine, which is distilled in an alembic still named 'Flo'.

HERNÖ

Unlike other Swedish distilleries, which are making some very distinguished whiskies, Hernö Distillery have their eyes firmly set on gin. It is Sweden's only dedicated gin distillery and, at the time of writing, the most northerly gin distillery.

Jon Hellgren is the founder of the distillery, which began producing in 2012 and already has seven different gins in stores. With that many, it's no wonder that Hernö claims to be the most highly decorated gin distillery in Europe over the past two years, having received 25 individual accolades. The packaging is beautiful, the liquid a delight, and the setting for it all perhaps tops them all: the village of Dala, just outside Härnösand, 'the gateway to the High Coast'.

The gin itself is of London Dry ilk (juniper, coriander seed, fresh lemon peel, cassia and black pepper), embellished with spice, fruit and flower: Vanilla gives a sweet, woodsy element to the aroma, which is pepped up by juicy lingonberries and some mossy meadowsweet. The effect is one of intensity, brightness and poise. The lingonberries are hand-picked, the meadowsweet hand-plucked, and the lemons are of course hand-peeled.

All of the botanicals in Hernö are organic-certified and the wheat spirit is organic, too. Juniper and coriander are macerated for 18 hours in said spirit then joined by the other botanicals. The still is a 250-litre (66-US gallon) Arnold Holstein and the gin is made according to the one-shot mantra. The standard botanical mix comes in three strengths (which I think is a record): Swedish Excellence (40.5%), Export Strength (47%) and Navy strength (57%), the latter of which is powerful enough to put hairs on the baldest of chests. There's an Old Tom too, sweetened with honey and heavy on the meadowsweet. It's predictably floral but not at the sacrifice of the juniper. Then there are two fruit gins, blackcurrant and sloe, and the juniper cask expression (47%). Hernö is not the only distillery playing around with gin matured in juniper wood, but I think I'm right in saying that they were the first to do it.

HERNÖ SWEDISH EXCELLENCE (40.5% ABV)

The aroma here is very much 'of the wild' where we find that mossy meadowsweet note, pepped up by honeyed vanilla. But juniper rides these other botanicals like a big blue wave, crashing around the place with Christmas tree sap, pine needle, and green juniper berries. The palate is no less exciting, pummelling juniper home with pepper and citrus derived, presumably, from the coriander. A marvellous gin. Makes a meaty Martini, but also delivers the goods in a Negroni.

HERNÖ OLD TOM (43% ABV)

The Old Tom from Hernö is in many respects a caricature of the standard release, where certain features have been grossly disproportioned. Juniper takes one step back (but is by no means missing) making way for more of that herbal meadowsweet and a big waft of pungent honeycomb. The taste is quite sweet, which softens the pepper while holding the length and delivering a pleasant mouthfeel. Makes a delightful Tom Collins or Gin Fizz.

HERNÖ JUNIPER CASK (47% ABV)

Building off the flavours of 'Excellence', the maturation notes are subtle, leaning towards preserved citrus fruits and gentle warm spices. Candied mandarin and ground ginger warm up the chilly juniper blast. It has just enough sweetness to keep the citrus dried and the spices soft and crumbly. The finish dries out quickly, making way for the next sip. Drink it neat, or with a splash of ginger ale over ice.

ABOVE Hernö Gin is bottled in refreshingly simple packaging that contrasts with the complexity of the liquid.

MONKEY 47

The picturesque Black Forest (or Schwarzwald), in South West Germany, is probably most famous for its gateaux, Kirsch (a cherry-based spirit), and Grimm's fairytales. Two things that do not spring to mind when speaking of the Black Forest are gin and monkeys. And indeed, if it weren't for the Royal Air Force (RAF) pilot, Montgomery Collins, it's quite likely that no one would ever have put them together. After World War II, Collins moved to the Black Forest to set up a watchmaking business. As with any profession that requires a huge amount of skill and patience, practice and experience is the key, of which Collins had neither. He subsequently ended up running his own guest house, which was named 'The Wild Monkey', apparently after a monkey he had adopted from the Berlin zoo (yes, this is a weird story). Collins' guest house did alright, and by the 1970s he had taken up the art of distilling fruit spirits. But given that he was a former RAF pilot, it would only be proper to distil some gins too, which he did, using locally sourced fruits and spices.

What became of Collins is not entirely clear, but given the diversity of his CV, he probably became an acrobat in the Russian circus, or founded a software company in Silicon Valley. What we do know is that he left behind a case of gin labelled 'Max the Monkey - Black Forest Dry Gin', which was discovered in 2007 by Alexander Stein, a man descended from a long line of German distillers. Stein decided to set up his own Black Forest distillery and requisitioned the help of distilling genius Christoph Keller in 2008. After two years of foraging ingredients and developing liquids, the pair released a limited run of 2,000 bottles of Monkey 47 gin in 2010. The following year it bagged the 'Best in Class' award at the International Wine & Spirits Championships in San Francisco.

Monkey 47 is made using no less than (wait for it…) 47 different botanicals, which is a record-breaking amount for anyone who's counting. And since you really need to be scraping the bottom of the botanical barrel to come up with that many unique ingredients, I doubt the record will be broken any time soon.

It's surprising to find that one of the most uncommon ingredients in this gin is the humble cranberry. Cranberry is actually a much more obvious choice for a botanical than you might think, imparting berry and citrus fruit qualities in the aroma of Monkey 47, and revealing the cranberry's trademark dryness when the gin is mixed with tonic. It's actually quite surprising that we don't see more of the cranberry in gin recipes.

BELOW LEFT An unconventional gin, made in an unconventional location by unconventional people.

BELOW Monkey 47 has proven to be a big hit with cocktail bartenders across the world.

Moving on to the other 46 botanicals, and besides all (and I mean all) of the usual suspects, there's quite a kooky arrangement of ingredients going on in this gin: Monarda didyma (also known as scarlet beebalm) is a crimson-coloured flower native to North America, deploying a fresh earl grey aroma in the distillate. Spruce shoots add a pine-y, citrus-y aromatic that helps to lift the greener notes from the juniper, which in this instance needs all the help it can get. The spruce shoots, along with lingonberries, acacia flowers, bramble leaves and angelica root are all sourced locally, as it happens.

With all these flowers and soft fruits it's not that surprising to hear that two distant extraction methods are used during distillation — a 36-hour maceration and boil for the hardier stuff, and vapour infusion for the delicate bits. This produces, in their own words 'a molecular aroma architecture' — if that pongs of an undesirable 48th botanical then you're not alone. But in all seriousness, 'architecture' is a suitable analogy for a product such as this, where many different materials come together in a single structure. The bottle's engraved metal ring that clasps the cork pays testament to this, the motto reading 'ex pluribus unum', translating as 'out of many, one'.

Speaking of the bottle, it really is a beauty. The brown medicine-style profile is a simple, squat affair, that is until you see the label. Based on an old colonial postage stamp, the purple details remind me of Black Forest cherries (which are curiously missing from the recipe!) and draws links between India, Great Britain and Germany.

Bump your Negroni (see pages 204–205) up to a 2:1:1 formula and Monkey 47 shines through nicely. Alternately enjoy with a generous slice of Black Forest Gateau.

MONKEY 47 (47% ABV)

Medicinal eucalyptus/camphor, mint and pine on the nose. Those are quickly challenged by an invasion of fruits (from the forest) along with citrus, angelica, tea and oak moss. Once in the mouth, the gin is complex, with bittersweet citrus notes accompanied by a smoked incense and a savoury edge that could be sage. The finish is all ripe berries and their associated foliage.

RIGHT Monkey 47 is a masterclass in spirits packaging and design. The label speaks of provenance and reliability without being pompous or overly serious.

NOLET

The Nolet Distillery, which sits alongside the Buitenhaven canal, in Schiedam, The Netherlands, possesses all the trappings of any other craft operation: old copper pot stills, a distiller dressed in a blacksmith-esque leather apron, and a history dating back 11 generations. But this is craft on a colossal scale. This distillery sprawls – towering above, tunnelling below, and stretching across both sides of the canal, today standing as a bona fide monument to the history and future of distilling in Schiedam. Among its long list of features is the tallest windmill in the world – or it would be if it were a mill rather than a turbine designed to look like a mill. The de Nolet windmill is home to a café, a 60-seater cinema, and some of the best views of the Schiedam skyline, including all six of the town's remaining [true] windmills.

While the windmill is a nod to the past, most of what goes on inside this distillery is focused on the future. After 325 years of distilling in Schiedam, the Nolets have more recently become famous for their Ketel One brand of vodka than for their gin and genever. So vodka is the cash cow, but it was 300 years of genever production that got them to this stage.

Looking at the operation today, it's hard to imagine that the Nolets were ever down on their luck but in 1977, during the midst of the genever price wars, it was the launch of Ketel One genever that saved them from certain ruin. Carolus Nolet (10th generation) the current CEO, took the decision to strip back the distillery's bloated portfolio from over 40 products down to just one. It was a relaunch of sorts at a time where only seven people were employed by the distillery. When genever prices were slashed it wasn't just the distilleries that struggled but the retailers, too, who could barely make a single guilder on the sale of a bottle. One of Nolet's shrewdest moves was to incentivize grocers by selling them genever at a price that could make them a good margin. In a market that was crowded with cut-price, poor-quality genever, Ketel 1 represented a return to *ambachtelijke* (a Dutch word meaning 'artisan' or 'craft') practices.

Ketel One genever is a jonge style, containing 'at least 3% malt wine'. The malt wine is, as with nearly all Dutch producers, sourced from Filliers in Belgium and made from a combination of wheat, corn and rye. When the malt wine arrives at the Nolet Distillery, it's matured for 12–18 months in 220-litre (58-US gallon) toasted French oak barrels, then re-distilled with 14 secret botanicals in still No. 1 or No. 7. The brick-jacketed, coal-fired, *Distileerketel No. 1* still is where the brand (as well as the Ketel One vodka brand) takes its name from. It's the oldest in the distillery, having been originally installed around 1853. The clear malt wine distillate is then blended with neutral wheat spirit and cut down to bottling strength with water.

The recent launch of Ketel One 'Matuur' represents the faith that the Nolets place in the future of barrel-aged genever. The liquid is a mixture of neutral wheat spirit combined with a blend of malt wines that have been matured for up to eight years in un-charred American oak casks. Some of the malt wine is re-distilled with a secret blend of botanicals. Caramel is added for colour, and a small amount of sugar is added to improve the mouthfeel.

Nolet's gin was, I suppose, an inevitability. The international success that Ketel One vodka achieved along with the resurgence of the gin category, not to mention a few centuries' worth of expertise in genever, meant that the Nolet's were perfectly placed to launch a gin. When 'Silver' and 'Reserve' were finally revealed

LEFT A shadow of intricate ironmongery at Nolet Distillery is cast on to a huge ceramic maceration pot.

in Miami, in 2007, it almost felt a bit late though, like that the family had (uncharacteristically) missed the boat on this occasion. But when you consider that these gins were seven years in the making, it appears to be more a case of making damn sure they were right, rather than any failure to pre-empt the renaissance.

The base for 'Silver' is a selection of classic London Dry botanicals, none of which are disclosed. These are each macerated individually in 50% ABV neutral wheat spirit at 50°C (122°F) for 24 hours. The spirit is allowed to cool during the maceration, eventually dropping down to room temperature. The botanical is then distilled in the 300-litre (79-US gallon) pot still. which has quite a long rectifying column attached to it, so the distillate comes off at over 90% ABV. The distillates are then mixed together according to the recipe and extracts of raspberry, rose and peach are added. It's then cut to bottling strength with water. The process for the 'Reserve' is even more shrouded in mystery, where almost any question you ask is met with a knowing smile and words to the effect of 'no comment'. Saffron and verbena are definitely involved and judging by the soft amber hue of the liquid I'd wager that they are macerated post-distillation. Judging by the aroma I'd say that rose, peach and raspberry are still present and correct. Besides that, I can't tell you much at all because they won't tell me!

KETEL 1 GENEVER ORIGINALE (35% ABV)

Musk, soft cereal, bread and hazelnut paste. Sweet and silky on the palate. Sponge cake, softly sweet. Vanilla. Pink peppercorn through to the finish.

KETEL 1 MATUUR (38.4% ABV)

Cacao butter and cacao nibs at first, then a suggestion of sweetness: spongey banana candy. Vanilla, ginger and clove. Water reveals waxy notes. Textured and slightly sweet. White chocolate. Gentle heat in to the finish.

NOLET'S DRY GIN 'SILVER' (47.6% ABV)

The aroma is like chalky sherbet 'Refresher' tablets. There are a lot of fruit elements that reside within that: raspberry, blackcurrant, red grape, orange and green apple. After a while, an incense-like smell wafts in, cedar and rose. The rose is more prevalent on the palate, but spice keeps it in check. The length is striking, slipping effortlessly in to sweet red berries, peach nectar, cinnamon and more of that smouldering sherbet. It's a gin like no other. Pop it in the freezer and drink it neat.

NOLET'S RESERVE (52.5% ABV)

Big, savoury, saffron at first, pungent, dry. The alcohol is expertly masked. Each return sniff slowly strips the saffron away however, revealing more elements present in the silver: rose, cardamom and sherbet. The palate is slick and oily, musky, intense and incensed. Second sip brings more rose, raspberry and green tea. Water reveals juniper. By the third sip it has transformed into a London Dry. Witchcraft! At £600 ($895) a bottle I suggest this one gets sipped… carefully.

ZUIDAM

There's an industrial estate on the outskirts of the southern Dutch village of Baarle-Nassau that looks just like any other industrial estate. But inside one of the shoebox-shaped buildings, a craft spirits revolution is taking place. Not the explosive kind of revolution, that waves its arms about like a lunatic, but the slower kind, the sort that takes careful arrangement and decades of quiet resolve. Nonetheless, the slow movements are often the most purposeful and in Zuidam we discover a mighty spirit in every sense.

Fred van Zuidam founded his distillery in 1976 having already forged himself a nice career as the master distiller at De Kuyper. Confident that he could do things… differently, Fred purchased a 300-sq. metre (3,250-sq. ft.) unit and installed a copper still. His wife, Helene, and two children, Patrick and newly born Gilbert, lived next door in what would soon become the barrel house. The business started by making boutique liqueurs, but after a while branched in to genever production. The boys grew up in the distillery – literally. The barrel house became their playground and the ricks their hiding place on the occasions that they swiped handfuls of fresh fruit intended for liqueur making.

Now the boys have grown up (mostly). Fred has retired and Patrick is the master distiller. Gilbert deals with sales, and Helene still has a hand in designing the packaging for all the products. The distillery has grown up too. It now covers 3,600 sq. metres (38,750 sq. ft) and features mash tuns, fermenters, maceration vats, six stills (two of which are a whopping 5,000 litres (1,320 US gallons) each), a bottling line, and over 5,000 casks of maturing spirit. On top of liqueurs and genever, the distillery now makes vodka, rum, whisky and, of course, gin. The operation is so big now that the family is building a brand new distillery.

As we walk around the distillery, Gilbert van Zuidam emits a relentless stream of passion and pride. Switching between misty-eyed nostalgia, bullet point facts and explosive humour, his excitement over the sound of mashing (Zuidam use equal parts of rye, corn and malted barley for their moutwijn) is infectious. He catches a glass of moutwijn directly from the spirit condenser, swills it around his mouth, then spits it on to the floor. 'Unbelievable!', he proudly declares, slapping me on the back (again).

Moutwijn undergoes a long, six-day fermentation here, using a brewer's strain of yeast. Once it has been distilled three times, it's mixed with neutral spirit, juniper distillate, liquorice/licorice and aniseed distillate, grain spirit and water to make either jonge or oude genever. Oude genever is available in standard 1-, 3- and 5-year-old expressions, along with limited single cask and extra old releases. Zuidam also make a range of Korenwijn genever and a 100% rye genever, 'Rogge', which comprises 50% malted rye and 50% unmalted rye. There's no age statement from Zuidam on the Rogge, but the liquid probably spends between 1–3 years in a cask. It's the only 100% rye genever on the market and at

BELOW LEFT Besides genever, there are also stocks of whisky and rum in the Zuidam warehouse.

BELOW The still house at Zuidam is a hive of activity and home to six copper pot stills.

€22 (US$24) for a litre, it's a bargain. These products are matured, as standard, in new or used American oak barrels, but Sherry casks are beginning to feature more on the warehouse racks, so expect to see things like Madeira-finished genever in the future. Yum.

The distillery launched Zuidam Gin in 2004, but have since changed the name to Dutch Courage. More recently, in 2012 and 2013, they have added an Old Tom and barrel-aged gin. The standard 'Dry Gin' expression is exactly what it says on the label. Each botanical (juniper, coriander seeds, orris root, orange peel, lemon peel, vanilla pod/bean, liquorice/licorice and cardamom) is distilled separately then combined together afterwards to the correct formula. According to the Zuidam brothers, this method (like Gin Mare on pages 160–161) guarantees that they are missing nothing at all in each botanical, 'capturing the ghost of the ingredients'. The 'Old Tom's' uses the same botanicals, but is briefly rested in cask, which, along with a touch of sugar, seems to bring out a clean, herbaceous, menthol quality in the liquid.

DUTCH COURAGE DRY GIN (44.5% ABV)

Punchy juniper, citrus, cool and clean on the nose. On the palate it's dry pepper, intense citrus and just enough forward, which continues through to the finish. As things dry out more the liquid becomes mineral, steely, metallic, copper… almost saline. Batten down the hatches and brace yourself for the driest Martini of your life. No garnish required.

DUTCH COURAGE OLD TOM'S GIN (40% ABV)

Herbal, warm, fennel, green cardamom at first – very much Chartreuse-y. Medicinal notes follow through, accompanied by vanilla, and a bright grassy, almost minty edge. Taste is slightly sweet, which carries the aroma through nicely to the palate. Soft and green. A very different take on an Old Tom. Sip it on ice.

AGED GIN 88 (44% ABV)

Light florals at first; creamy. Then some pleasant soft tropical notes: papaya, vanilla, lemon curd. More spice on the palate, melding with the fruit nicely. Wood through the finish, with a nicely oxidized, herbal edge. Makes for an interesting Martinez (steady on the vermouth) and an equally tasty Negroni

ROGGE GENEVER (35% ABV)

Pâtisserie on the nose, with dry cacao, sweet glaze, white chocolate and the faint hint of raisins. More peppered notes on repeat visits. Rye holds the spice on the palate even despite the lower ABV. Mossy, herbal flavours develop through the finish.

SINGLE BARREL KORENWIJN 5 YEAR OLD (38% ABV)

Vanilla butter on toasted fruit loaf. Malty, cereal notes, with the sweet banana and vanilla. Dry at first, soft, clean fruit on the palate. The liquid drifts in to coconut and fruit fudge territory, before settling down to a pleasing, beer-like finish.

FOUNDERS RESERVE 25 YEAR OLD OUDE GENEVER (38% ABV)

Soft apricot, prune and date subside in to marzipan, tobacco pouch, pipe smoke and dark fruits. The taste is concentrated, long and complex. More tobacco, fig pudding, dried mango and apple. Sweetness is soft and tannins manageable, so while it's rich, it's also quaffable. Released to commemorate Fred van Zuidam's 80th birthday, it's the oldest packaged genever available… or it would be if it weren't already sold out!

BOLS

For most of us, our first encounter with Bols is something blue or something minty. Or perhaps one of the other 37 colourful flavoured liqueurs that the company makes. Liqueurs have always been a part of the company's portfolio, but it was genever that established them in the first instance.

The story begins with the Bulsius family, who arrived in Amsterdam around 1575 and changed their name to Bols. They are thought to have established the Bols brand the same year, which comfortably makes Bols the world's oldest surviving spirits company.

Things were fully up and running by 1634, when Pieter Jacobzoon Bols is registered in Amsterdam town papers as the operator of *'t Lootsje* ('The Little Shed'). The first Bols distillery was, as the name suggests, little more than a shed. All the distilling was done outside, rain or shine, and water from the nearby stream was used to condense the spirit. It's not known exactly when genever production at Bols began, but Bols' earliest record is from an accounts ledger that details the purchase of juniper berries in 1664. Shortly after that Lucas Bols, the third generation of the family, began working at the distillery and it would be under his watch that the company would go global.

It was the dawn of the Dutch Golden Age, where the VOC (Dutch East Indies Company) would transform the nation in to an international super power. One of the VOC's many functions was the trade and transport of exotic spices, many of which could be used in genever and liqueur production. Lucas Bols must have recognised the importance of such a thing to his business; he became a major shareholder and through that gained the attention of the VOC's 17-man council, who appointed him the VOC's exclusive supplier of 'fine waters'. This granted him unparalleled access to fruits and spices, which allowed Bols to grow his range far beyond that of his competitors. It's arguably this period, where items like cinnamon, nutmeg and cardamom became more common, that has shaped the flavour of genever and gin through the centuries. By 1700 Bols were producing over 200 different liqueur recipes and distributing them across a network of Dutch colonies.

Lucas Bols' death, in 1719, signified the beginning of a century of slow decline for the Bols organisation. The company was sold in 1819 to Gabriël Van 't Wout, head of a family of accountants and financiers based in Rotterdam. The Van 't Wouts saved Bols, got the books in order, and even wrote their own book, *Distillers and Liqueur makers Handbook by an old patron of The Little Shed*. It's this book that Bols refer to for many recipes.

The third significant family, the Molters, took over the business in 1868. During their tenure, they opened eight international distilleries and expanded export trade, especially into the lucrative American market. Bols became a publicly listed company in 1954, and ended up under the watch of premium spirits company Rémy Cointreau, in 2000. Five years later and Bols was in a much healthier financial position, but distilleries had closed and copper pot stills were transported to Filliers in Belgium (see pages 156–157) or ripped apart

FAR RIGHT Bols have liqueur bottles dating back 150 years with fanciful names, like 'Lift Your Shirt'.

RIGHT Some of the oldest materials relating to genever production are housed in Bols' archives.

and sold for scrap. Bols' master distiller and blender, the legendary Piet van Leijenhorst, still remembers that day with a tear in his eye. In 2006 a takeover took place. The new leadership has been responsible for the many and varied new releases of the past ten years, as well as the House of Bols museum in Amsterdam and the opening of a small, craft distillery in the city centre.

Bols still mix and make a vast range of products these days. Their colourful liqueur range owns a big slice of that pie, in addition to their genever range and the other genever brands that they have acquired over the years: Bokma, Claeryn, J.H. Henkes, Hoppe, Hartevelt, Wijnand Fockink – all once independent companies that are now under the Bols umbrella. Malt wine for the Bols genevers is produced in four original Bols stills after a five-day fermentation, all taking place at the Filliers distillery, in Belgium. It's mixed with neutral spirit, *habaida moutwijn* (juniper berry malt wine), a herbal malt wine (flavoured with coriander and caraway among others) and water. This forms the basis of Bols' range of young, old and corenwijn genevers.

BOKMA JONGE GRAANJENEVER (35% ABV)

Light and faintly malty. Soft digestive biscuit, dry straw, vanilla and hemp. Muscular on the palate, well-assembled heat carries cereal notes while alcohol gives just enough freshness. Rich and beefy in to the finish. A great liquid to revisit light, citrus-led gin classics with.

BOLS GENEVER (42% ABV)

Pungent farmyard smells (in a good way): horse sweat, silage, warm hay, saddle leather. Grain mash. Dried plums and apricots lurk under the surface. On the palate it's sweet and drying. Stone fruits are back, this time stewed with a gentle fennel and menthol shimmer. Texture is big and oily. This is one of the best un-aged genevers out there. It works fantastically well in a Gin Fizz or in an inverted Martini.

WIJNAND FOCKINK ROGGE JENEVER (38% ABV)

Spiced apple strudel served on freshly cut oak… with toffee sauce. Some scorched red fruits and plenty of pepper complete the nose. Drier than expected on the palate, with no shortage of prickly pepper to carry the flavour through. Drink 50 ml/2 fl. oz. from the bottle, then top it back up with sugar syrup and store in the freezer - Genever Sling!

ABOVE Bols' range of aged genevers are bottled in traditional stone crocks, while unnamed products tend to go into glass bottles.

BOLS BARREL-AGED GENEVER (42% ABV)

Soft mints and grape juice top the smells list on this light and breezy genever. There are rooty, oak notes lurking behind that, but the maturation has cleaned the spirit up if anything. Oak is more persistent on the palate, where gentle red fruits and tannins bolster the breadth of the liquid. Over time the oak tightens up further, gripping tightly to the palate.

BOKMA OUDE FRIESCHE GENEVER (38% ABV)

Cereals meet millstone in this warm yet mineral genever. Brown bread and nutty mash smells give an altogether wholesome quality to the aroma. Herbaceous and fruity on the palate, a touch of piña colada about it even? Warm spice fills the finish.

BOKMA DE VIJF JAREN 5 YEAR OLD (38% ABV)

Juicy and deep. Mirror polished oak, fresh blackberry, mulberry wine and crème brûlée. Bourbon-esque on the palate, but forest fruits are not lost easily. Gentle and finessed, the fruits dry and eventually become jammy in that rancio Cognac finish.

BOLS CORENWYN 6 YEAR OLD (40% ABV)

Peachy and fragrant initially, there's a pastel-y, floral, elegance to the nose. The palate is beautifully designed, balanced and full, sweet and hot. It drifts from bright tropicals: mango, melon; then on to crème caramel and malty ferment flavours. The finish is long and damn tasty.

STOKERIJ VAN DAMME

In 1843, there were 455 farm distilleries in Belgium. For a farmer, distilling booze was a sensible means of converting excess cereals from the summer in to an essential cash reward in the winter. Rivers and springs churned out icy water in the winter, too, which made the distillery condensers more efficient, and a hot copper still provided a very welcome heat source as the weather turned frosty. Spent cereals were used to feed the farm's livestock, which in turn provided the necessary fertilizer to farm the land and grow more cereals for the following year. But the powerhouse jenever distillers that emerged in the late 19th century forced the farms out of business. By 1913 there were only 24 left and today there are no remaining farm distilleries in Belgium or The Netherlands. Except one.

Stokerij Van Damme sits on the outskirts of the Belgian town of Aast, around a 45-minute drive west of Brussels. The farm and distillery were founded in 1862 by the distant ancestors of Ludo Lampaert and have remained in the Lampaert family ever since. Since 2010, Van Damme has been recognized by the Belgian government as a site of national heritage, but from the outside it appears to be nothing more than a medium-sized, quite pretty farm. There's a coffee room and a modest guest house, too.

One of the barns houses the distillery, however – a distillery like no other in the world. Entering Van Damme's still house is like stepping through a wormhole that takes you all the way back to the mid-

19th century. All of the equipment save the column still is original, dating back over 150 years. The original column was only retired recently, however, and can be seen leaning up against the barn wall in a crumpled, undignified state. The entire distillery is run on a wood- and coke-burning furnace that heats a grease- and oil-caked steam engine. The engine is rigged up to a series of huge overhead pulleys than turn the mash tun, fermentation vat, and even power the pumps which route the liquid from one stage to the next. Only the lights and the bottling line run on electricity. In accordance with tradition all of the distilling is done between the months of November and April, where a typical day for Ludo and Dominique Lampaert sees them up at 5am to feed Van Damme's 200 cows, cooking breakfast for guests at 7am, making up and cleaning the rooms of the guest house through the remainder of the morning, then into the still house to mash, brew and distil jenever all afternoon.

The jenever is made from a combination of rye and malted barley. The farm grows all the rye it needs, but the barley is bought in as they don't have facilities to malt their own. There are three different genever recipes made here, each with a slightly different mash recipe

THIS PAGE There are a few farm distilleries featured in this book, but none go so far as Stokerij Van Damme, where even the cows have a role to play in the jenever-making process.

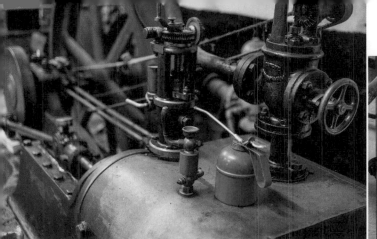

ABOVE A steam-powered solid fuel-burning steam engine provides all the power this distiller needs.

RIGHT Most of the distillation equipment on the farm belongs in a museum.

and each bottled at a different alcohol strength: 30%, 41% and 54%. After distillation it is rested in huge oak vats, of between 4,000 litres (1,055 US gallons) and 10,000 litres (2,640 US gallons). This wood is original too, and long past its 'use by date', so very little flavour is imparted in to the product. It's at this stage that a tiny amount of juniper essence is added, but this is for conformity with jenever regulations rather than to adjust the flavour. This feels like a category that wants to become a whisky, but remains inextricably tethered to its 'jenever' name and therefore the juniper berry.

Stokerij Van Damme produce a healthy 50,000 bottles of jenever a year, including their flavoured lemon and cherry jenevers. With additional income from the farm and the guest house, plus subsidies from the Belgian government, the future looks good for them. The Lampaerts have three daughters who help with work on the farm, but there are no plans in place as to who will manage the distillery once Ludo and Dominique retire. For a budding young Belgian distiller that surely makes the Lampaert sisters three of the most eligible women in all of Belgium!

BELGEMSCHE (31% ABV)

The nose is a combination of warm, farm aromas, like hay, silage, and rye bread, coupled with intense strawberry fruit esters and acetone. The palate is delicate, broad and lightly spiced, finishing with more of that airfix-glue acetone, which lingers.

BELGEMSCHE (41% ABV)

The fruit is beginning to dominate, but in a perverse kind of manner. It's beyond fruit. Whacky solvent aromas pervade, with faint elements of banana and red fruit coming through, too. In the mouth it's surprisingly well structured, grippy and hot. But it's difficult to ignore the rawness of the product.

BELGEMSCHE (54% ABV)

The most refined of the three. More neutral on the nose, with white pepper, soft vanilla, blackcurrant and prune. The palate is surprisingly soft considering the strength, spicy, but not astringent.

USA

After the Philippines, the US is the world's biggest gin market, attracting sales of over 120 million bottles in 2014. About one-third of that is imported stuff (mostly from the UK) which a sizeable chunk of the pie for domestic brands. Seagram's is the USA's top selling native brand, which actually has its origins in Ontario, Canada. Then there's Gordon's, which, if you're buying it in the US, is actually bottled in Connecticut and distilled in Canada. The truth is that proper American gin brands (the born and raised variety) have had a rough ride over the past 100 years, which has seen a well-established industry crumble under the weight of the temperance movement and pretty much die a death altogether. Thankfully things have changed, and what a change it has been.

And why not? After all, this was a nation founded from the colonies of the Dutch, Spanish and British – all known associates of the juniper juice. Genever was among the first spirits to be produced in North America and by the 19th century the nation was importing more genever than any other country in the world. When tastes got drier, gin got drier, too, and Americans adopted the ice-white highly tuned new style as the golden child of the cocktail hour.

Then Prohibition happened. Illegally imported gin arrived by the boat and truck-load offering a superior product to moonshine. When Prohibition ended it was the bootlegged brands that people were faithful to, which also happened to be the ones best placed to set up shop on US soil. The market that Seagram's and Gordon's leveraged in the 1930s was only available to them thanks to Prohibition. These distilleries and a handful of others became the dirty secrets of the American gin market; nobody wanted to face up to the fact that America was making gin, because it wasn't American gin that they were making

There's no shortage of American gin being produced nowadays – oh no. The number of craft distilleries in the USA will have topped 1,000 by the time this book goes to print, which would have been an inconceivable number had it been suggested 10 years ago.

Aside from the spread of products, there has been a coming of age to gin styles here, too. The rise of the New Western Dry style offers an alternative to juniper for new gin distillers, but has also altered the playing field for producers all over the world, stating clearly that 'It's ok not to be juniper forward.' By some measures (including the legally defined ones) some of these gins are not gin at all. New definitions are needed – there is no doubt – but one thing I am quite sure of is that the US needs its own style. Only 12% of all the gin in the US goes in to Gin & Tonics (in the UK it's 74%) whereas 44% of it gets consumed neat or in cocktails. And since there are no products that offer a truly one-size-fits-all solution, these different applications demand a different style of liquid.

THIS PAGE AND OPPOSITE America has a longstanding relationship with the juniper berry. Modern American gins tend to either leverage that history (like New York Distilling Company), or take a more contemporary route.

ANCHOR

To the American gin market, Junípero really was the second coming – in much the same way that Miller's or Blackwoods were in the UK. And just like those products, Junípero has become a bit of a martyr to its cause, allowing other brands to carry the message of gin and continue the important work that began in the late 1990s, while it watches (confused) from the sidelines.

Junípero is made by Anchor Distilling, who are the spirits arm of the Anchor Brewing Company, based in Potrero Hill, California. The brewery, which traces its roots back to the 1890s, is probably best known for its 'Steam beer' brand. The early years were unkind to Anchor, with the sudden death of two owners in 1906 and 1907, a fire in 1933 and numerous location changes and upheavals. Then, in the 1950s, Anchor's full-flavoured style of beer suffered badly. The brewery was finally saved from closure when it was bought by Frederick Louis Maytag III in 1965. It moved again in 1979 to its current location, and the distillery was set up in 1993. Anchor Distilling's first product was a rye whiskey, called Old Potrero, which was followed by the launch of Junípero, in 1997, which takes its name from Saint Junípero Serra, a Franciscan friar and an important figure in the history of San Francisco and California.

Junípero is almost boastful in its uncompromising juniper-forward character. There are over a dozen undisclosed botanicals used to supplement the juniper, but it's clear who the winner of this contest is.

JUNÍPERO GIN (49.3% ABV)

Various facets of juniper are at play here, from floral lavender to Christmas tree warmth and even a touch of leather shoes. It's not all about the juniper though; a crumbly ginger note is lurking around too, and warm mossy notes similar to sage or rosemary. Citrus is restrained on the nose, but cleans the palate up well as alcohol assaults the tongue. Long and spicy into the finish as juniper reverb bounces back and forward. It's too much for a Martini - stick to a G&T.

RIGHT It looks more like a bottle of wine or *eau de vie* than a premium gin, but there can be little doubt that it smells and tastes like gin.

AVIATION

Those of you who know your Margaritas from your Marguerites may already be aware that this gin shares its name with a classic gin cocktail. Pale violet in colour, and bracingly citric to drink, the Aviation has the ability to slap your senses in to order. The first recipe for the Aviation was penned in 1916 just as the temperance movement was hotting up and called for dry gin, lemon juice and crème de violette (violet liqueur). But with scant time to develop a significant following before Prohibition put the brakes on in 1920, the Aviation became a bit of a forgotten classic and crème de violette all but vanished from liquor store shelves. David A. Embury lists an Aviation in his cocktail book, *The Fine Art of Mixing Drinks* (1948), but by that time the drink was using maraschino (cherry liqueur) instead, and needless to say, it was quite a different encounter. Such was the way, right up until 2007, when finally, after a long vacation, crème de violette returned and we could all go about making Aviations once again.

It could just have been coincidence that the year before crème de violette made its comeback, Aviation Gin was launched in America. Originally the brainchild of bartender Ryan Magarian, Aviation gin came about thanks to a partnership between Ryan and Portland's House Spirits Distillery – the first of its kind between bartender and distillery… so the story goes. Ryan was on the hunt for a new, more mixable, style of gin that could be used in classic cocktails other than the Martini. No such gin existed, so they developed Aviation gin and named it after one of Ryan's favoured classic cocktails.

The botanicals for Aviation gin (in no particular order: juniper, coriander seed, anise seed, green cardamom, lavender flower, sarsaparilla and sweet orange peel) are steeped together in neutral grain spirit, then the solids are removed prior to distillation in a 1,500-litre (400-US gallon) stainless steel pot.

Everything is bottled in-house, and what a delightful bottle it is! As Art-Deco as they come, it's probably my favourite thing about the product.

From day one, the team have been quite unblushing when it comes to talking about the role of juniper (or lack thereof) in their gin. 'Botanical Democracy' is how Ryan phrases it, where juniper no longer gets to be the dictator of style. These days it seems a moot point, but in 2006, Aviation Gin caused quite the controversy. I remember tasting it for the first time and with great disdain remarking 'it's not gin'. In the context of gin in 2016, where some gins have barely touched a juniper berry, it's positively classic. In some circles, juniper is quickly receding from view; in others, it's already left. Modern gins are falling in to new flavour camps of floral, spicy, herbal and even fruity. The once extraneous flavours of the category's traditional style are now a genre of gin unto themselves. New Western Style gin (a term originally coined by Ryan Magarian) is a thing that we cannot choose to ignore, but for me that isn't just a case of giving contemporary gins the respect that they deserve; it's also about preserving what little integrity 'London Dry' has left. Hell – it might be too late already.

AVIATION AMERICAN GIN (42% ABV)

Heavy-set and round on the nose, with a generic herbal note that seems to swallow everything else around it. After a few attempts, you'll find the lavender, which is in the form of powdered cosmetics, bolstered by that medicinal sarsaparilla hue. On the palate it feels a bit flabby - unfocused and indistinct. As the purple haze dissipates, you're left with a pleasant spice and brief fluttering of juniper. Well suited to a Ramos Gin Fizz, where the florals lift the creaminess of the drink's body.

ABOVE Aviation is perhaps better known for progressing the American gin category than for the gin itself.

DEATH'S DOOR

Washington Island, Wisconsin, and the neighbouring islands are separated from mainland Door County by a seven-mile stretch of water known as Death's Door Passage. The name dates back to the time when a war party of 300 Indians tried to cross in canoes on a stormy night. They all lost their lives and thus began the legend that the waters were infested with an evil spirit. Death's Door Distillery was established in 2005, and takes its name from the Passage. That year, Brian Ellison was running a sustainable agricultural project for the island with farming brothers Tom and Ken Koyen. In 2005, they planted 2 hectares (5 acres) of a specific strain of hard winter wheat, testing the water to see if there was a space for a new farming industry.

Their intention was for the wheat to be turned into bread flour, but it attracted the attention of the Washington Island's Capital Brewery who, in partnership with Ellison, used the cereal to make a wheat beer. Ellison decided that beer was only half the journey to a finished project, so began taking distilling courses at Michigan State University. That's where he met the future Head Distiller at Death's Door, John Jeffery, who was studying food science, specializing in fermentation and distillation, and consulted with Death's Door while writing his thesis.

Ten years on, and at least 485 hectares (1,200 acres) of wheat is growing on Washington Island. Death's Door also have a new, upgraded distillery. And they're not messing about. A 9-m (30-ft) column takes care of the neutral spirit production (which is made from organic certified 'hard red' Washington Island winter wheat), and a 2,000-litre (530-US gallon) pot still makes all the gin. This distillery is capable of outputting 250,000 cases of spirit a year, and the products are carefully put together and beautiful to look at.

It's quite exceptional for a gin to faithfully reflect its immediate environment with locally sourced botanicals. But that's exactly what Death's Door Distillery does with its three botanicals: juniper, coriander and fennel. The juniper is sourced from Washington Island, and the fennel and coriander come from mainland Wisconsin – predictably they're working towards growing that on the island, too.

DEATH'S DOOR (47% ABV)

Cool, green, juniper on the nose, like mint and pine. Botanicals play out in quick succession on the palate. Juniper cracks a whip, soft and green, then big spiced coriander explodes. The finish is green, fresh and anise as the fennel seed takes hold. Try a 2:1:1 Negroni (in favour of the gin) and marvel as the Campari and vermouth attempt to overcome it!

LEFT Few distilleries can match Death's Door for commitment to provenance in their immediate area.

FEW

The FEW distillery is on 918 Chicago Avenue, in Evanston, Illinois. Evanston is town synonymous with the temperance movement. A state of quasi-prohibition was in effect here from the 1850s onwards. Northwestern University, which was set up in 1855, took it upon themselves to protect the moral, Christian sensibilities of their students, and amended the university charter on February 14th to provide that:

'No spiritous, vinous, or fermented liquors shall be sold under license, or otherwise, within four miles of the location of said University [...] except for medicinal, mechanical, or sacramental purposes, under a penalty of twenty-five dollars for each offense.'

When the 18th amendment that enforced nationwide Prohibition in 1920 was passed, it was barely noticed in Evanston. When Prohibition was repealed in 1933, Evanston voted in 1934 to maintain the four-mile alcohol-free zone until 1972, when liquor was finally permitted to be sold by the glass.

The Women's Christian Temperance Union has its roots in Evanston, basing their headquarters here from 1910 onwards. It's been suggested that one of their founders, the suffragist Frances Elizabeth Willard, might have loaned her initials to the FEW Spirits Co., but owner, Paul Hletko, claims it's just coincidence. I suspect there might be a degree of backtracking going on here though. The WCTU is now every bit the global operation and with their headquarters still in Evanston, I don't imagine they would like the idea of the initials of one of their founding heroines being paraded across the front of liquor bottles.

The real reason that Paul decided to call the distillery FEW, was simply because there was so little of it – very little alcohol in Evanston historically, but also very little of his product, because FEW is a small distillery. Before setting up FEW Paul had been a keen home brewer for most of his life. His Czech family had a history in owning and operating breweries in former Czechoslovakia. His working background was as a patent lawyer, which must have come in handy when he was attempting to get a distilling licence in one of America's driest towns. It took 15 separate hearings before the law was changed and the licence was finally granted, in 2011.

FEW have a grain to glass approach to whiskey and gin making. Corn, wheat and barley are mashed and fermented on site, before being converted into spirit. The kit list comprises a rectifying column attached to a 350-litre (92-US gallon) pot, a configuration that is typical of American whiskey, plus a 150-litre (40-US gallon) pot still used to make the gin. Neither still is capable of making pure, 96% ABV, neutral spirit. So the gins here use a base of 'white whiskey', which really comes through in the finished product.

Gin comes in three forms. American Gin, which used Tahitian vanilla and Paul's home-grown hops among other conventional botanicals. Standard Issue is the Navy Strength version of the above. Then there's the Barrel Gin, which has a juniper-heavy gin base and is aged for four months in 22-litre (6-US gallon) new American oak casks.

FEW AMERICAN GIN (40% ABV)

This gin smells more like an unaged whisky at first, with cereal notes developing in to soft apples, marzipan, citrus zest and fermentation aromas. There's a subtle, sweet, juniper note underlying it, however. The palate is bizarre. Starting with peppery cereal notes, it develops into a savoury nutmeg and saffron character, before dipping in to more traditional gin territory. Good in a Martinez, or in a Holland's Punch.

FEW BARREL GIN (46.5% ABV)

Sweet and chilly dessert-like qualities emanate from this glass. There's lacquered cedar and alpine sawdust, followed up by grated nutmeg, mace and cloves. Big nutmeg hit in the taste too; it's gently spiced and softly sweet, developing into vanilla, with pine-y juniper notes filling the finish. It's a benchmark aged gin. Drink it neat, or with a splash of soda.

LEOPOLD'S

Todd and Scott Leopold originally set up a craft brewery in Ann Arbor, Michigan, back in 2009. A couple of years later they added a micro-distillery to the operation. Todd brought the brewing and distilling expertise to the table, having earned his Diploma in Malting and Brewing in 1996 and then interning at a number of German breweries in the years that followed. He later attended a distilling school in Kentucky (yes, such a thing exists). Scott Leopold brought the sustainability factor, he was formerly an environmental engineer, so scrutinized every element of the distillery's design to ensure it was as carbon neutral as possible. The brewery and distillery became quite well known for their 'eco' approach to things, which included the uses of organic cereals and effective management of waste water by-products.

The distillery has since re-located to Denver, Colorado, the original operation having closed down and the brewing side of things put to bed for good. Today, Leopold Bros is a sizeable mass of buildings spread across a 1.5 hectare (4 acre) campus. There's a still-house with seven stills including a column that's used to make neutral spirit, a 2,000 capacity barrel store and most impressive of all – the largest floor malting of any North American distillery.

Of course this is all a bit much for a few bottles of gin – the brothers only produce 50 cases of gin a year! It turns out that they make over 20 products here, though. Diversity, innovation, sustainability and environmental awareness. What's not to love?

RIGHT It's unusual to see a bottle of Leopold's outside the US, so try it if you get the chance.

FAR RIGHT The new Leopold's Distillery has big production capacity for a craft operation. It's just a shame that they don't make more gin!

Two types of gin are made here, 'American Small Batch' and 'Navy Strength American'. For each expression the botanicals are macerated and distilled in isolation of one another. This is becoming a more and more common approach to gin making, Todd explains the logic behind it, 'when boiled together, certain botanicals are overworked, resulting in the extraction of tannin-like flavours which dry out the gin, while other flavours are not fully realised.' For the standard 'American Small Batch', Todd uses juniper, coriander seed, pummelo, orris root and Valencia oranges, plus another four undeclared ingredients. It's the ones that are declared which seem to shine through. The 'Navy Strength American' is rarer than hen's teeth, and uses a souped-up formula containing more juniper and coriander seed, but also including cardamom and bergamot peel among the botanical mix.

SMALL BATCH AMERICAN GIN (40% ABV)

Soft on the nose with a slightly confected, bready note. This gives way to forest floor, cardamom, green pine needles and some woodsy herbal elements. On the palate it's clean and green, with good citrus presence and a mild pepper finish. I liked this gin in a Fizz – the citrus softens some of the more savoury elements nicely.

NEW YORK DISTILLING CO.

My first encounter with the NY Distilling Co was during a holiday with my wife in 2012. We had arranged to meet good friend and gin guru, Angus Winchester, at a Brooklyn bar called The Shanty. A cab dropped us off in a dismal-looking alley, and we hurried toward a glowing warehouse door. Once inside, the contours of small bar came into focus, busy with the sounds of cocktail making. Then, to the right, we saw two huge windows that – to our surprise – looked out over a huge distillery.

The NY Distilling Company started with Tom Potter, co-founder of Brooklyn Brewery and one of the patriarchs of the East Coast craft brewing fraternity. Potter sold most of his shares in Brooklyn Brewery in the mid 2000s, planning a gentle retirement process. But the craft distilling scene was gathering pace and after visiting a handful of distilleries on the west coast he hatched a scheme to open his own in New York. Potter and his son Bill teamed up with Allen Katz, a renowned spirits educator, who would go on to become master distiller and frontman of the NY Distilling Co.

The distillery makes two gins as well as a rye-based, genever-style spirit modelled on an 1809 recipe for 'Holland Gin'. It was developed in partnership with spirits historian David Wondrich who discovered the recipe in Samuel McHarry's *The Practical Distiller*. First of the gins is Dorothy Parker, named after the New Yorker whose wit made her one of the roaring 20s' best-loved celebrities. One of her most enduring remarks relates to the Martini cocktail and explains why the name of Dorothy Parker is well placed on the front of a bottle of gin: 'I like to have a martini, two at the very most. After three I'm under the table, after four I'm under the host'.

Dorothy Parker is one of the only gins I can think of that excludes both coriander and angelica – two of juniper's most favoured playmates. It's pleasing to see that you can make a delicious gin without them, though: juniper, elderberry, dried hibiscus flower, lemon peel, grapefruit peel and cinnamon are the union of flavours that make this gin tick.

Perry's Tot was, when it was launched, the first American Navy Strength gin. It remains a good'un, and is named after Commodore Matthew C. Perry, who was commandant of the New York Navy Yard in Brooklyn. Botanicals are a more classic mix of juniper, orange peel, lemon peel, grapefruit peel, coriander seed, angelica root, cinnamon, anise, cardamom and wild flower honey from upstate NY. It's one of the best overproof gins out there.

Chief Gowanus is representative of the kind of spirit that was drunk in Brooklyn in the early 19th century. It's made from a rye whiskey base (similar to a malt wine), which is then re-distilled with 'a couple of shovel-fulls of juniper and a handful of hops.' It's named after the chief of the Canarsie Native Americans, who sold the area that would later become Brooklyn to the Dutch.

DOROTHY PARKER [44% ABV]

Zingy juniper jumps up at you first on the nose of this sprightly gin. There's an herbaceous element to it, too, plus a (curiously alluring) rubber/latex quality. Great juniper presence in the mouth, the alcohol carries it for some time. There's perhaps a touch of cinnamon; a lick of grapefruit; a dot (excuse the pun) of hibiscus. This gin loves being mixed.

PERRY'S TOT [57% ABV]

Surprisingly relaxed on the nose, which makes it all the more worrying. Snuffed candle, bread crust and plenty of earthy spices: dandelion root and angelica. Medicinal. The taste is bold and well structured. It builds first with peppered juniper, then as it drops: cassia, nutmeg, grapefruit peel, jasmine-like florals and coriander seed. Lovely in a Martini. Just as at home in a Gimlet.

CHIEF GOWANUS [44% ABV]

Pungent and malty, this old genever-style liquid positively stinks of malt loaf, pumpernickel, pipe tobacco, leather and hops… with just a tickle of juniper cruising through the middle of it all. In the mouth it's thick and lively. Cask character creeps in, providing just a touch of caramel, menthol tobacco and pomegranate molasses. Try it in a punch, or, if you can't be bothered, just drink it straight.

ST. GEORGE SPIRITS

St. George Spirits are based on the former Alameda Naval base, on Alameda island, in San Francisco Bay. The distillery was set up in 1982, which makes it the oldest of the new-wave 'craft' distilleries in this book. Lance Winters, a long-time employee of the distillery, took over the reigns in 2010 and the company launched three gins in 2013.

The first thing you notice about the gin is that the labels look like dollar bills, which is a clever bit of subliminal marketing. Two of the three gin expressions are quite contemporary in their style ('Terroir' and 'Botanivore'); the third ('Dry Rye') is more a recreation of what 17th century genever might have tasted like. All St. George gins are distilled in a 1,500-litre (395-US gallon) pot still, often using a combination of distillates and, in some cases, vapour infusion.

St. George's 'Ode to the Golden State' is 'Terroir'. This product sees Douglas fir, bay laurel and sage, brought together to mirror the smells and tastes of the forest and patches of vegetation near the distillery. There are nine further botanicals including 'wok-toasted coriander seeds', which apparently capture the aroma of the surrounding area. Two distillations are performed for this gin: one for the Douglas fir and sage, then a separate one for the rest of the botanicals where the bay leaf and juniper are vapour-infused.

'Botanivore' by name, and digester of nature by nature. The gin uses 19 botanicals, the most notable of which are fresh coriander/cilantro, hops, dill seed, fennel seed, caraway seed, ginger and bay leaf. This one is made in a single distillation, which, like 'Terroir' sees the juniper and bay leaf, plus the coriander leaves/cilantro, added to a botanical basket for extraction by spirit vapour.

'Dry Rye Gin' is made from 100% pot-distilled rye, (effectively an un-aged rye whiskey, or 'white dog') re-distilled with six botanicals, with the emphasis on the juniper berry. It's full-on, and I don't think I can put it more eloquently than St. George do, 'this is a gin for whiskey lovers – and for gin impurists who don't mind malty, warm rye gettin' all up in juniper's grill.'

I've heard it said that St. George's 'Terroir' really sets the standard for the current generation of New Western style gins. While it's always my aim to keep tasting notes as objective as possible, I'll go out on a limb on this occasion and say that the St. George range of gins are among the best – American or otherwise.

ST. GEORGE 'TERROIR' (45% ABV)

The nose has a lively incense note from the sage that persists; spiced, but equally fruity and sweetly floral. After a while it turns greener, like Irish moss. There's a subtle fermented tropical note there, too. The palate is dry and spicy at first, drifting into a chalky, maritime note, with some salinity seemingly apparent. It drifts in to more soft fruit, but the real backbone is the herbaceous notes and florals. An impressively complex distillate. Drink it neat, or try stirring it down over ice with a drop of your favourite honey. Too potent for a G&T.

ST. GEORGE 'BOTANIVORE' (45% ABV)

Damp grass and misty mornings. Warm hay, a slight waft of fennel, dried spice, and definitely a touch of hops. The palate is more fruity, with the heat of the alcohol playing nicely with that bright herbaceous quality. There's black pepper, cinnamon, citrus, and a fleeting appearance from those hops again. Good for an ice cold 50/50 G&T. Garnish with grapefruit peel and drink it quick.

ST. GEORGE 'DRY RYE' (45% ABV)

Well here's something different. Big pear drops lead the charge, seasoned with hot spices – caraway and fennel seeds. There's a nutty, malty quality there, too, but the fruit is huge, although still clean and fresh. The botanicals push through on the palate, which is unctuous and juicy. A gentle nudge from juniper is flooded by soft spicy notes that couple with the bigger ones coming from the rye itself – completing the spectrum of flavour nicely. This is fantastic in a Martinez – 2 parts Dry Rye, 1 part sweet vermouth, plus a dash of your favourite bitters.

GINEBRA SAN MIGUEL

Gin is probably not the first thing you might think of on a visit to Manila, but the local juniper juice, known as 'Ginebra San Miguel', is incredibly popular there.

This product has been in production since the founding of the Spanish-owned Destileria y Licoreria de Ayala y Compañia in 1834 and was purchased by its current owners (then known as La Tondeña) in 1924. San Miguel, who are actually the biggest company in all of the Philippines, typically produce 200 million litres (52.8 million US gallons) of Ginebra a year. This makes it by far and away the biggest gin brand globally, with second place Gordon's outputting only around one-sixth of the volume. In fact, Ginebra San Miguel accounts for just under 50% of all the gin in the world and 1% of all the spirit in the world, which isn't bad going for a product that is scarcely seen outside of the Philippines.

There are a number of reasons that can be attributed to gin's success and popularity in the Philippines. Tax on spirits is low for a start, meaning that a litre of gin costs about the same as a litre of beer, thus the liquor store decision-making process is that little bit easier. Low tax also means bigger revenue for the manufacturers and a good chunk of this is thrown in the marketing and advertising budget. Gin advertising is everywhere in the Philippines, from baseball and soccer games to magazines and soap operas. Hell – San Miguel outrightly own the Barangay Gin Kings basketball team.

A typical night out on the streets of Manila usually consists of bucket loads of Ginpo, an aptly named and quite delicious mixture of gin and powdered pomelo juice, served over great mounds of crushed ice. Another version of the drink uses pineapple juice instead, but if that all sounds too civilized then there's always the Expired cocktail, which – with a nod of a minty hat to the Victorian 'Gin & Pep' – ranks up there as one of the most disgusting drinks I have ever tasted, combining gin, beer and menthol candies, and named after the fact that it tastes like off-beer. Now, before you go rushing out to buy a pack of Fox's glacier mints, remember that it's customary in the Philippines to pour the first shot of a new bottle of gin on the floor as a sign of ancestral respect. Although less common now, if the ritual was properly policed, a little maths suggests that a larger volume of gin would end up on Philippine floors every year than is manufactured by a medium-sized western distillery, like Hendrick's.

RIGHT The San Miguel Corporation's Corporate Center in Manila, in the Philippines, features many advertisements of its food and drinks products. Among them, Ginebra San Miguel is imbedded in the nation's fabric. The brand even owns its own basketball team and media network.

GIN COCKTAILS

DRY MARTINI

45 ML/1½ FL. OZ. TANQUERAY TEN
10 ML/⅓ FL. OZ. DOLIN DRY VERMOUTH

Add the ingredients to a chilled mixing beaker (kept in the freezer) and stir with lots of ice for at least 90 seconds. Strain into a chilled Martini glass or coupe.

This makes quite a small drink. It's far better, in my opinion, to keep things civilized and keep the Martinis cold. It shouldn't take more than five minutes to drink it in its entirety, which gives you plenty of time to make another round.

A perfect union of two ingredients in any context – food, drink or otherwise – is a thing worth celebrating. Where the Martini is concerned it would appear that we have achieved just that. The cultural significance of this drink is something that most people are aware of, but the true genius of its making is the preserve of a lucky few. A good Martini is potent, but subtle; complex, but clean; cool, but spicy. Most importantly, perhaps, is the beauty that can be found in its brevity. A Martini cannot (and should not) be savoured if it is to be enjoyed properly. It's an all or nothing affair. Get stuck in quickly, or lose forever that fleeting chill which softens alcohol, crisps up citrus, and consorts to thicken the texture of the drink on the palate.

The history of this drink is a confusing and often contradictory mess. Essentially, the Dry Martini is a riff on the Martini, which first made its appearance in the 1890s. The Martini was itself nearly identical to the Martinez cocktail, the name having likely been changed to indicate the Martini brand of vermouth that was being used to make the cocktail at the time. Cocktail books from the late 19th century seldom list both the Martini and Martinez, which leads many of us to conclude that they were Siamese twins of sorts – different names but put together the same way. The Martinez of 1884 was effectively a gin-based Manhattan consisting of two parts Italian vermouth to one part Old Tom gin, bitters and a splash of sugar syrup. The Martinis that landed during the 1890s were the same, most of them made with sweet vermouth and Old Tom gin.

Other drinks from around that time toyed with the idea of dry gin and French (dry) vermouth. The 'Marguerite', published in 1904 called specifically for Plymouth gin, which was mixed with equal parts French vermouth, orange curaçao and orange bitters.

Then there was the Turf Club (first appearing in the 1880s) which opted for sweet vermouth, and Harry Johnson's 'Martine' cocktail, which could have been a misspelling of either Martini or Martinez! The world had to wait until the early 1900s for a Dry Martini recognisable by today's standards; Bill Boothby's *The World's The Drinks and How to Mix them* (1908) calls for equal parts French Vermouth and 'dry English Gin', orange bitters, and to garnish with a squeeze of lemon peel and an olive. There are other references to the drink before Boothby's book, but his is the first I can find that uses French vermouth and dry gin after the modern fashion. Boothby also includes a recipe for a 'Gibson', which is the same drink but without the bitters. Interestingly, we now call a Dry Martini garnished with a silverskin onion a 'Gibson', but Boothby opted for the olive.

Even Boothby's Dry Martini wasn't all that 'dry' when compared with what was to come. The gradual nudging of ratios between gin and vermouth meant that the drink became stronger and less sweet as time went on. As the Martini reached peak dryness in the 1950s – where the slightest glance at a bottle of vermouth, or as Churchill liked to put it, 'a phone-call to France', would suffice – its cold-blooded disposition was the perfect test of a hard-nosed businessman's resolve. Three martini lunch, anyone? You bet.

As vodka took over, gin died out, and conservative tastes moved on, too. But far from being ignored, the Martini was brought back to life (kicking and screaming) in the 1980s when any drink served in a Martini glass was called an '*insert flavour here* Martini' – ironically, the only things that tended to be absent from the glass were gin and vermouth!

With cocktail culture now firmly back on track, bartenders have revisited the Martini story and paid homage to this, the holiest of all cocktails. I have spent much time mulling over the multitude of variables that make this seemingly simple drink so frustratingly difficult to get right. The truth is that there's a perfect Martini out there waiting for everyone; the difficulty is fathoming out what's right for you. It's probably for this reason that the Martini has stood the test of time. It's more of a concept than a drink in its own right, primed and ready for customization to each drinker's requirements. Ask a bartender to make you a Martini and you should have at least five questions fired back at you. Walk away if you don't.

Here are but a few of my own observations that I think are worth sharing with you. Take them as you will, as they are not gospel, but merely an insight from someone who, over the years, has imbibed and deliberated over their share of Martinis.

Don't assume that drier is better; for me the sweet spot is somewhere between 3:1 and 6:1 in favour of the gin. Use dry ice cubes (i.e. preferably straight from the freezer), otherwise the drink becomes too diluted and a bit flabby. Do dilute the drink enough; a Martini shouldn't be a chore to get through. Martinis generally need stirring for 90 seconds to reach the best possible temperature, and dilution is a part of that process. It's surprisingly difficult to over-dilute a Martini by stirring too long, so take your time. Shaking is fine if you like it that way and it's certainly a lot quicker. Don't go crazy with the garnish. I think it's debatable whether a Martini needs a garnish at all, but a very small piece of lemon peel or an olive is fine – I've been known to say that it's easier to ruin a Martini with a piece of lemon peel than it is a cocktail shaker.

Or take the superstition, for I cannot dignify it as a heresy, that the Martini must not be shaken. Nonsense. This perfect thing is made of gin and vermouth. They are self-reliant liquors, stable, of stout heart; we do not have to treat them as if they were plover's eggs. It does not matter in the least whether you shake a Martini or stir it. It does matter if splinters of ice get into the cocktail glass, and I suppose this small seed of fact is what grew into the absurdity that we must not 'bruise the gin'.

Bernard de Voto, author of *The Hour: A Cocktail Manifesto*

GIN & HOMEMADE TONIC

TONIC SYRUP
1 LITRE/34 FL. OZ. WATER
60 G/2 OZ. FINELY GROUND CINCHONA BARK
30 G/1 OZ. GRAPEFRUIT ZEST
3 G/⅛ OZ. GROUND ALLSPICE BERRIES
3 G/⅛ OZ. PINK PEPPERCORNS
15 G/½ OZ. CITRIC ACID POWDER
3 G/⅛ OZ. SALT
1 KG/4 CUPS SUGAR
100 ML/3½ FL. OZ. VODKA

Makes 2 litres/½ US gallon – enough for 40 G&Ts

Add the water, cinchona bark, grapefruit zest, ground allspice and pink peppercorns to a pressure cooker, then seal and heat to maximum pressure according to the manufacturer's instructions. After 20 minutes, allow the pressure to release, then strain the liquid through muslin/cheesecloth, removing as much sediment as possible. Allow the liquid to rest in the fridge for 6 hours, then carefully pour into a clean saucepan, leaving any insoluble matter behind. Gently heat the infusion and add the citric acid, salt and sugar. When the liquid clarifies, remove it from the heat. Finally, add the vodka, which isn't essential, but will double the lifespan of the syrup (and is good to add to any refrigerated syrups).

To make your Gin & Tonic, I recommend equal parts of gin and tonic syrup, topped up with a splash of soda and plenty of ice.

There was a time, believe it or not, when a bar call for a Gin & Tonic would have had heads turning. I cite that period as being between 1970 and 1990 – although I'm happy to have my authority questioned on this occasion since I was either not alive or not of legal drinking age throughout the entire period. For two decades (give or take), the gin and tonic was a well-kept secret, safeguarded mostly by ladies of a certain age, who opted for refreshment and flavour over a natural compulsion to eschew the beverage that had filled their parents' highballs. Given that the list of alternatives at the time included the likes of the Blue Lagoon cocktail and sweet German wines, one would think the humble G&T an obvious choice, but trends are capricious things and hindsight a wonderful benefit.

For me, the G&T works thanks to the balance of bitter and sweet. Many of the botanicals found in gin are inherently bitter and some, namely juniper and liquorice/licorice, have a good helping of sweetness, too. But the distillation process neglects to include most of these compounds in the final bottle – physics disallows it. So when bittersweet tonic is mixed with gin, it is like a coming of age or a rediscovery of old values. Throw some bubbles in there too and you have a buoyant, prickly heat that penetrates the tongue with all the aforementioned aromatic and taste qualities. Spices are restored, roots rekindled and fruits and herbs reanimated to their original form. In some respects you could argue that gin is an incomplete package without tonic water – neither product reaching their full potential until mixed with the other.

I've been making tonic water for over a decade now, and first tried my hand at it while working at Jamie Oliver's Fifteen restaurant, back in 2005. This was before the G&T revolution had really gathered pace, and I'm not at all ashamed to say that we approached the task with a certain degree of irony. Today, there are over 50 varieties of tonic water available across Europe and the US. That's about 48 more than were around when I became a bartender. When matched with the grand multiplicity of gins that are now around, the number of unique Gin & Tonics that can be potentially mixed reaches into the tens of thousands.

The tonic must be bittersweet and the gin must be aromatic and in most cases taste of juniper and citrus. Beyond that, the extremities of style within the two categories can result in some very disparate drinks. Take Hendrick's, Aviation or G-Vine Floraison and mix it with Fever Tree Elderflower Tonic Water and you will have a gently floral and softly sweet drink that cower under the concentrated force of Gin de Mahón or Sipsmith VJOP mixed with Schweppes Tonic.

If you've read the history section of this book, you'll know by now that quinine, the bitter element of tonic water, can be found in the bark of the cinchona tree. In fact, cinchona remains the only economically practical means of sourcing quinine naturally, and since the synthesis of quinine has proven to be quite tricky, nearly all of the world's quinine still comes from cinchona.

I found it quite difficult to buy cinchona bark back in 2005, but eventually stumbled across an online source that specialized in herbs and spices for witchcraft! We ground the red bark down into a fine powder, then heated it with water to extract the quinine. This was then sweetened and taste-tested. Since we had no real means of measuring the quinine levels – which can be dangerous in high doses – we gauged the right strength based on taste alone, attempting to match the bitterness with Schweppes' offering. What followed was a succession of prototype tonics, until we finally concocted the finished product. These days I've taken to using a pressure cooker for the cinchona extraction, as this extracts more of the bitterness and basically makes your bark go further. It's not essential however, but you may need to use more cinchona than stated to get similar levels of bitterness.

Finally, quinine levels do seem to vary from one batch of bark to the next, and like any natural product the tree and its constituents are subject to the whims of terroir and climate. Remember this, and always err on the side of caution when it comes to developing your recipe. As a general rule, bitter things tend to be dangerous and in large enough doses, quinine is no exception. In fact there is a medical condition unique to quinine, known as cinchonism, characterized by a ringing in the ears, headache, abdominal pain and sweating. In the US, the Food and Drug Administration (FDA) regulates tonic water and permits no more than 85 parts of quinine per million, which works out as 0.0085% quinine. If in doubt, you can always send your tonic water off to a food testing lab to have its quinine levels analysed.

ᕤ WHIPPER GIN FIZZ ᕥ

200 ML/7 FL. OZ. GIN (TRY AN OLD TOM)
350 ML/12 FL. OZ. MINERAL (BOTTLED) WATER
110 ML/12 FL. OZ. DE-PULPED LEMON JUICE · 60 ML/2 OZ. SUGAR SYRUP
(MADE WITH 2 PARTS SUGAR TO 1 PART WATER)
30 G/1 OZ. EGG WHITE

Makes 750 ml/25 fl. oz./3 cups, or approx. 6 small serves

Mix all the ingredients together thoroughly in a large jug/pitcher or blender. Pour carefully into a 1-litre (34-fl. oz) soda siphon (adjust the recipe proportionately for smaller or larger siphons) and place in an iced water bath for an hour. Once fully chilled, charge the siphon once with carbon dioxide (CO_2). Once charged, shake the siphon, then turn upside-down and release a blast of gas. Charge again, shake, then put it back on ice for five minutes. Shake again before dispensing into ice-cold highball glasses.

There a number of ways to pimp this drink. A pinch of salt goes down a treat, as does a splash of olive oil and a dot of good quality vanilla extract.

One of the marks of a truly great cocktail is resilience, and I mean that in two senses. Firstly, that the drink is abiding in its design, capable of merrily riding out trends and leading the charge in better times. Secondly, the drink must be resistant to creative hazards. Whether dressed up with exotic ingredients or festooned with an elaborate garnish, the conceptual standards of the cocktail must remain in place at all times. The Martini failed in the latter, having been bastardized beyond all recognition. The Margarita is a good example of a drink that has aged quite gracefully, but there is perhaps no other drink that does it so well as the Gin Fizz.

But there is one skeleton lurking in the Gin Fizz's cocktail cabinet: the Tom Collins. From an ingredient perspective, the Tom Collins and Gin Fizz are identical. Only their construction differs. For years now the bartending elite and cocktail historians have debated over whether the drinks should be stirred, shaken, include egg white, and be served over ice or not.

The historical similarities of these drinks have necessitated some gentle deviation from their original forms. With that in mind, a Tom Collins should be built over ice and simply stirred. A Gin Fizz should be shaken and served with no ice, topped with soda and, crucially, contain egg white. The inclusion of the egg white (for texture) means you have to shake for decent periods of time, and to shake the drink twice. In past times, bartenders would call upon a 'dry shake' to achieve the best possible degree of aeration. This involved shaking the drink without ice first, to whip the cocktail up, then shaking with ice afterwards to make it cold. Over many years of bartending I became uneasy around this practice of aerating then chilling. Then, in 2011, after some tests in my London cocktail bar, The Worship Street Whistling Shop, I discovered that the better practice was to shake with ice first, then without afterwards, to avoid knocking all the air back out of the drink. Henceforth, the 'reverse dry shake' became the way. I now see bartenders all over the world doing it.

Better still than dry shaking is blending or foaming the drink. This kind of technology wasn't available in the 19th century but there's no reason why we shouldn't take advantage of it today. Blending creates a super creamy, super cold version of the Gin Fizz. Aerating the drink in a cream whipper is even better though, as it's easier to control the dilution and maximize fizz.

✥ FRENCH 75 ✥

35 ML/1¼ FL. OZ. G'VINE FLORAISON GIN
10 ML/2 TEASPOONS LEMON JUICE (PULP REMOVED)
5 ML/1 TEASPOON SUGAR SYRUP
CHAMPAGNE

Method 1
Premix the gin, lemon and sugar then pop it in the fridge for 1–2 hours.
This means that no ice is needed, alleviating any dilution of flavour. Once cold, measure the
premix into the glass and top up with chilled Champagne.

Method 2
If you have a soda siphon to hand, it's worth the effort of premixing and chilling
(see method 1), and then carbonating everything (except the Champagne) by charging the
siphon with CO_2. Mix the two fizzy (and chilled) components together in the correct
proportions to finish the drink.

Method 3
Don't worry if the ingredients are warm or cold, simply build everything into the glass then
add a few pellets of dry ice. The dry ice will chill and carbonate the cocktail without inflicting
any dilution at all. A few things to be wary of though; dry ice will add a very subtle acidity to
the drink as it releases carbonic acid during the sublimation process – you can account for
this by using 10% less lemon juice. Also, you must wait until all the dry ice has 'dissolved'
away before enjoying the cocktail – don't eat it!

Garnish with a twist of lemon, or a cocktail cherry. Or both. Or neither.

Let's get one thing straight: Sparkling wine is not an easy ingredient to mix with.

Be it Champagne, Cava, Prosecco or indeed any other regionally delineated bubbly – these wines tend not to play nicely with others. This is partly down to the simple fact that sparkling wines are designed to be stand-alone ingredients, not intended for jumbling-up with extraneous flavours. And on this matter they tend to be fairly inflexible, playing on their reputation as the highest-calibre of liquid refreshment: pristine and untouchable. It is ironic then, that the other reason that Champagnes and other fizzy wines don't mix well with other ingredients is because they actually don't taste that great in the first place.

No need to re-read that last bit. Most people recognise the fact that Champagne isn't especially tasty stuff, but choose to happily push on knocking it back because it's the socially correct thing to do. Wait, you don't like Champagne?! No – not especially.

Sure, I'll drink it – because it's wet, contains alcohol, and I get a sadistic kick out of knowing that someone (who isn't me) spent a lot of money buying a bottle of liquid that is, on reflection, of quite inferior quality and complexity to a similarly priced whisky, rum, brandy, Tequila or gin. Or a similarly priced flat wine for that matter. But the truth is, in this author's opinion at least, Champagne is not worthy of either the reverence or the price tag that it receives.

With that little rant behind us, you might now be wondering what to do with that no-longer-so-appealing 'save it for a celebration' bottle of fizz that's been lurking in your cooler for months now. The simple solution is to make a French 75. Or make a few.

There are only a handful of decent sparkling wine-based cocktails known to mankind, and while I'd be happy to concede that the Bellini and Kir Royal are also both good drinks, the simplicity of their construction makes for a less than credible claim of cocktail-hood. The French 75 on the other hand is without doubt a cocktail, and perhaps the only cocktail containing sparkling wine that can truly be deemed delicious. Indeed, the ingredients in this drink don't just pair nicely with one another, they actually taste better than the sum of their parts. Gin, lemon and sugar transform sparkling wine into the liquid that you'll probably end up wishing was in the Champagne bottle in the first place.

There's no particular genius behind this marriage of flavours – the drink is the forehead-slappingly obvious evolution of the Fizz and Sour. Here though, the wine takes the place of the soda. Sounds innocent enough, but when you consider a world where soda water has an alcohol content in excess of 16%, you don't need to be a mathematician to realise that a French 75 packs a bit of a punch.

Putting the theory to the test, after your third French 75 it becomes worryingly evident why the drink was named after a 75-mm (3-inch) field gun. Used to great effect by the French during World War I, and more of a canon than a gun, 'Soixante-Quinze' would fire noxious gas canisters the size of your forearm into enemy trenches. Perhaps it was the explosive and intoxicating effects of Champagne and gin that caused Harry McElhone, the bartender generally credited with the drink's invention, to name his cocktail after the most deadly weapon of the era.

Temperature and fizz are the two major obstacles to overcome when mixing one of these, and with that in mind, there are three different methods that can be employed here, all of them simple but some requiring specialist kit. Naturally the fizz will be softened by the non-carbonated ingredients (yet another reason that sparkling wine cocktails tend to be a let-down), so using a fresh bottle of Champagne is paramount.

⸙ GIMLET ⸙

60 ML/2 FL. OZ. PLYMOUTH NAVY-STRENGTH GIN
20 ML/⅔ FL. OZ. ROSE'S LIME CORDIAL OR FRESH LIME JUICE

Shake and strain into a freezing cold Martini glass then devour like you've just been diagnosed with scurvy. You may choose to garnish it with a lime wedge, but I find one an unnecessary distraction.

Back in 1740 a British Admiral by the name of Vernon took the unprecedented step of watering down his sailors' rum rations with citrus juice. While initially (and quite understandably) not a hit with the men, this simple act went on to save countless lives. Seven years later, in 1747, a Scottish surgeon named James Lind discovered that incorporating fruit juice into the sailors' diets dramatically reduced the chances of them contracting a potentially lethal bout of scurvy. It turned out that scurvy was a result of vitamin C deficiency, so all ships began carrying citrus juice. In 1867 it became mandatory for British ships to carry lime juice rations.

The problem was that the juice tended to go off after a week or two sitting in a barrel. Another enterprising Scotsman, Lauchlan Rose, developed and patented a new method of preserving lime juice by concentrating it. Crucially though, the medicinal properties of the juice were retained and the vitamin C remained intact. Rose's Lime Cordial was born – the world's first concentrated fruit juice.

Drinking lime cordial on its own is no fun at all, so a (very large) spoon-full of gin is necessary to help the medicine go down. The story goes that it was Sir Thomas Gimlette, a surgeon in the Royal Navy, who allegedly introduced this drink as a means of inducing his messmates to take lime juice as an anti-scurvy medication. There's very little in the way of evidence to actually back this story up, though, and it's more likely that the drink simply takes its name from the sharp handheld tool used for punching holes in

things – a description that is just as apt for the drink as it is for the tool.

There's an elephant in the room among bartenders when it comes to mixing gimlets, and that is whether to use fresh lime and sugar, or lime cordial?

As we have already learned, the original calls for Rose's cordial, but the nomination of cordial was driven more by circumstance than by the pursuit of deliciousness. I'd wager lime juice would have been preferable if it were as practical and readily available as it is today. So with that in mind it's fair to consider a lime juice an upgrade. But this is beginning to sound a lot like a 'Gin Daiquiri', and in the Gimlet we have a cocktail that deserves its own name and its own terms and conditions. For me this is one occasion where nostalgia wins the day, and I'm happy to sacrifice a little freshness in a Gimlet to know that I am drinking a simple union of ingredients that have remained relatively unchanged for over 250 years. A win for Lauchlan Rose!

Now that we have settled upon the ingredients, ratio remains the final point of contention. *The Savoy Cocktail Book* (1930) suggests 50/50 gin and lime cordial, backed up by the 1953 Raymond Chandler novel *The Long Goodbye*, which stated that 'a real gimlet is half gin and half Rose's lime juice and nothing else'. But I urge you to consider what your dentist might say, and lower the lime cordial a little. Three parts gin to one part cordial is a sweeter (or not) spot to aim for.

ᵒᵉ SALTED LIME RICKEY ᵉᵒ

**50 ML/2 FL. OZ. PLYMOUTH GIN · 15 ML/½ FL. OZ. LIME JUICE
1 G/¹⁄₃₂ OZ. SALT · SODA, TO TOP UP**

This drink needs to be cold – like, really cold. If possible use glasses from the freezer
and make sure that your ice is dry. Fill a highball glass with chunks of ice; add the gin, lime
and salt, then give it a good stir with a bar spoon. While still stirring, pour the soda water
in, leaving a small space at the top. Add more ice, stir some more, then finish
with a wedge of lime.

On page 57 of *Daly's Bartender's Encyclopedia*, published in 1903, a passage reads: 'This drink was devised by the late Colonel Rickey, whose fame as a congenial friend and dispenser of hospitality, as well as a judge of appetizing edibles and liquid refreshments, is worldwide, and it is universally conceded that for a drink containing an alcoholic ingredient it is the most refreshing known.'

This was the first book to publish a recipe for a Gin Rickey but, as the author alludes to, it was already a very popular drink by then and quite possibly the most popular gin-based cocktail of the 1890s. Today however, the Rickey is not known by many and very rarely called for, at least in my experience. It has faded into obscurity, and I'll be the first to admit that for a great deal of my early bartending career, I spared very little thought for the Rickey. It's a Collins or a Fizz made with lime juice, I thought. That's not to say I didn't think it was tasty – gin, lime and soda is a union of ingredients that makes as much sense on paper as it does swishing down your throat – but the thought of drinking one didn't exactly fill me with excitement. My opinion changed during a trip to India in 2011.

The Rickey is one of the most popular cocktails in India which, given the country's past dealings with gin and the favourability of its climate to citrus fruit growers, should come as no great surprise. But Rickeys are not made in the Western manner out there, oh no. In India, there's either little or no sugar in the recipe

and salt is added instead. Salt has the effect of buffering the acidity of the lime juice (in the same way as sugar), but also exposing some minerality from the gin and lime oil. Removing the sugar also makes the drink less cloying and circumvents that nauseating sugar overload that typically happens after about your third or fourth sour/fizzy drink. Putting flavour to one side, forgoing the sugar altogether is an attractive proposition for some, making the drink a friend of diabetics and those counting calories. Although your doctor may question the logic of replacing sugar with salt, Indians swear by the drink's hydrating power during hot summer days.

The Rickey was probably first made with Bourbon, which is a little odd since Bourbon and soda are not especially enthusiastic bedfellows and it'll need a lot more than a squeeze of lime to change that. Nonetheless, George A. Williamson of Shoomaker's bar in Washington thought the marriage a loving one, and at some time in the 1880s conceived the Rickey, naming it after the Democratic lobbyist, Joe Rickey, who may or may not have had some part to play in the drink's creation. One thing is for sure, though: Rickey was quite displeased at having loaned his name to a popular cocktail, once saying that 'I was Col. Rickey, of Missouri, the friend of senators, judges and statesmen and something of an authority on political matters... But am I ever spoken of for those reasons? I fear not. No, I am known to fame as the author of the "rickey," and I have to be satisfied with that.'

PURL

FOR THE BOTANICAL INFUSION
**150 ML/5 FL. OZ. PLYMOUTH GIN • 3 G/¾ OZ. CRUSHED BLACK PEPPER
3 G/¾ OZ. BAY LEAVES • 3 G/¾ OZ. SAGE • 1 G/¹⁄₃₂ OZ. GENTIAN ROOT
1 G/¹⁄₃₂ OZ. WORMWOOD • 1 G/¹⁄₃₂ OZ. STAR ANISE
1 G/¹⁄₃₂ OZ. NUTMEG • 1 G/¹⁄₃₂ OZ. DRIED ROSEMARY**

For the botanical infusion, macerate all the ingredients in a jam jar (or similar)
for 2 weeks, then strain and reserve. You can speed this process up a little by pressurizing the
ingredients in a hand-held cream whipper, charged with a nitrous-oxide cartridge.

FOR THE DRINK [MAKES 700 ML/24 FL. OZ.]
**150 ML/5 FL. OZ. BOTANICAL INFUSION [SEE ABOVE]
500 ML/17 FL. OZ./2 CUPS BROWN ALE
50 G/¼ CUP DEMERARA SUGAR • 50 G/¼ CUP CASTER/SUPERFINE SUGAR**

For the drink, build all the ingredients into a glass bottle or a large jar, allowing the sugar to dissolve.
The cocktail can be enjoyed cold, straight from the fridge, or warmed up in its bottle. Adjust the sugar
according to taste and feel free to play around with different styles of beer.

I could hardly pen this book without sparing a thought for Purl – the drink that leant its name to my first cocktail bar. Before Purl opened in 2010 you would have been hard-pressed to find a bartender who had heard of this drink. Hendrick's Gin saw the genius in the mixture, though, and collaborated with us on a promotion that gained the drink some traction. But its brief period of fame was a far cry from the mid-18th century, where it would have been difficult to walk past moored boats on the Thames without the aroma of warm Purl.

The drink's original form pre-dates English gin by at least 100 years, becoming popular some time around the turn of the 17th century. The use of hops as a preservative (and bittering agent) for ales was highly uncommon back then, which meant that beer spoiled quickly and tasted quite bland. Resourceful folk pepped up their beers with other herbs and spices, and wormwood was amongst the most common of these pre-hop seasonings. Beer with wormwood was often called 'Purl' – a 16th century word used to describe the twisting and meandering of a brook or stream.

In the winter, it became trendy to warm this mixture up, and sometimes seasonal spices and sugar were added, too. Then, as you might expect, those early, debauched years of the 18th century saw it necessary to fortify Purl with a healthy measure of the ubiquitous spirit of the age: gin. The drink is celebrated in a handful of Charles Dickens novels, most notably *The Old Curiosity Shop* (1840) where the character, Dick Swiveller, serves a mistreated maid 'a great pot, filled with some very fragrant compound, which sent forth a grateful steam, and was indeed choice purl...'

The recipe itself is amenable to some poetic license and, like mulled wine, can be tailored to your desired level of sweetness and spice. Truthfully, the only ingredients that you must use are beer, gin and wormwood, but I'd certainly suggest some sugar to balance the bitterness, and some choice fruits and spices wouldn't go amiss either.

Try to avoid holding the liquid on the heat too long and certainly don't boil it. I suggest mulling the beer together with sugar and other seasonings for 10 minutes with the lid on, then adding the gin to temper the heat and fortify the mixture. Perhaps the best way is to batch a mixture in sealed bottles, then warm it up in a hot water-bath or pan.

CLOVER CLUB

FOR THE RASPBERRY SYRUP
250 G/2 CUPS FRESH RASPBERRIES · 2 G/¹⁄₁₆ OZ. SALT
250 G/1¼ CUPS CASTER/SUPERFINE SUGAR
250 ML/1 CUP WATER

Toss the raspberries in the salt and sugar then place in a 1-litre (35-fl. oz.) mason jar (you can also use a zip-lock bag) and pop it in the fridge overnight. In the morning add the water to the jar. Using a temperature probe, bring a saucepan of water up to 50°C (122°F) and turn the temperature right down so that it holds there. Pop the mason jar in the water and leave it for 2 hours, giving it the occasional wiggle. When the 2 hours are up, carefully remove the jar then strain the contents through a sieve/strainer. You may need to strain a second time using muslin/cheesecloth. To prolong the lifespan of your syrup it's often useful to add a splash of gin or vodka. Store in the fridge for up to 1 month.

CLOVER CLUB
40 ML/1½ FL. OZ. GIN (DARNLEY'S VIEW OR ANY GIN WITH A SPICY KICK)
15 ML/½ FL. OZ. LEMON JUICE · 15 ML/½ FL. OZ. RASPBERRY SYRUP
15 ML/½ FL. OZ. MARTINI EXTRA DRY VERMOUTH · 15 G/½ OZ. EGG WHITE

Shake all the ingredients with ice then strain into a separate mixing glass or shaker and shake again with no ice. This 'dry shake' has the effect of whipping air into the cocktail. Strain into a chilled coupe glass and drink it quickly. You can leave the egg white out if you prefer, but it adds a lovely sherbet effect to the palate.

Part gin sour, part Martini, part raspberry liqueur, the Clover Club is fruity, dry, delicate and fiendishly addictive. I think it has something for everyone and, had it been given a chance, it could quite possibly have single-handedly saved the 1980s from the depths of drinking depravity.

The cocktail was named for and enjoyed by the eponymous Philadelphia-based lawyers' and writers' club founded in 1882. Like many other gentleman's clubs of the time, a signature drink was an essential component of congenial gatherings. The Clover Club drink dates to 1896, as seen in the 1897 book, The Clover Club of Philadelphia.

When I first became a bartender, the Clover Club was still dragging itself out of 70 years worth of obscurity. We used to make them with gin, grenadine, lemon and egg white. It was basically a pink gin sour, and even though it tasted nice enough, it wasn't going

to be winning any awards for innovation. The earliest recipe in fact calls for raspberry syrup, not grenadine, and also a splash of vermouth. Slowly, we bartenders began to embrace the classic version, and like the unfurling of pink petals the beauty and balance of the true Clover Club blossomed.

And for me it's the addition of a splash a vermouth that really sets the Clover Club apart, where aromatics of thyme and the bitterness of wormwood intercept the raspberry before it becomes overly fruity. That said, the raspberry syrup is probably the most important ingredient. As is often the way with off the shelf syrups, most taste more like the devil's confectionery than the carefully concentrated essence of a piece of fresh fruit. Fortunately, raspberry syrup is super-simple to make at home, so I've included the only recipe you'll ever need above. It's a game changer as far as the Clover Club is concerned.

❧ NEGRONI ❧

30 ML/1 FL. OZ. GIN
(avoid citrus-forward gins, they get lost)

30 ML/1 FL. OZ. CAMPARI · 30 ML/1 FL. OZ. NARDINI ROSSO VERMOUTH

A good Negroni should be served over big chunks of freezer-temperature ice, and there's nothing wrong with building the whole thing in a rocks glass. Stir for a full minute, then garnish with a small strip of grapefruit zest or a slice of orange.

For new initiates it's wise to start with Aperol instead of Campari – it's like Campari's better-natured, mawkish cousin. If the bitterness is still too much you can always drop the ratio slightly, or do what I do and just up the gin!

It's a fairly well-kept secret that bartenders don't usually drink cocktails when sat on the receiving end of the bar, preferring instead to swig a beer or down a shot. It's an act of martyrdom, graciously sparing their fellow bartender the ordeal of cocktail mixing and the indignity of being observed by a keeper of the craft. The Negroni is one acceptable deviation from this rule however. Uncomplicated, yet challenging; strong, yet quaffable, the Negroni is hallowed ground to the bartender – an impeccable decoction of spirit, wine and bitter; blood red and ice cool.

If the significance of the Negroni should ever come in to question, one need only observe the openness of bar room discussion about the drink. Everyone has an opinion on its components, method of mixing, garnish and ice; those that swear by it will do so until their dying sip, those that come to dislike it will lay down their lives to avoid a single drop. And even though the brazen character of the Negroni may divide opinion, it is a drink that all cocktail enthusiasts desperately want to appreciate to its full extent. Regardless of preference, there remains a right of passage, or entitlement when it comes to the Negroni. Like your first face-scrunching sip of wine or beer, the conspiracy that surrounds this drink demands that you try, try again until life become incomplete without it. Here, in the Negroni, is the drink that, beyond all others, has become the Ferrari-red pin-up of the craft cocktail movement.

My understanding of the origins of the Negroni comes from the book *Sulle Tracce del Conte* (On the Trail of the Count) (2002) by Luca Picchi. Backed up by considerable historical documentation, it intimates that the drink is named after ★deep breath★ Camillo Luigi Manfredo Maria Negroni, who originally asked Fosco Scarselli, bartender at Café Casoni, to fortify his Americano (a bitter Italian aperitivo mixed with sweet vermouth and a splash of soda) with gin. This happened at some time in 1919 or 1920. One of the ways in which the story is qualified is by a letter sent from Frances Harper of London to [the evidently unwell] Negroni on October 13th 1920:

'You say you can drink, smoke, and I am sure laugh, just as much as ever. I feel you are not much to be pitied! You must not take more than 20 Negronis in one day!'

Nobody can drink that many Negronis in a single day, so it's fair to assume that the early version of the drink was either quite small or contained proportionately less gin – or both. These days we default to a Negroni made with equal parts gin, bitter liqueur/amaro, and sweet vermouth. The exact ratio can be tweaked (I prefer it slightly in favour of the gin, but with plenty of dilution) along with the brand of gin, bitter and vermouth. It's the simplicity of the drink coupled with the potential for customization that makes it a prevailing classic.

GIN & JUICE

40 ML/1½ FL. OZ. GIN
100 ML/3½ FL. OZ. CINOTTO

Stir the ingredients with plenty of ice in a highball glass. Garnish with a wedge of
blood orange, or a normal orange if you can't be bothered.

'What the hell is gin & juice?'

That was the question I asked myself before tackling this recipe. It seems like a stupid question, but when you contemplate it, the whole concept seems a bit odd – like lathering tomato ketchup on your sushi.

To me, Gin & Juice has always felt like an amusing piece of alliteration rather than a drink that you would actually mix, let alone order. When, in 1999, the drink was catapulted to stardom by rapper Snoop Dogg's rhythmic utterance of the immortal words 'sippin on gin and juice, laid back, with my mind on my money and my money on my mind', I immediately assumed that Gin & Juice was a metaphor for something sexual or drug-related. It turns out it wasn't. It also turns out that America loves Gin & Juice and that, as a nation, America mixes more gin with juice than it does with tonic water.

Of course mixing gin with fruit juices is no new thing. Gin Palaces were known to sell a drink called a 'Gin Twist', which was made with lemon juice garnished with a lemon twist, and the near 150-year-old Gimlet (pages 196–7) is little more than gin and fruit juice concentrate mixed together. Then there's the Red Snapper (essentially a Bloody Mary with gin), which finds its origins in the mid-20th century. And the Spanish 'Pomada', which sees gin traditionally mixed with lemon juice. Gin gets mixed with juice in Fizzes, Collins, Daisies, Rickeys, Punches and so on. But with those drinks, it is always as a measured souring agent, rather than a lengthener or mixer.

Delving deeper into the practices of Gin & Juice advocates, I found that gin gets mixed with all kinds of different juices, but grape, grapefruit and orange are the most popular choices. Orange and grapefruit make a good fit in theory, given that they crop up regularly in the botanical bill of many London Dry gins. But it doesn't work, or at least not how I would hope it would. The juice kills the gin so that it might as well be vodka that you're mixing, leading back to the conclusion that it's the alliteration on the 'g' and the 'j' that has popularized this drink rather than any deep affinity between the ingredients.

So now it's time to own up, dear reader. I will not be furnishing you with a recipe for gin mixed with fruit juice because it doesn't taste very good. Instead I am suggesting you mix your gin with cinotto. Now, cinotto is not a fruit juice, but it isn't all that far off. Bright red in colour and lightly sparkling, cinotto is a non-alcoholic Italian aperitivo that is also sold under the brand name 'Cino'. It's made from a combination of bitter spices, fruit and sugar and sits somewhere between Campari, blood orange juice and tonic water on the flavour spectrum. Sounds delicious, right? Well, it is. And it's a great match for gin, especially when sat on the porch in your high-tops.

The drink pictured opposite was one of my early attempts to emulsify fruity essential oils in to gin, sugar, acids and water, effectively constructing a soft drink from scratch. After hitting upon a formula that worked really well, I was struck by the realisation that I had created a soft drink that already existed (albeit with a different colour) – cinotto!

HOLLAND HOUSE

50 ML/1¾ FL. OZ. BOLS GENEVER
20 ML/⅔ FL. OZ. DRY VERMOUTH
10 ML/⅓ FL. OZ. LEMON JUICE
5 ML/1 TEASPOON MARASCHINO LIQUEUR

Shake all the ingredients with ice and strain into a punch glass. Add an ice cube from a shaker, or use a chunk of clear ice. Garnish with a lemon twist.

Those readers old enough to remember the manned Moon landings might recall the Holland House brand of cocktail mixer. These popular bottles of 'Whiskey Sour' and 'Daiquiri' mix sought to simplify cocktail mixing at home by giving you all the ingredients you needed (except the alcohol) in one bottle. They saw quite a bit of success in the 1950s and 1960s until people realised that they tasted dreadful. And so began two decades of Dark Ages for the cocktail.

In this book, with its select collection of cocktails, the Holland House serves as a handy mashup of at least three other classic gin cocktails. The first of those is the Martinez, the elder sibling of the Martini and cocktail that I featured in *The Curious Bartender: The Artistry & Alchemy of Creating the Perfect Cocktail*, where the Holland House borrows vermouth and maraschino liqueur. The second is The Aviation, a drink that also featured in my first book, which sees gin combined with lemon juice and maraschino or violet liqueur. The third is the Corpse Reviver No. 2 (favoured child of the Corpse Reviver family), where we find gin, lemon, orange liqueur and dry vermouth in concert with one another. Fourth − if I may − is the Clover Club and you can turn to page 203 to discover the similarities for yourself.

All of the aforementioned drinks are, in isolation, quite different beasts, despite having a few similar ingredients. The Holland House is like a missing link between them all, probably pre-dating all but the Martinez. In fact, some cocktail buffs argue that the Holland House *is* a Martinez, given the similarities between the widely accepted modern recipe and Jerry Thomas' original Martinez recipe from 1862, which called for: maraschino, Old Tom gin, vermouth, bitters and a slice of lemon − forgo the bitters and up the lemon and you have yourself a Holland House right there. However a more likely explanation for the similarities between the two drinks is that most mundane of rationales: coincidence.

For the Holland House Cocktail (if you hadn't guessed already) it's the use of genever in place of gin that makes all the difference. The boldness of a nice oude genever or corenwijn, really stands up to the lemon and liqueur, while the vermouth offers some welcome dilution and finesse to the ensemble. I've heard the Holland House described as a 'malty Aviation' in the past, which is a fair description but also an injustice to a cocktail that deserves fair recognition in its own right, rather than loose comparisons to better known, classic cocktails (as I have just done).

⚜ SLOE GIN ⚜

SOUS VIDE/OSMOSIS METHOD
500 G/1 LB. 2 OZ. SLOE BERRIES
(You can flash-freeze them to soften the skins, but it's not essential)
250 G/1¼ CUPS CASTER/SUPERFINE SUGAR
10 G/⅓ OZ. MALIC ACID · 5 G/1 TEASPOON SALT
500 ML/17½ FL. OZ. GIN

Using a large zip-lock or vacuum bag, add the sloes, 100 g/½ cup of the sugar, the acid, and salt. Give it a good shake and a bit of a squash and leave to sit in the fridge overnight. In the morning you'll find a lot of the juice has leached out. Add the rest of the ingredients, including the gin, then seal the bag and drop it into a water bath set at 65°C (150°F). Leave to cook for 3 hours. You can go hotter and quicker, but this is the best balance of flavour and efficiency for me. Remove the bag and filter the liquid through a fine-mesh filter and muslin/cheesecloth. Pour the filtered liquid in to a sterile bottle. It should keep for years.

BLENDER METHOD

500 G/1 LB. 2 OZ. SLOE BERRIES · 100 ML/3½ FL. OZ. WARM WATER
500 G/17½ FL. OZ. GIN · 200 G/1 CUP SUGAR · 10 G/⅓ OZ. MALIC ACID ·
5 G/1 TEASPOON SALT

Makes approximately 1 litre/34 fl. oz./4 cups

Start with the sloes at room temperature, as they tend to give up their juices more readily. Add them to the blender along with the water and most of the gin. Blend on a high speed in 10-second bursts for 1–2 minutes. The aim is to purée everything without the liquid heating up too much. Pass the purée through a coarse sieve/strainer using the back of a spoon to push all the juice out. Then pass through a finer sieve/strainer, doing the same, followed by muslin/cheesecloth. Use what's left of the gin to 'wash' any flavour out of the leftover fruit pulp. Add the sugar, acid and salt and bottle the liqueur. Keep in a warm place for a few hours until the sugar has completely dissolved. Serve chilled.

Not so long ago the home kitchen was a veritable hive of booze-based activity, as household cookbooks like those published by The Women's Institute will testify to. Homemade wines, cordials and liqueurs were as commonplace as homemade bread and jams. Gin was a popular candidate for all manner of fruit infusions, both at home and at the big distillers of the day, who sold lemon- and orange-flavoured gins with some success. These days, flavoured gins have all but died out and despite the emergence of some contemporary gin brands choosing to flavour and sweeten their product (see *The Gin Tour* chapter), it is only sloe gin that has truly stood the test of time. And the manufacture of sloe gin stands as one of the few alcohol-based culinary crafts that remains a homemade British staple.

Before we dive in head first, though, it's important to stress that on the subject of manufacturing sloe gin, we must tread very carefully indeed. There is no other line of conversation that can send handbag ripples through a Women's Institute tea room like the finer

points of gin/fruit infusions. What began as a wholesome household craft is now seen by some as a classical art form, shrouded in superstition and mystery. As for the sloe berry itself, there is a fruit that, to some, holds a position of near divine reverence, reflected in the manner in which it must be treated prior to and during sloe gin preparation.

Some older recipes for sloe gin suggest waiting until after the season's 'first frost' before picking the berries. At first this might seem an attempt at some biodynamic strategy (allowing the heavens to align before foraging for the fruit) and explained away by most as nature's way of softening the fruits skin prior to infusion. Science tells us that the hydrogen cyanide (natural antifreeze) content of the fruit increases during cold snaps and imparts a desirable almond character to the liqueur, similar to bitter almond kernels of apple pips. If hydrogen cyanide sounds a bit dangerous to you, that's because it is. In my experience, the first frost generally lands a little too late in the year anyway and runs the risk of losing the crop altogether. One option is to make your own frost by picking the ripe fruit and briefly freezing them before infusion. I've heard of others who choose to prick the sloe berries one by one before mixing them with the gin, in a process so arduous that it has been clinically proven to gradually erode the mind of its physical capabilities and is now officially classified under the Human Rights Act as a form of prolonged mental torture. Traditionally this is done with one of the thorns from the blackthorn tree from whence the sloes

were picked, but a needle will do it just fine, so long as it is made from silver (naturally).

The point is that everyone has their own method that's been handed down from one generation to the next. For better or worse, most people are fairly stubborn when it comes to cherished family recipes and as quaint as this may sound, traditions such as these are often tough nuts to crack when it comes to enforcing some logical culinary processes in to the mix.

I make sloe gin using two different methods. Both work very well and both require very little time. The first is to cook the sloe berries, in gin, sous vide. This means packing both fruit and liquor into a ziplock bag (or vacuum-packing bag) and holding it in a temperature-controlled water bath for a few hours. Afterwards the mixture is strained-off and sweetened. This method extracts more bitterness than a cold infusion, which means the liquor can take a touch more sugar, resulting in a more concentrated shot of juice.

My second technique is a 'cold' method and it calls for the use of a blender. It isn't pretty or particularly efficient, and it certainly isn't the way your mother would do it, but it gets the job done quickly and easily. It also makes for a good talking point around the Christmas table. Blending the sloes and gin together makes a fine purée that requires only a short infusion followed by a slightly longer filtering process.

In both methods you'll find you need comparatively fewer sloes and far less finger tapping than in the traditional recipes.

✤ FRUIT CUP ✤

FOR THE FRUIT CUP SYRUP

300 G/1½ CUPS CASTER/SUPERFINE SUGAR
200 G/7 OZ. STRAWBERRIES, THINLY SLICED
150 G/5 OZ. CUCUMBER, SKIN REMOVED, SLICED
30 G/1 OZ. GRAPEFRUIT PEEL
10 G/⅓ OZ. FRESH MINT LEAVES
SEVERAL SPRIGS DRIED LAVENDER FLOWERS
300 ML/10 FL. OZ. WATER

Sprinkle the sugar over the strawberries, cucumber, grapefruit, mint and lavender and place in the refrigerator overnight – this helps to draw the moisture out of the fruit. Add the water, then pour everything into a resealable plastic bag. Heat a pan of water and use a temperature probe to hold it at a steady 55°C (130°F). After 4 hours, remove the bag from the pan and strain the contents through a fine mesh sieve/strainer.

FOR THE FRUIT CUP

200 ML/7 FL. OZ. FRUIT CUP SYRUP
400 ML/14 FL. OZ. GORDON'S GIN OR ANY OTHER JUNIPER-FORWARD GIN
400 ML/14 FL. OZ. GANCIA ROSSO VERMOUTH
LEMONADE OR GINGER ALE
SLICED STRAWBERRIES, ORANGES, LAVENDER SPRIGS
AND BAY LEAVES, TO GARNISH

Once the fruit cup syrup has cooled, mix it with the gin and vermouth. Your Fruit Cup will keep best when stored in the fridge and should remain in good shape for up to 6 months.

To construct the finished drink, mix one part fruit cup with two parts lemonade or ginger ale (or both) over plenty of ice. Garnish as if your life depends on it.

At first glance the 'fruit cup' appears to be a family of mixed drink still patiently waiting for their renaissance. But when you consider that the Pimm's brand of aperitif is actually a fruit cup, and indeed, the originator of the genre, it's clear that this category needs no help from anyone. In the UK, Pimm's is associated with sitting outside on a summer's day and specifically the Wimbledon tennis tournament, where drinking the stuff, along with eating strawberries and cream, is more or less mandatory.

The Pimm's No. 1 Cup (known simply as Pimm's) is of particular interest to gin drinkers because it's gin-based. Of course it doesn't taste much like gin, that is, until you try the other Pimm's Cups and learn that each have their own unique character driven by different base spirits.

The garnishing of Pimm's has more recently become a point of contention between purists and the 'more is better camp'. The doctrinaires will tell you that Pimm's should only be decorated with the blue flowers or leaves of the borage shrub, and perhaps a slice of lemon if you're really pushing the boat out. But there is an enormous temptation with Pimm's to throw as much fruit at the drink as possible, and I am certainly guilty of this myself (see right).

My recipe calls for a fruit cup syrup, which is best made sous vide, using a heated water bath, although a pan of hot water and a digital thermometer will do the job just as well. The syrup is then mixed with gin and sweet vermouth for the finished fruit cup.

Now, we might not think of it as such, the Pimm's No. 1 Cup, or just 'Pimm's' as it is more commonly known, is in fact a bottled cocktail. The 'Cup' family of drinks were defined on paper by Jerry Thomas in his book *How To Mix Drinks* or the *Bon Vivant's Companion* (1862), but James Pimm actually developed his recipe back in the 1820s, shortly after opening his first oyster bar in 1823. The fruity, herbal infusion was intended as a digestive aid for patrons who had overindulged on shellfish. It proved popular, as did his growing chain of restaurants, and in 1859 he launched a version of the product that could be sold to other restaurants. That product was called the No. 1 Cup, a name which had stuck on account of Pimm serving the drink in large cups in his restaurants.

No. 6 (vodka) is probably the second most common after No. 1, and it has a much lighter colour to match its less spicy taste. Then there's the No. 3 Cup, which was re-released as the warming 'Pimm's Winter' back in 2008. Finally, there's the No. 2 Cup (Scotch whisky), No. 4 Cup (rum) and No. 5 cup (rye whiskey). If you can find an unopened bottle of the latter three you should buy it – they have been out of production since the 1980s. More recently, Pimm's have released numerous other iterations of the product, featuring other fruity combinations.

Looking at the original No. 1 Cup, we find that it performs a clever flavour balancing act, being dark, warm and spicy, as well as crisp, refreshing and fruity (the only product I can think of that does this better is Coca Cola). When mixed with lemonade, ginger ale, ginger beer or a combination thereof, the liquid really comes alive and it's quite astonishing how jugs of the stuff can be demolished over a sunny afternoon's picnic bench. Cucumber sits near the top of that list for me, with its cooling qualities and fresh aroma, British supermarket shelves are often cleared of cucumbers when it turns Pimm's-o-clock.

GLOSSARY OF DISTILLERIES

It's a fact worth celebrating that it's no longer possible to cover all the world's gin brands, in detail, in one book. There is some fascinating work going on out there though, particularly in the smaller brands that are still striving to establish themselves. This appendix recognizes the big and the small that didn't make it in to the final cut and hopefully gives you an introduction into the continued depth and breadth of gin making going on around the world. Having said all that, even this list – comprehensive as it is – is by no means exhaustive.

UNITED KINGDOM

7 Dials (46% ABV) – Produced by Atom brands on behalf of The London Gin Club, 7 Dials takes its name from the seven-pointed crossroads in London's Covent Garden. The gin is made from seven botanicals: juniper, coriander, angelica, mallow root, clementine peel, cardamom and almond, and is cold-distilled in a rotary evaporator before being cut with neutral spirit and water.

Ancient Mariner (50% ABV) – Ancient Mariner is a juniper-forward gin, owned by the Hebridean Spirits & Liqueurs company, but produced at Thames Distillers in London. It takes its name from Coleridge's famous poem, 'The Rime of the Ancient Mariner'.

Anno (43% ABV) – This Kentish gin was founded by two retired big-wigs from drug mega-corporation GlaxoSmithKline, and uses a whole array of fresh and flavourful ingredients from the 'Garden of England', including hops, rose hips, elderflowers, lavender (from the National Lavender Collection at Downderry Nursery), and samphire from Romney Marsh. It's tasty stuff. They also make a sloe gin and an elderflower vodka.

Bath Gin (40% ABV) – Bath gin is made on behalf of the Canary Gin Bar, on Bath's Queen Street, by Thames Distillers. The label is straight out of a Victorian fashion catalogue (it's actually an image of a winking Jane Austen) and the liquid includes a classic array of ingredients, plus wormwood and kaffir lime leaves.

Beckett's (40% ABV) – This gin is made at the Kingston Distillery, in Kingston-Upon-Thames in the south-western suburbs of London. The gin is made from juniper, lime, orris root, sweet orange peel, coriander and fresh mint. Beckett's use juniper sourced from Box Hill in Surrey and are involved in a juniper conservation programme in partnership with the National Trust in England.

Blackdown (37.5%) – Sussex's answer to the gin boom, Blackdown is distilled from 11 classic botanicals then charcoal-filtered before being mixed with locally sourced silver birch sap. It's good juice, but at 37.5% you're left wanting a little more structure and persistence from the product.

Blackwoods (40% ABV) – Shrouded in a bit of mystery on account of the fact that nobody knows where Blackwoods is made (my belief is that it is at Balmenach Distillery) this Shetland Islands inspired gin uses an ever-changing list of foraged botanicals, including wild water mint and sea pink flowers, which makes for an every evolving product called 'Blackwoods Vintage'. The original Blackwoods brand was an early entry in to the new gin market, but after falling in to administration in 2008 the brand was saved and relaunched by the Blavod Wines & Spirits Co.

Boë (41.5% ABV) – This gin is another Scottish entry, coming from the Deanston Whisky Distillery near Stirling. Interestingly, the master distiller, Ian Macmillan, once worked in the now closed Booth's Gin Distillery, which is as good a CV entry as I've seen where it comes to gin. I'm not all that keen on the packaging, which uses a 'tag cloud' effect to display the 11 classic botanicals – but the gin is a good'un.

Boodles (40% ABV) – The Blades Club that features in the James Bond novels is said to be based on London's legendary Boodles gentleman's club, which dates back to 1845. It only seems correct, then, that they should have their own gin. Boodles is made at G&J Distillers and includes nutmeg, sage, rosemary and juniper among its botanicals.

Boxer (40% ABV) – It's got a boxer on the bottle, but the real reason why this gin is called Boxer is because you can buy it in boxes. The idea is that you buy a bottle then refill it from the box, which means the cost per litre goes down, but it's also a more environmentally sound investment. The gin starts as a classic London Dry, produced at the Langley Distillery, which gets mixed with distillates of fresh Himalayan juniper distillate and cold press bergamot extract.

Brecon (43% ABV) – Produced by the Penderyn Whisky Distillery in Wales. The botanicals in their 'Botanicals' gin are undeclared, though the label and clear glass bottle offer up nice illustrations of juniper, orange, angelica and coriander. Also available is a standard 'Brecon Gin', which uses 11 classic botanicals in its formula.

Brockmans (40% ABV) – Produced at G&J, this gin is flavoured with a post-distillation blueberry and blackberry composite, which gives it a rather distinctive and pervasive berry aroma.

Bulldog (40% ABV) – This was another relatively early entry in to the growing gin market when it was launched back in 2008. Bulldog is made at G&J and despite its quintessentially British name, it includes Eastern ingredients like poppy seeds, lotus leaves and longan fruit among its botanical bill. The packaging is black, broad shouldered, and slightly S&M, with a spiked dog collar circling the neck.

Cambridge (42% ABV) – This distillery uses a rotary evaporator to distil botanicals under low pressure. Cambridge's Will Lowe famously made a gin for the NOMA restaurant in Copenhagen, which included wood ants among its botanicals – although under EU law ants are technically not a botanical. Cambridge's own gin is released seasonally and can include, amongst other things, blackcurrant leaf, lemon verbena, angelica seed, rose petals, violet petals, and basil and rosemary from the distillery's gardens. It's a great product.

Chilgrove (44% ABV) – A Sussex-based gin distilled from wine with a selection of 11 botanicals including wild water mint. The gin is suitably winey, with soft lemon and floral notes to back up a decent juniper base.

City of London (40% ABV) – This distillery and cocktail bar first opened in 2013 and is now a popular pit stop for wandering gin aficionados. Jamie Baxter consulted on the set-up and what with shoes that big to fill COLD have begun bringing in guest distillers of the highest calibre. The first of those is the former Tanqueray and Gordon's master distiller, Tom Nichol, who recently partnered with COLD on a special edition 'Christopher Wren' gin that complements their four other expressions.

Colonel Fox (40% ABV) – This gin is allegedly based on an 1859 recipe discovered by the celebrated war hero, Colonel Fox. The formula is simple: juniper, coriander, angelica, cassia, liquorice/licorice and bitter orange peel. It's distilled by Thames in London, who also make a sloe gin version called Gentleman Badger (who was not a real person).

Conker Gin (40% ABV) – Presumably named after the practice of distilling conkers to make industrial acetone during war, this is the first offering from Dorset. Locally sourced elderberries, samphire and gorse flower (among others) go in to the pot and the result is a soft, woodsy gin contained within a nice, understated bottle.

Cotswolds (46% ABV) – This distillery is set to focus more on whisky in the future, but right now Cotswolds use a combination of 'steep and boil' and 'vapour infusion' to produce a rather tasty gin. The bottle looks more like a wine or liqueur offering but gets a big thumbs-up from me. Expect to find bright grapefruit and fresh pine notes on the nose. Definitely one to watch.

Dà Mhile (42% ABV) – Dà Mhile (da-mee-ay) has an interesting story. It begins with whisky, which the owner John Savage-Onstwedder commissioned Scotland's Springbank Distillery to make back in 1992. The whisky was named after the Gaelic for 'two-thousand', to commemorate the millennium. Then, in 2010, John was successfully granted a licence to distil on Glynhynod Farm in south west Wales. Their organic 'Farmhouse' gin is made using 20 botanicals and sits in the cool, floral, citrus, herbal flavour camp. They also make a seaweed gin, which undergoes a post-distillation maceration with Newquay seaweed.

D1 Daringly Dry London (40% ABV) – A product of Langley Distillery, D1 is made by distilling juniper, coriander orange and lemon peel, angelica root, cassia bark, almond, liquorice/licorice root and nettles. The nettles are selected by a master tea blender and do give the gin a slightly herbal, citrus character.

Daffy's (43.4% ABV) – Another gin brand who are a touch secretive when it comes to divulging where the product is actually made, although they do admit that they are based in Scotland and use 'an old still' from one of the Scottish Islands. The brand take a 'slow cook' approach towards distillation, which is a 9.5-hour process and only conducted after 4 days of botanical steeping. Nine traditional botanicals are used along with Lebanese mint.

Dr J's (45% ABV) – Founded by a Dr. John Walters, who has a doctorate in biochemistry from Oxford University under his belt, Dr J's is made by the English Spirit Distillery, on the outskirts of Cambridge. Besides making grappa, flavoured vodka, Sambuca and even rum, Dr. John also makes a gin from a combination of juniper, five different varieties of coriander, fresh lemons, limes, oranges, macadamia nuts and grated angelica root. The distillery has five alembic stills all called 'Fanny'.

Durham (40% ABV) – Durham Distillery claims to be the first in the county since the reign of Henry VIII. They also claim to employ the youngest female master distiller in the country. The botanicals used to make Durham gin are undisclosed, but juniper and pink peppercorn are among them. The aroma is quite floral, with chai spices suggesting that cinnamon or cassia plays a part in this gin.

Fifty Eight (43% ABV) – An excellent London Dry style gin from East London's Hackney Downs and produced in a Portuguese alembic still in batches of only 80 bottles at a time.

Forest (42% ABV) – With glorious stone crock bottle screen-printed with paper-cut artwork that is straight out of a Julia Donaldson picture book, Forrest gin promises a lot. Created by Lindsay and Karl Bond, the pair forage some of their botanicals (including wild bilberries, gorse flowers, raspberries and moss) from nearby Macclesfield Forest in the Peak District.

Gin Lane 1751 (40% ABV) – Another bottling from Thames Distillery, produced in partnership with the Bloomsbury Club. The gin features eight classic botanicals and is housed in a rather tasty looking bottle too. They also bottle an Old Tom, 'Victoria' Pink Gin (infused with cocktail bitters) and a 'Royal Strength', bottled at 47%.

Japanese Gin (42% ABV) – Another product of the Cambridge Distillery, this gin is a composite of traditional botanical distillations along with low temperature, vacuum distillates of shiso leaf, sesame and yuzu.

King of Soho (42% ABV) – Thames Distillery in south London make this gin, which is owned by Howard Raymond, son of the property and porn tycoon of Soho, the late Paul Raymond. The packaging is overt to say the least, highly stylised and very much un-gin-like. The liquid on the other hand is – slightly disappointingly – fairly standard stuff, made from 12 botanicals.

Liverpool (42% ABV) – Liverpool's first gin distillery for over 100 years produces a range of three 'complex organic gins', including a 'Rose' flavour and 'Valencian Orange' flavour in addition to their standard release. The distillery is a joint venture between the landlord of the Belvedere Pub and Liverpool Organic Brewery.

Makar (43% ABV) – Glasgow's answer to the gin renaissance. Makar comes from the Glasgow Distillery Company, which was originally founded in the 1770s, then raised from the dead in 2013. The bottle proudly states that it is 'superior juniper-led dry gin' which is more than most bottles give away and for that we should be grateful. The current consulting master distiller is David Robinson, who used to make whisky for The Macallan. The gin is as promised, very juniper forward and as staunchly classic as they come.

Masons (42% ABV) – Masons are another brand getting in on the juniper foraging scene, which is sourced from somewhere in their home county of Yorkshire. Packaging is refreshingly simple and the taste is reflective of this, but in a good way. Masons are one of only a handful of English gin brands that claim to make their own neutral spirit (from sugar beet).

Mayfair (40% ABV) – Another Thames Distillery product, Mayfair uses juniper, angelica root, coriander seed and orris root. The packaging is square and dumpy. I hate it, but I suspect I'm not the target market. The liquid, however, is nice and classic.

Mombasa Club (41.5% ABV) – Probably the most atypical piece of gin packaging around, Mombasa looks more like a flagon of mead than it does a bottle of gin. This gin is named after a famous social club in Mombasa, where British ex-pats used to enjoy a gin or five. It's fittingly spicy, earthy and dirty. All in a good way.

NB (42% ABV) – NB stands for North Berwick, which is a town northeast of Edinburgh. It's the creation of couple Steve and Viv Muir, who gave up successful careers as corporate lawyers to realise their dream of making booze. The packaging is simple and the liquid inside could be classed the same way. The 9 classic botanicals form the basis of a tasty gin, but this might be one gin that has perhaps played things a little too safe.

No. 1 London Original (47% ABV) – Ironically, this is not technically a London Dry gin and you won't see much of this gin in London, even though it's made in London at the Thames Distillery. No. 1 London is a popular choice in Spain (the brand is owned by the Sherry house Gonzalez Byass) and one that I see often lining the shelves in the Spanish Duty Free. It's faintly blue in colour on account of a post-distillation infusion of gardenia flowers.

Pinkster (37.5% ABV) – Bottling a pink coloured gin strikes me as a none too subtle marketing strategy. It's made by Thames Distillers and undergoes a post-distillation maceration with fresh raspberries. I was very pleasantly surprised when I first tried it, as the raspberry is not as potent as it might have been. Underneath all the pink there is a tasty gin – I almost feel sorry for it.

Poetic License (43.2% ABV) – From Sunderland, Poetic License 'Northern Dry Gin' is made in the Poetic License Distillery Bar at the Roker Best Western Hotel. The gin is made using Persian limes and cardamom, for a green Middle Eastern twist. They also produce an Old Tom.

Rock Rose (41.5% ABV) – Nice, ceramic-style packaging from one of Scotland's most northerly gin distilleries. The liquid features a healthy dose of foraged botanicals, including rhodiola rosea, rowan berries, sea buckthorn, blaeberries and verbena.

Shortcross (46% ABV) – Distilled on the Rademon Estate, County Down, Northern Ireland using locally foraged wild clover along with elderflowers, elderberries and green apples. This gin is made by David and Fiona Boyd-Armstrong, the latter being the daughter of property tycoon Frank Boyd, who is one of the richest people in Ireland.

Steam Punk (40% ABV) – This gin is made by the Northumberland Gin Co. using 'peculiar botanicals' and based on an 1892 recipe from someone called Sir Raleigh Holmes-Dunson – who might be fictional… I'm really not sure.

Stovell's (42% ABV) – Stovell's 'Wildcrafted' gin comes from the award-winning Stovell's restaurant in Chobham, Surrey. The team use a rotary evaporator to make concentrated low-pressure distillates of a whole range of foraged botanicals, including oak moss, red clover, sweet flag, rosehips, fennel, woodruff and nettles. The gin has a touch of local honey added to it prior to bottling.

Strathearn (40% ABV) – From one of Scotland's newest and smaller distilleries, based only an hour north of Edinburgh. Strathearn have already released what they call a 'classic gin' made with kaffir lime leaves and star anise, along with a heather and rose infused gin and an 'Oaked Highland Gin' that is matured in small oak casks.

SW4 (40% ABV) – A fairly standard London Dry sale gin, made at the Thames Distillery, from whence it also takes its name, after the postcode.

Trevethan (43% ABV) – Based in Saltash, on the Cornish side of the border between Cornwall and Devon, Trevethan uses a 220-litre (58-US gallon) Portuguese alembic still. The recipe is based on a 1920s gin recipe created by Norman Trevethan, who was a kind of Cornish socialite who obviously felt the need to make his own gin. The present-day Trevethan gin has been re-imagined by Trevethan's grandson, Robert Cuffe, using a range of classic botanicals, along with locally foraged items.

Two Birds (40% ABV) – Two Birds comes from Leicestershire (is there an English county without a gin?) and is made by Mark Gamble in a 25-litre copper still, which size-wise puts it on a par with the still at Thames that is used to make Oxley (it's tiny). The gin is juniper-rich, oily and resiny – in other words, not at all as contemporary as the packaging suggests. Two Birds also bottle a gin geared specifically at cocktails, which ramps the juniper up even more.

Twisted Nose (40% ABV) – Coming from the capital city of the ancient Kingdom of Wessex, Winchester, Twisted Nose make a range of flavoured spirits and a gin. The botanical selection includes juniper, grapefruit zest, cassia bark, fennel seed, orris, angelica, lavender and, most notably, locally-grown watercress. Interestingly, the Romans used to call watercress 'nasturtium', which means twisted nose.

EUROPE

Audemus Pink Pepper (44% ABV) – Situated in the heart of Cognac, this distillery produces a spicy Pink Pepper gin using low-pressure distillation that captures all the aromatics of peppercorn, but keeps the other botanicals (which include honey, vanilla and cardamom) in play too. Audemus also make an umami spirit by distilling capers.

Berlin Dry Gin (42% ABV) – Challenging Christian Jensen for simplicity of packaging, the white space on this bottle is a fair representation of the ethereal softness of the gin inside. The recipe is designed to capture 'the soul of Berlin' and uses fresh cucumber, mallow and sweet woodruff, among others. Each batch is individually numbered from 1 to 9999.

Blackwater No. 5 (41.5% ABV) – Ireland's Blackwater Distillery was founded by whiskey writer Peter Mulryan in 2015. The Blackwater Valley, just north of Cork, was an important area for spice shipping during the 19th century, which was the inspiration for the No. 5 recipe. Gin is made using a 300-litre (79-US gallon) still and on the nose, the cardamom and juniper notes prevail. Blackwater have also recently released a juniper cask-aged gin matured in a 50-litre (13-US gallon) custom-made barrel.

Bobby's Schiedam (42% ABV) – Dutch Courage mixed with Indonesian spice is how owner and distiller Sebastien van Bokkel describes this gin. The gin is named 'Bobby' after an Indonesian immigrant to The Netherlands, who settled in the 1950s and had a passion for infusing spices from the East in to Dutch spirit. Made at the Herman Jansen Distillery in Schiedam, it uses organic juniper, fennel and rosehips among other botanicals. The packaging is a nice fusion of traditional and modern Dutch design, and a little Indonesian thrown in for good measure.

Buss (40% ABV) – The Buss No.509 range of gins is made by Belgium's Buss Spirits, which was created by Serge Buss. The company also produce Raspberry, Persian Peach, and Pink Grapefruit flavoured gins, but for their White Rain expression the botanicals include juniper, coriander, angelica, liquorice/licorice, vanilla, cardamom, iris, verbena, orange and lemon - among others. It also features a hearty hint of marjoram at its core, bringing full herbal notes to the fore.

Cork (40% ABV) – Cork Dry Gin has supposedly been in production in Cork since 1793. These days it is manufactured in the enormous Irish Distillers production plant at Middleton Distillery, which is a subsidiary of Pernod Ricard. Around half of all the gin consumed in Ireland is Cork Dry. It's of the compounded denomination, of questionable quality, cheap as hell, and available everywhere throughout the Emerald Isle.

Cockney's (44.2% ABV) – Although this gin sounds like it's from London, it is in fact made in Aalst, Belgium. The recipe is purportedly from a Londoner who set up a distillery in Ghent, in 1838, and it features 15 secret botanicals. The gin is citrus led, mineral and razor-sharp.

Dingle (42.6% ABV) – Dingle is a Irish whiskey distillery based in County Kerry, but they also make a vapour-infused gin. Rowan berry, bog myrtle, chervil and heather are among the botanical checklist. The gin takes on a cooked berry character with undertones of juniper and eucalyptol.

Elephant (45%)- Taking some design cues from a certain primate themed gin that also comes from Germany, Elephant uses a selection of unusual African botanicals like Baobab, the Buchu plant, Devil's Claw and African Wormwood. Fifteen percent of profits made from this gin goes towards the preservation of elephants in Africa.

Ferdinand's Saar (44% ABV) – Any product containing Schiefer Riesling wine gets my vote. This gin from the Avadis Distillery, Wincheringen, Germany, also uses 30 different organic botanicals (only Monkey 47 uses more). The ones that stand out the most are the florals: lavender, lemon thyme, hop blossom and rose. Others include sloes, rose hip and thyme. Definitely one to watch.

Glendalough (40% ABV) – This new Irish distillery is focusing on the history of Irish distilling and mainly on whiskey and poitín, but they also make a gin. It's really worth visiting their website and watching the video that shows the distillery's historical inspiration – it has a level of production quality normally only seen in Hollywood blockbusters. Their gin changes seasonally (four releases a year) based on whatever forgeable matter they can recover from the Wicklow countryside.

Granit Bavarian (42% ABV) – Another German gin with an emphasis on raiding the local larder. Granit is made by the Penninger family, in Hauzenburg, and uses (among others) lemon balm, melissa, bald money (similar to lovage) and gentian root foraged from the Bavarian forest. It's rested in earthenware pots and filtered through granite rubble – hence, the name – before bottling. You even get a lump of granite attached to the bottle (no, really).

Helsinki (47% ABV) – This Finnish distillery was set up in 2014 to make whisky, but the team of experienced distillers are also making a gin that flavoured with Finnish lingonberries, Seville orange, lemon peels, fennel and rose petals. The lingonberries take on a cooked flavour after a long maceration and distillation, which is tempered by the rose and green fennel notes.

Isjford (44% ABV) – Greenland's only gin is, as you might expect, cut with water from melted icebergs. There are 12 botanicals in the recipe and the emphasis here is on smoothness (thanks to the water) rather than botanical complexity. The gin is mineral, sweet, and slightly saline. The packaging is nicely understated.

Larios (40% ABV) – Larios is Spain's biggest selling gin brand. Despite the bargain price tag (around € 10 for a 1-litre/¼-US gallon bottle), it's surprisingly good stuff and has recently been joined by Larios 12, a more premium offering that aims to tap in to Spain's lucrative quality gin market.

Mikeller (44% ABV) – From Copenhagen, Denmark, this gin is made using a level helping of Simcoe hops, which gives it an earthy floral aroma. Unlike some hopped gins this one is subtle enough to sit in the 'modified classic' flavour camp.

Napue (46.3% ABV) – Hailing from the Kyrö Distillery company (a former cheese factory) in Isokyrö, Finland, this gin is based on a sourced rye spirit and is distilled with birch leaves, sea buckthorn, cranberries, spruce wood and meadowsweet, along with another seven more traditional botanicals.

Nginious! (45% ABV) – With some of the most 'out there' packaging of any spirit I have ever seen, this Swiss gin is likely to divide opinion. It's the carefully conceived brainchild of Oliver Ullrich and Ralph Villager, who first met on a spirits training course in London. Distillation of the 18 botanicals is done in four separate batches where aromatically similar ingredients are grouped together. The result is a fruity, sweet-smelling gin. I love it.

Nordisk Brænderi (44.8% ABV) – Anders Bilgram's Danish gin is inspired by his adventures sailing around the Arctic Circle. It uses qajaasat, a low-growing flower native to Greenland, Swedish cloudberries, sea buckthorn from Denmark, wild rose flowers and so on… The base spirit is distilled from fermented molasses and Danish cider. Distillation is by vapour infusion and is done in 3 batches that combine similar ingredients.

OMG (45% ABV) – The Žufánek family are based in the Czech Republic and produce two gin expressions: OMG (Oh My Gin) and OMFG (Oh My Finest Gin). I'm not even kidding you. OMG uses 16 botanicals including lavender flowers and blossoms from the Czech national tree, the small-leaved linden. OMFG builds upon the work of OMG, adding in damiana, a chamomile-like flower known for its aphrodisiacal properties (OMFG!).

Saffron (40% ABV) – Guess what this gin is flavoured with? If the name didn't make it obvious enough the colour certainly will – it looks like orange soda. The gin is made by respected Dijon-based liqueur producer, Gabriel Boudier, who are masters of maceration. This is apparent in the gin, which, while being saffron dominant, is not the hailstorm one might expect. This is a largely a juniper and coriander driven product, but I still find the day-glo orange a bit off-putting.

Sloane's (40% ABV) – Named after the botanist Sir Hans Sloane, who was largely responsible for the Chelsea Physic Garden and loaned his name to the London's Sloane's Square, this London Dry Gin is made at the Toorank Distillery in the Netherlands. The gin is a composite of 10 separate botanical distillations and sits comfortably in the London Dry flavour camp.

Spirit of Hven (40% ABV) – One of the world's most experimental whisky distilleries is also dabbling with gin. Master Distiller Henric Molin set up his distillery on the island of Hven in the Öresund Strait between Denmark and Sweden back in 2008. He has since established a groundbreaking oak laboratory for assessing the effects of maturation in spirits. No surprise then that their Organic Gin undergoes a short ageing before the final distillation run. The gin is intense with citrus character, which translates to bright spice on the palate.

Strane (47.4% ABV) – This gin from Pär Caldenby at the Smögen Distillery, in Sweden, is made from a combination of three distillates: citrus, herbal and juniper. The gin is, as stated on the label, 'London Dry' in style, and can be purchased at the standard 47.4%, 'Navy Strength' (57.1%), or ludicrous 'Uncut Strength' (76%).

Santamania (41% ABV) – This distillery in Madrid, Spain, is sometimes compared to Sipsmith in London. They're in the process of upgrading their operation right now as demand is quickly outpacing production capacity. The gin is made from a base of Tempranillo grapes and includes a range of classic botanicals along with raspberry and, unusually, Spanish pistachio. Santamania have also released a limited run of 'Reserva' gin, which is aged in French oak barrels.

Sylvius (45% ABV) – The fact that 'Dr. Sylvius' categorically did not invent genever was clearly no deterrent to Distilleerderij Onder de Boompjes, in Schiedam, when it came to naming their product. The gin uses 10 botanicals, all classic examples except for the caraway, which is perhaps the one that shines through the most along with cinnamon and lemon.

Three Corner (42% ABV) – A product of the legendary A. Van Wees distillery in Amsterdam, this gin uses only two botanicals: juniper and lemon (you have to wonder why it isn't called 'Two Corner'). You can be forgiven for thinking that more goes in there though, the juniper is heavy, spicy and oily, and the lemon comes through bright and floral.

Vilnius (45% ABV) – If you've brushed up on your legal classifications, you might remember that gins from the Lithuanian town of Vilnius are protected under EU law. Vilnius Gin happens to be the only gin from that town right now and it is mostly citrus driven but pepped up by the inclusion of dill seeds.

Vincent Van Gogh (47% ABV) – This gin was launched by Royal Dirkzwager Distilleries, in Schiedam, The Netherlands, in 1999, which makes it positively ancient. It uses the same ten botanicals as Bombay Sapphire, but in this instance they are distilled separately in small pot stills before being blended together with neutral spirit.

Vor (38% ABV) – Made at the Eimverk Distillery in Gadabær, Iceland, Vor gin is a fantastic example of how local terroir can shape spirits. Everything, from the barley used to make the neutral spirit, down to all of the botanicals, is grown in Iceland. The quirky list of local flavours includes Icelandic moss, rhubarb, angelica, creeping thyme, sweet kelp, kale and crowberries. The packaging is equally interesting and despite the relatively low alcohol content it almost seems a shame to mix this gin.

NORTH AMERICA

Aura Gin (40% ABV) – This gin is made in at the Yukon Shine Distillery in Whitehorse, Yukon Territory, amidst Canada's vast northern expanse. Potato spirit is used as the base (made from the famous Yukon Gold variety). The gin is vapour infused and citrus-forward on account of the three types of citrus in the 12 strong botanical list.

Barr Hill (45% ABV) – Todd Hardie is a beekeeper by trade, but the need to diversify his Vermont-based operation, located on the banks of the Lamoille River, plus an interest in his extended family's whisky operation in Scotland meant that a future in distilling was on the cards. Head distiller Ryan Christiansen makes two Barr Hill expressions; Barr Hill Gin, which is slightly sweetened with a wonderfully floral raw honey, and Barr Hill Reserve Tom Cat, which is matured in oak casks. Both of them are excellent.

BIG Gin (47% ABV) – Produced by Captive Spirits based just outside of Seattle, the name of this gin is in reference to its BIG flavour, but also for distiller Ben Capdevielle's nickname for his dad - Big Jim. The still is made by Vendome, who are famous for their bourbon stills. The flavour is heavy on the juniper, with some soft spicy notes and a kick of pepper provided by the Tasmanian pepper berry.

Black River (43% ABV) – Based at the Sweetgrass Farm Winery in Maine, Black River is a London Dry style gin that also uses locally foraged Maine blueberries in its recipe. The nose is as blue as they come, with sweet juicy juniper and soft forest fruit notes. Black River also make a 'Cranberry Gin', wherein the cranberries are infused into the gin after distillation.

Bluecoat (47% ABV) – American gin doesn't get more patriotic than this. Bluecoat is named after the jackets worn by the American forces during their fight for independence. It's made by Philadelphia Distilling and was launched way back in 2006. The gin is quite contemporary in style, being largely citrus driven. You can taste the dulcet tones of Walter Cronkite in every sip.

Boreal (45% ABV) – The Vikre distillery in Duluth, Minnesota, make three gin expressions: Juniper, Cedar and Spruce. Despite all being a type of tree, each expression follows a different path from the relatively classic 'Juniper' which is made with rhubarb through to sappy and spicy 'Cedar' and finally on to the herbaceous and evergreen 'Spruce'.

Brooklyn (40% ABV) – If it's an attractive bottle you're after you could do a lot worse than Brooklyn gin from, yes – Brooklyn. From the brass disc on the front to the mottled blue glass Art-Deco-inspired bottle, this product certainly looks the part. The gin is made from fresh citrus peels and 'hand cracked' juniper berries – which sounds a lot better than saying 'squashed', I suppose. It's citrus-forward, medium-bodied and good for mixing with.

Breuckelen Glorious Gin (45% ABV) – Pronounced 'brook-len' it's not hard to imagine where this gin takes its inspiration from (it's the original Dutch spelling of Brooklyn). It was close enough to create a legal dispute between Breuckelen gin and Brooklyn Distillery back in 2011, which appears to have been settled now. These days the official line is that this 'Glorious Gin' is produced by the Breuckelen Distillery, which ironically isn't in Brooklyn – it's made at the Warwick Valley Winery in the Hudson Valley, NY. The gin is made using grapefruit and rosemary among others, and is cut with NY tap/faucet water.

Cold River (47% ABV) – This Maine-based distillery was once toured by the Chase family and became the inspiration for setting up their own vodka brand in England. Cold River Gin looks like a bottle of expensive olive oil, but it's definitely gin inside. The product is made from a base of potato spirit then redistilled with seven botanicals that all sit within the 'old favourites' category of ingredients.

Corsair (44% ABV) – This distillery is making a good name for itself in whiskey, but they have also released two 'gin' expressions (and I do use the term loosely) – Corsair Genever is malty and warm smelling, with hints of citrus peel and spice. Corsair 'Steampunk' gin has smoked grain and hops added to the botanical list, which turns it into a kind of 'gin-with-a-cigarette' sort of experience.

Four Peel Gin (44% ABV) – Guess what? This gin is made from four types of citrus fruit: orange, lemon, grapefruit and lime. It's more a citrus vodka than a gin, but it's a good one at that and should fit the bill for all your citrus-led gin needs. The Watershed Distillery is based in Columbus, Ohio.

Greenhat (41.6% ABV) – New Columbia Distillers are one of handful of American gin distilleries that are making an impact in Europe. The packaging helps, which seems to have taken images from a 1930's hat catalogue. The standard expression is decidedly green, with fennel, celery seed, cardamom and lime all coming to the fore. Greenhat also bottle a Navy Strength expression (57%) plus seasonal releases that include a hybrid spirit called Ginavit – a combination of gin and, caraway-scented akvavit.

Greenhook (47% ABV) – This Brooklyn-based distillery is one of only a handful of US operations using a copper vacuum still to make their gin. Their 'American Dry Gin' is more floral than a classic London Dry, with punchy aromas of Asian spices and clean citrus. Water reveals bags of sweet spices. They also bottle an Old Tom, which undergoes a short maturation, and a gin-based plum liqueur.

Halcyon (46% ABV) – The Bluewater Distillery is run by John Lundin in Everett, Washington. And (if you'll allow me) it's very much 'Lundin Dry' that we're looking at here, and a great example of it too. The gin uses the same 8 botanicals as Beefeater and also undergoes a 24-hour maceration prior to distillation. The still is a tiny copper alembic and direct-fired.

Koval (47% ABV) – Chicago's Koval Distillery is better known for its range of Scandinavian looking and sounding whiskies, but they have recently launched a gin. The packaging is reminiscent of Dodd's Gin being geometric and achingly cool. The gin is grassy eucalyptus, citrus peels and menthol.

Long Table (44% ABV) – This Vancouver-based distillery bottles three gin expressions and their 'London Dry' is a great example of a classic-style Martini gin. They also make a 'Bourbon Barrel Aged Gin', which is matured quickly in 30-litre (8-US gallon) casks, as well as a 'Cucumber Gin' made with fresh cucumbers.

Okanagan (40% ABV) – This distillery in Kelowna, British Columbia, has a history of producing eau de vie and fruit liqueurs. Four botanicals go in to Okanagan Gin: juniper, coriander, spruce and rose. The effect is an earthy yet ethereal liquid that sits between classic and contemporary.

Seagram's (40% ABV) – Still the biggest selling American gin, Seagram's is cheap but not half bad. Weirdly it has a slightly yellow hue to it which used to be attributed to a short period of barrel ageing, but now simply goes unmentioned. Of course there are a range of Seagram's flavours to choose from too: peach, pineapple, apple, lime…

Smooth Ambler (40% ABV) – This 'Appalachian distiller', based in West Virginia, primarily focus on rye and bourbon whiskey, but they also make two expressions of gin. Smooth Ambler use a classic botanical formala but the focus of their Greenbrier gin shifts to spice and citrus over traditional juniper characteristics. Smooth Ambler also make a barrel aged gin that is matured in 180-litre (47-US gallon) bourbon casks for 3-months. The distillery produces its own neutral spirit from a mash bill of locally grown corn, wheat and malted barley.

Spring 44 (40% ABV) – A Colorado based distillery making juniper-forward gin (as indicated by the huge macro-shot of a juniper berry on the label) using Rocky mountain spring water.

Victoria (45% ABV) – Probably Canada's best known craft gin, Victoria gin is made from 9 classic botanicals and one secret 'wild-gathered' botanical. The distillery was sold in Summer 2015 to the Marker Group, who, in the near future, plan to move production to a larger facility.

REST OF THE WORLD

9 Botanicals Mescal (45% ABV) – From Pierde Almas Distillery in Mexico's Oaxaca region. A botanical Mescal is not something you see every day and this product reminds us why. It's largely the charred and smoky Mexican spirit that wins this battle, with perhaps some fruit and burnt juniper husk coming through in the finish.

Botanic Australis Gin (40% ABV) – This gin is made in Northern Queensland, Australia at the Mt. Uncle Distillery (there is a Mt. Aunty too) which was founded in 2001. All 14 botanicals are native to Australia and most of them I have never heard of – they include: riberry, finger limes, bunya nut, river mint and no less than three different varieties of eucalyptus. The taste is green, clean and very herbal.

Four Pillars (41.8% ABV) – Perhaps the Southern Hemisphere's best known gin, the Four Pillars Distillery is located in the Yarra River Valley, outside Melbourne. Among an array of classical botanicals, Four Pillars include Australian Lemon myrtle and Tasmanian pepper, both of which are well represented in the finished products, which seem to have a eucalyptus streak running through them. Four Pillars also bottle a Barrel Aged Gin (43.8% ABV) and a navy-strength 'Gunpowder Proof' at 58.8% ABV.

Lighthouse (42% ABV) – I first encountered this gin at a Brooklyn restaurant called Lighthouse, but it turned out to be coincidence as this gin is made on New Zealand's northern island. The Greytown Distillery uses a selection of botanicals, some of which are specific to New Zealand, from New Zealand navel oranges to the lesser-known 'kawakawa' and 'yen ben lemon' (!)

Rogue Society (40% ABV) – Rogue Society is another great New Zealand gin with awesome presentation (with a nod to Holland) and a rather lovely website to boot. It uses 12 classic botanicals and a John Dore to produce a spiced juniper-themed gin. The team has also produced a handful of special releases, too.

Principe De Los Apostles Mate Gin (40% ABV) – I tried this gin on a recent trip to Argentina (where it comes from) and enjoyed it a lot. It's minty, grapefruit and slightly nutty thanks to the inclusion of yerba mate in the botanical list. Pretty label too.

Vaiõne (40.2% ABV) – With a base spirit distilled from whey on equipment salvaged from a milking parlour, Vaiõne gin is more a celebration of New Zealand's dairy industry than its flora and fauna. Vaiõne 'Pacific' gin has a lemon meringue colour to it thanks to a post-distillation maceration with fresh citrus. The flavour is citrus-dominant, feeling more like a citrus vodka than a gin.

West Winds (40% ABV) – Based on the Margaret River in western Australia, Gidgie Distilleries produce West Winds Gin in three expressions. The flagship 'Sabre' is made using 12 botanicals that include lemon myrtle, lime peel and wattle seed – it's citrus-forward with nice baking spices tethering it back down to earth. 'Cutlass' is cut to 50% and includes the native bush tomato in its botanical make up. Finally, there's 'Broadside' – their navy-strength offering, bottled at 58% ABV.

GLOSSARY

Botanical Anything that grows (fruit, root, bark, seed, herb, flower). Used to flavour London Dry Gin, Distilled Gin and Genever.

Bourbon cask 180–200-litre (48–53-US gallon) charred American oak cask.

Charred (cask) A barrel or cask that as been burnt on the inside with an open flame. This process caramelizes wood sugars and opens the grain of the cask, typically speeding up the maturation process and imparts 'brown' or burnt flavours in to a spirit.

Cut/Cutting Can be used in relation to 'cutting' the Heads or Tails of a distillate, or when cutting a distillate with neutral spirit, water etc.

Ester A chemical compound formed by the interaction of an acid and an alcohol. Typically smells fruity and floral.

Floor Malting Traditional process of malting barley, where the grains are spread evenly across a large floor space and regularly turned over typically a week long period (but variable).

GNS Grain Neutral Spirit (see Neutral Spirit).

Heads The first liquid distillate to flow off a still; typically 3–10% of the entire run. The heads are usually discarded because they contain dissolved oils that can make a spirit cloudy in appearance.

Heart The drinkable body of a gin distillation run that comes after the Heads and before the Tails (ie. the good stuff).

Moutwijn/Malt wine A triple-distilled spirit made from a fermented mash of barley, corn, wheat, or rye, or combination thereof. Malt wine is generally distilled first in a column-style still, then redistilled twice in a pot still. Malt wine can be used in a number of different ways to create jonge, oude, corenwijn, or 100% moutwijn genever. It can also be distilled a fourth time, with juniper or other botanicals.

Neutral Spirit Spirit distilled above 96% ABV and made from cereal, potato, grape, molasses, or any other sugar or starch source. Can be denoted as Grain Neutral Spirit, which infers that cereal is the base product.

Reflux The (repeated) condensing of vapours within a still before it has reached the condenser proper. Reflux is controlled by temperature and time and is one way of producing a lighter spirit.

Supercritical CO_2 extraction A process used to extract essential oils and distillates. Carbon dioxide is forced through the medium to be extracted (such as a botanical in solid or liquid form) under very high pressure. The gas becomes too warm to be a liquid and too squashed together to be a gas, so it sits somewhere in the middle: a supercritical fluid. Carbon dioxide in this state is an incredibly powerful solvent and its extremely high pressure – comparable to the pressure at the bottom of an ocean – ensuring that it is forced deep within the cell structure of organic materials.

Tails The low alcohol leftovers of a gin distillation run. Sometimes the Tails are distilled over until the pot is run nearly dry; other times they refer to the slushy mix that is left in the still.

Toasted (cask) A barrel or cask that has been grilled on the inside over a period of time (typically over a minute) by means of radiant heat. This is a less intensive process than charring that imparts softer, baked, nutty, and toasted flavours in to a spirit.

Tannin/tannic Coloured substance extracted from wood that gives a sensation like a drying bitterness on the tongue. Derivatives of gallic acid.

Vapour Infusion A method of botanical flavour extraction wherein spirit passes through a botanical rack or chamber in its vaporous form.

Virgin (wood/oak) A cask/barrel that has not previously held any spirit or wine (i.e. Bourbon, Sherry).

Volatile Molecules with evaporative tendencies that distil easily and, assuming they are not odourless, can also be smelled easily.

Wash Alcoholic beer produced from the fermentation of mashed cereals.

INDEX

7 Dials 216
9 Botanicals Mescal 220

Adnam's 48, 69, 78–9
alcohol by volume (ABV) 48, 55, 70
Anchor 176
Ancient Mariner 216
angelica 66–7
Anno 216
Argentina 221
Atom 80–2
Audemus Pink Pepper 218
Aura gin 219
Australia 220, 221
Austria 150
Aviation 69, 177

Barr Hill gin 219
barrels 18, 31, 43, 56, 221
bartenders 38–9, 43
Bath gin 216
Beckett's 216
Beefeater 42, 53, 68, 76, 83–4
beer 30, 31, 32, 41, 200
Belgium
   distillation methods 33
   genever classification 72
   genever history 14, 16–17
   legislation 40, 41
   malt wine 16, 56
   modern production 56, 156–7, 172–3, 218
   World War II 40
Berkeley Square 69, 93–4
Berlin Dry gin 218
BIG gin 219
Black River gin 220
Blackdown 216
Blackwater No. 5 gin 218
Blackwoods 132, 216
blending 54
Bloom 69, 94–5
Bluecoat 220
Boë 93, 216
Bols 17, 170–1
Bombay Sapphire 42, 53, 68, 85–7, 93
Boodles 93, 216
Boord distillery 29
Booth's gin 28
Boreal 220
Borovi ka 72
Botanic Australis gin 220
botanicals 57–67, 221
   aroma 55, 57
   foraged 132
   genever 56
   low-pressure distillation 52
   macerating and boiling 49
   modern usage 43, 47, 71
   one-shot/multi-shot gin 53
   use in recipes 32, 33, 70
   vapour infusion 50
The Botanist 69, 149
bottling 55
Boxer 216
Brecon 216

Breuckelen Glorious gin 220
Bristol 29
Britain 42, 216–18
Brockmans 93, 216
Brooklyn gin 220
Bulldog 93, 216
Burleigh's (West 45) 68, 131
Buss range 218

Cambridge 216
Cameron Bridge Distillery 132, 139
Canada 220
Caorunn 68, 134
cardamom 61
cassia 64–5
Chase 48, 68, 69, 88–9
Chilgrove 216
Cinchona bark 34–5, 82, 189
cinnamon 64–5
Citadelle 42, 68, 152–3
City of London 216
Clover Club 202–3
Cockney's gin 218
cocktails 36, 37, 38–40, 43
   Clover Club 202–3
   Dry Martini 186–8
   French 75 194–5
   Fruit Cup 213–15
   Gimlet 196–7
   gin & homemade tonic 189–91
   Gin & Juice 206–7
   Holland House 208–9
   Negroni 204–5
   Purl 200–1
   Salted Lime Rickey 198–9
   Whipper Gin Fizz 192–3
Cold River gin 220
Colonel Fox 216
compounding 54, 55
Conker gin 217
corenwijn 56, 73, 150
coriander 49, 60
Cork gin 218
Corsair geneva 220
Cotswolds 217
Cruikshank, George 26–7, 31
cut/cutting 49, 53, 55, 221
Czech Republic 150, 219

Dà Mhile 217
Daffy's 217
Darnley's View 69, 121
De Kuyper 154–5
Death's Door 69, 178
Denmark 219
DI Daringly Dry London 217
Dingle Distillery 218
distillation 51–3
   craft distilling 43, 51, 88, 112, 174
   early gin recipes 20, 21
   laws 17, 19, 26–8, 30–1
   low-pressure 52
   neutral spirit 48
   origins 10–11, 14
   re-distillation 47, 70
   steep and boil 49

still development 29, 32–3
distilled gin 70
Dodd's 53, 68, 127–8
Dr J's 217
dry gin 33, 38–9, 71
Dry Martini 186–8
Durham Distillery 217
Dutch Courage 20
Dutch East Indies Company (VOC) 17, 18, 170

East London Liquor Company 68, 69, 90–1
Eden Mill 69, 135–6
Edinburgh gin 69, 137–8
Elephant gin 218
England 42, 76–131, 216–18
   see also London
Europe 150–73, 218–19

feints 49
Ferdinand's Saar 218
FEW Distillery 69, 179
Fifty Eight 217
Fifty Pounds 68, 121–2
Filliers Distillery 56, 69, 156–7, 171
Finland 218, 219
flavour 47, 54, 57, 68–9
Fleischmann's gin 38
Ford's 68, 122–3
Forest 217
Four Peel gin 220
Four Pillars 221
France 14, 48, 72, 150, 152–3, 162, 218, 219
French 75 cocktail 194–5
Fruit Cup 213–15

G&J Distillers 55, 92–6
genever
   in America 38–9
   Belgian ban 40
   birth 15, 16–18
   classification 72, 73
   in London 19–20, 21
   manufacture 56
geographical indication 72
Germany 14, 72, 150, 164–5, 218
Gilbey's Distillery 28, 39
Gilpin's 69, 123
Gimlet 196–7
gin
   classification 70–3
   consumption figures 42, 183
   early recipes 20, 21–2
   gin craze 23–5, 30
   & homemade tonic 189–91
   loss of popularity 40–1
   manufacture 47–73
   modern revival 42–3
Gin Acts 26–7, 28
Gin de Mahón 68, 72, 158–9
Gin Fizz, Whipper 192–3
Gin & Juice 206–7
Gin Lane, etching 25
Gin Lane gin 217
Gin Mare 69, 160–1
Gin palaces 30–1, 37
Ginebra San Miguel 183

ginger 22
Glendalough Distillery 218
GNS (Grain Neutral Spirit) 21, 47, 48, 79, 221
Gordon's 29, 39, 42, 48, 53, 68, 139–41, 174
graanjenever 73, 150
Granit Bavarian 218
Greenall's 68, 95, 120
Greenhat 220
Greenhook 220
Greenland 219
G'Vine 48, 68, 69, 162

Halcyon 220
Half Hitch 69, 97
Hayman's 42, 68, 98–9, 120
heads 49, 221
Helsinki Distillery 218
Hendrick's 42, 48, 54, 69, 144–5
Hepple gin 68, 108–9
Hernö 68, 163
history of gin 7, 10–43
Holland House 208–9
Holland's gin 38, 39, 73

Iceland 219
industrial production 17–18, 28–9, 32, 35, 38
Ireland 218
Isjford 219
Italy 150

Japanese gin 217
Jensen's 53, 68, 71, 100–1
Jonge genever 56, 73
juniper 58–9
    distillation process 49
    medicinal uses 12–13, 17, 20
    use in spirits 14–15, 16, 21, 43, 70, 72
Juniper Green 68, 123–4
Junípero 42

King of Soho 217
korenwijn 16, 56, 73
Koval 220

The Lakes Distillery 68, 102–3
Lamplighter gin 28
Langley 48, 53, 69, 97, 104–7
Larios gin 219
legislation 17, 19, 26–8, 30–1
Leopold's 180
Lighthouse gin 221
liquorice/licorice 62
Lithuania 72, 219
Liverpool 29, 33, 217
London
    genever introduction 19–20
    Gin Acts 26–7, 28
    gin craze 23–5, 30
    gin making 21–2, 28–9, 83, 97
The London Distillery Company 127–8
London Dry Gin 71
    manufacture 33, 41, 49, 53–5, 132
    modern revival 43
Long Table 220
Luxembourg 14

maceration 47, 49
Makar 217
Malt wine (Moutwijn) 16, 21, 33, 56, 73, 171, 221
Martin Miller's 42, 68, 106
Martini 39, 40, 41, 186–8, 203
Masons 217
Mayfair 217

medicinal uses 12–13, 15, 17, 34, 36
Mexico 220
Mikeller 219
Minorca 72, 158
Mombasa Club 217
Monkey 47 gin 69, 164–5
Moorland Spirit Co. 108–9
Moutwijn (Malt) wine 16, 21, 33, 56, 73, 171, 221
multi-shot gin 53, 54, 55

Napue 219
NB gin 217
Negroni 204–5
the Netherlands
    consumption figures 42
    distillation methods 33, 41
    genever production 14, 16–18
    immigrants to America 38
    malt wine 56
    modern revival 17, 48, 56, 154–5, 166–71, 218, 219
    World War II 40
neutral spirit 21, 47–8, 79, 221
New Western style 43, 72–3, 174
New York Distilling Co. 181
New Zealand 221
Nginious! 219
No.1 London Original 217
Nolet Distillery 48, 69, 166–7
Nordisk Brænderi 219
North America
    cocktails 38–9, 40
    gin classification 55
    modern production 43, 174–82, 219–20
    New Western gin 43, 72, 174
    Prohibition 39, 40, 174
    spread of gin 38–9

Okanagan 220
Old Raj 68, 146
Old Tom Gin
    cocktails 38, 39
    loss of popularity 41
    modern revival 43, 71, 100–1, 163, 169
    origins 29, 32–3
OMG gin 219
one-shot gin 53
Opihr 69, 95–6
orris 63
Oude genever 56, 73
Oxley 69, 124–5

Philippines 42, 183
Pickering's 68, 69, 147–8
Pinkster 217
Plymouth Gin 29, 33, 35, 68, 72, 110–11
Poetic License 217
Poland 150
Portobello Road 68, 125–6
Portugal 43, 150
Principe De Los Apostles Mate gin 221
proof spirit 21
pubs 31
punch 36–7, 213
Purl 200–1

quinine 34, 32

Rickey, Salted Lime 198–9
Rock Rose 217
Rogue Society 221
Romania 150

Sacred 54, 69, 112–13
Saffron gin 47, 219
St. George Spirits 69, 182
Santamania 219
Scandinavia 150, 163, 218
Scotland 29, 32, 132–49, 216–19
Seagram's 42, 174, 220
Shortcross 218
Silent Pool 68, 114–15
Sipsmith 42, 53, 68, 116–17
Sloane's gin 219
Sloe gin 79, 99, 130, 210–12
Slovakia 42, 72, 150
Smooth Ambler 220
Southwestern Distillery 118–19
Spain 42, 72, 150, 158, 160, 219
spice trade 15, 17, 22
Spirit of Hven 219
Spring 44 gin 220
Steam Punk 218
Steinhäger 72
stills
    Carterhead 50, 92
    column 32, 48, 50, 56, 78
    continuous 56, 71
    development 29, 32–3
    pot 56, 84
    rotavap 52
Stokerij van Damme 172–3
Stovell's 218
Strane 219
Strathearn 218
supercritical CO_2 extraction 221
supermarket gin 54, 55, 93
SW4 Gin 218
Sweden 163, 219
Switzerland 150, 219
Sylvius 17, 219

tails 50, 221
tannin/tannic 221
Tanqueray 42, 48, 53, 68, 69, 139, 141–3
Tarquin's 53, 68, 118–19
Thames 120–6
Thomas Dakin 53, 69, 92–3, 96
Three Corner 219
tonic water 34–5, 41, 189–91
Trevethan 218
Twisted Nose 218
Two Birds 218

Vaiōne gin 221
vapour infusion 50, 221
Victoria gin 220
Vilnius gin 72, 219
Vincent Van Gogh gin 219
vodka 41, 42, 47, 48, 53
Vor gin 219

Warner Edwards 68, 129–30
water, adding 55, 56
West 45 Distillery 131
West Winds 221
Whipper Gin Fizz 192–3
World War II 40

Xoriguer Distillery 72, 158

Zuidam 56, 68, 69, 168–9

ACKNOWLEDGMENTS

The biggest thanks, as always, must go to Laura and Dexter for allowing me the time, space and patience to make this book happen.

Big thanks to Tom as well – my other partner in life.

Thanks to the teams at Whistling Shop and Surfside for being generally awesome and for being curious bartenders.

Addie and Sari for tasty photos and their boundless energy for these books.

Thanks once again to Nathan, Geoff and the team at RPS: Julia, Leslie, Christina, Gordana and Cindy.

Jake Burger, Jose Carlos, Sam Carter, Hannah Lanfear, Duncan McRae, John Parsons, Tim Stones, Dennis Tamse and Dan Warner, and to Ginge Warneford for putting the 'badass' in to ambassador. Thanks to all the distillers and producers who allowed me to poke and probe their at their operations, in particular: Jamie Baxter, Jared Brown, Kris Dickenson, Nik Fordham, Tarquin Leadbetter, John McCarthy, Charles Maxwell, Tom Nichol, Desmond Payne, Darren Rook, Nick Strangeway and Gilbert Van Zuidam. Phillip Duff for help with Genever.

Finally, Walter and Lucy Riddel, thanks for allowing me in to your home and serving me lobster. Ian and Hilary Hart, for allowing me in to your home and serving me cyanide.

ABOUT THE AUTHOR

Tristan Stephenson is an award-winning bar operator, bartender, barista, chef, some-time journalist, and bestselling author of the *Curious Bartender* series of drinks books. He is the co-founder of London-based Fluid Movement, a globally renowned drinks consultancy firm, and half the brains behind the drinks programs at some of the world's top drinking and eating destinations. In 2009 he was ranked 3rd in the UK Barista Championships. He was awarded UK bartender of the year in 2012 and in the same year was included in *London Evening Standard*'s 'Top 1000 most influential Londoners'.

Having started his career in the kitchens of various Cornish restaurants, Tristan was eventually given the task of designing cocktails and running bar operations for Jamie Oliver's Fifteen restaurant (in Cornwall) back in 2007. He then went on to work for the world's biggest premium drinks company, Diageo, for two years. After co-founding Fluid Movement in 2009, Tristan opened two bars in London – Purl, his first, in 2010, and then the Worship Street Whistling Shop in 2011. Worship Street Whistling Shop was awarded *Time Out London*'s best new bar in 2011 and has been placed in the 'World's Fifty Best Bars' for three consecutive years. *Time Out London*'s top 25 bars roundup in 2012 included all three Fluid Movement venues, including Dach & Sons, a New York inspired hot-dog, beer and bourbon restaurant that opened in 2012. In 2014 Fluid Movement opened their next venue, this time outside of London. Surfside, a steak and lobster restaurant on Polzeath beach in North Cornwall, was awarded the No. 1 Position in the *Sunday Times* 'Best alfresco dining spots in the UK 2015'. Tristan served as head chef there for the first year and continues to manage the food and beverages menu.

Tristan's first book, *The Curious Bartender: The Artistry & Alchemy of Creating the Perfect Cocktail* was published in October 2013 and shortlisted for the prestigious André Simon Award. His second book, *The Curious Bartender: An Odyssey of Malt, Bourbon & Rye Whiskies* hit the bookshelves in October 2014. In Spring 2015 he published *The Curious Barista's Guide to Coffee* (having previously successfully harvested, processed, roasted and brewed the first cup of UK grown coffee from the Eden Project in Cornwall, achieving international press coverage). This, *The Curious Bartender's Gin Palace* is his fourth book. During the course of his research, Tristan has travelled to over 150 distilleries around the world, in over 20 countries, including Holland, Scotland, Mexico, Cuba, France, Lebanon, Italy, Guatemala, Japan, America and Spain.

Tristan is husband to Laura and father to Dexter. In his very limited spare time he rides a Triumph motorcycle, takes photos, designs websites, bakes stuff, cooks a lot, attempts various DIY tasks beyond his level of ability, and collects whisky and books.